U.S.
IMMIGRATION
STEP
BY
STEP

Edwin T. Gania

Attorney at Law

SPHINX® PUBLISHING
AN IMPRINT OF SOURCEBOOKS, INC.®
NAPERVILLE, ILLINOIS
www.SphinxLegal.com

First Edition, 2002

Published by: **Sphinx® Publishing, An Imprint of Sourcebooks, Inc.®**

Naperville Office
P.O. Box 4410
Naperville, Illinois 60567-4410
630-961-3900
Fax: 630-961-2168
www.sourcebooks.com
www.SphinxLegal.com

This publication is designed to provide accurate and authoritative information in regard to the subject matter covered. It is sold with the understanding that the publisher is not engaged in rendering legal, accounting, or other professional service. If legal advice or other expert assistance is required, the services of a competent professional person should be sought.

From a Declaration of Principles Jointly Adopted by a Committee of the American Bar Association and a Committee of Publishers and Associations

This product is not a substitute for legal advice.

Disclaimer required by Texas statutes.

Library of Congress Cataloging-in-Publication Data
Gania, Edwin T.
   U.S. immigration, step by step / Edwin T. Gania.
      p. cm. -- (Legal survival guides)
Includes index.
   ISBN 1-57248-218-4 (alk. paper)
  1. Emigration and immigration law--United States.--Popular works. I.
Title. II. Series.
   KF4819.6 .G36 2002
   342.73'082--dc21
                                                    2002026997

Printed and bound in the United States of America.
VHG Paperback — 10 9 8 7 6 5 4 3 2 1

CONTENTS

SECTION 3: THE PERMANENT RESIDENCE APPLICATION PROCESS

USING SELF-HELP LAW BOOKS

Before using a self-help law book, you should realize the advantages and disadvantages of doing your own legal work and understand the challenges and diligence that this requires.

THE GROWING TREND

Rest assured that you won't be the first or only person handling your own legal matter. For example, in some states, more than seventy-five percent of divorces and other cases have at least one party representing him or herself. Because of the high cost of legal services, this is a major trend and many courts are struggling to make it easier for people to represent themselves. However, some courts are not happy with people who do not use attorneys and refuse to help them in any way. For some, the attitude is, "Go to the law library and figure it out for yourself."

We at Sphinx write and publish self-help law books to give people an alternative to the often complicated and confusing legal books found in most law libraries. We have made the explanations of the law as simple and easy to understand as possible. Of course, unlike an attorney advising an individual client, we cannot cover every conceivable possibility.

COST/VALUE ANALYSIS

Whenever you shop for a product or service, you are faced with various levels of quality and price. In deciding what product or service to buy, you make a cost/value analysis on the basis of your willingness to pay and the quality you desire.

When buying a car, you decide whether you want transportation, comfort, status, or sex appeal. Accordingly, you decide among such choices as a Neon, a Lincoln, a Rolls Royce, or a Porsche. Before making a decision, you usually weigh the merits of each option against the cost.

When you get a headache, you can take a pain reliever (such as aspirin) or visit a medical specialist for a neurological examination. Given this choice, most people, of course, take a pain reliever, since it costs only pennies; whereas a medical examination costs hundreds of dollars and takes a lot of time. This is usually a logical choice because it is rare to need anything more than a pain reliever for a headache. But in some cases, a headache may indicate a brain tumor and failing to see a specialist right away can result in complications. Should everyone with a headache go to a specialist? Of course not, but people treating their own illnesses must realize that they are betting on the basis of their cost/value analysis of the situation. They are taking the most logical option.

The same cost/value analysis must be made when deciding to do one's own legal work. Many legal situations are very straight forward, requiring a simple form and no complicated analysis. Anyone with a little intelligence and a book of instructions can handle the matter without outside help.

But there is always the chance that complications are involved that only an attorney would notice. To simplify the law into a book like this, several legal cases often must be condensed into a single sentence or paragraph. Otherwise, the book would be several hundred pages long and too complicated for most people. However, this simplification necessarily leaves out many details and nuances that would apply to special or unusual situations. Also, there are many ways to interpret most legal questions. Your case may come before a judge who disagrees with the analysis of our authors.

Therefore, in deciding to use a self-help law book and to do your own legal work, you must realize that you are making a cost/value analysis. You have decided that the money you will save in doing it yourself outweighs the chance that your case will not turn out to your satisfaction. Most people handling their own simple legal matters never have a problem, but occasionally people find that it ended up costing them more to have an attorney straighten out the situation than it would have if they had hired an attorney in the beginning. Keep this in mind if you decide to handle your own case, and be sure to consult an attorney if you feel you might need further guidance.

Immigration law is federal, which means that the same law and forms will apply to all INS offices across the country. However, there may be important differences in filing procedures depending on the particular local INS office. For example, a few office require that an adjustment application is filed in person rather than mailed in. If unsure, it may be wise to confirm a procedure by visiting the web site for that office or dropping by the INS building and asking someone in the lobby.

You should not necessarily expect to be able to get all of the information and resources you need solely from within the pages of this book. This book will serve as your guide, giving you specific information whenever possible and helping you to find out what else you will need to know. This is just like if you decided to build your own backyard deck. You might purchase a book on how to build decks. However, such a book would not include the building codes and permit requirements of every city, town county, and township in the nation; nor would it include the lumber, nails, saws, hammers, and other materials and tools you would need to actually build the deck. You would use the book as your guide, and then do some work and research involving such matters as whether you need a permit of some kind, what type and grade of wood are available in your area, whether to use hand tools or power tools, and how to use those tools.

Before using the forms in a book like this, you should check with your court clerk to see if there are any local rules of which you should be aware, or local forms you will need to use. Often, such forms will require the same information as the forms in the book but are merely laid out differently, use slightly different language, or use different color paper so the clerks can easily find them. They will sometimes require additional information.

CHANGES IN
THE LAW

Besides being subject to state and local rules and practices, the law is subject to change at any time. The courts and the legislatures of all fifty states are constantly revising the laws. It is possible that while you are reading this book, some aspect of the law is being changed or a court is interpreting a law in a different way. You should always check the most recent statutes, rules and regulations to see what, if any changes have been made.

In most cases, the change will be of minimal significance. A form will be redesigned, additional information will be required, or a waiting period will be extended. As a result, you might need to revise a form, file an extra form, or wait out a longer time period; these types of changes will not usually affect the outcome of your case. On the other hand, sometimes a major part of the law is changed, the entire law in a particular area is rewritten, or a case that was the basis of a central legal point is overruled. In such instances, your entire ability to pursue your case may be impaired.

Again, you should weigh the value of your case against the cost of an attorney and make a decision as to what you believe is in your best interest.

INTRODUCTION

Immigration is one area of life prone to false rumors. Too often, the truth of a rumor bears no relation to the speed with which it disseminates. I have seen too many instances where people have wound up in immigration court because they applied for permanent residence based upon a non-existent *amnesty*, for example.

The popular media sometimes unwittingly fuels the fire. The details of a new immigration statute may not make interesting reading or may be difficult to understand, so they are left out of the article. By making the story simpler, details are left out that may affect a significant number of people.

Hopefully, this book can assist in separating fact from fiction. More than just a description of the eligibility requirements for a particular category, much of which can be obtained elsewhere, this book will hopefully provide a feel for the reality of the process itself and where it might go awry.

The process of applying for a green card is a notoriously challenging undertaking. For the potential immigrant, it is no small accomplishment to understand this country's evolving eligibility requirements. It is equally difficult to file the correct forms and supporting documents and then guide the application through the INS. Indeed, one veteran INS trial attorney told me that the INS regulations are more confusing to her now than when she first started prosecuting INS cases.

Many immigration cases can just be filed, go through the system and end up being granted. But there is an incredibly fine line between an easy case and an impossible one. If an alien files a case for which he is not eligible, then he has just turned himself in to a federal law enforcement agency along with all relevant information needed to deport him. Imagine a thief filing with his local police station a signed confession, copies of his ID documents and other personal information, tax returns, photos and fingerprints, paying $500 in filing fees and then saying hurry up and schedule me for an interview. Sounds funny, but many thousands of hopeful aliens do the equivalent each year.

However, immigration cases vary widely in complexity. At one end of the scale are probably naturalization cases, which are typically straight forward, especially where the applicant has good command of the English language and no criminal background. (See Chapter 21.) Further, the stakes are lower for the naturalization applicant who already has a green card and can in any event normally reapply for naturalization if something goes unexpectedly wrong. If there is no criminal record, a naturalization applicant cannot be deported.

At the other end of the scale, are those who are in immigration court. (See Chapter 19.) Such persons really should not proceed without expert advice. At the very least, one who is in immigration court must consult with an immigration attorney or competent organization so that their right to relief is confirmed. Mistakes made in immigration court may prove fatal. See Chapter 22 for information on attorneys.

In the broad middle area of the immigration scale, are those seeking to apply for the green card through one of the eligibility categories listed in Chapters 4 through 12. Some cases are easier than others. The easiest of these cases are probably the family based applications if there are no complicating factors. A key aspect of this book is to identify where the applicant can proceed without outside assistance. Chapters 13 through 20 give you this information, while Chapter 23 will help you predict any future action in immigration law.

USING THIS BOOK

The U.S. immigration system is essentially a *closed system*, meaning you have to qualify in a specific category in order to obtain a green card. A person cannot normally *self-petition*. An excellent contrast is the Canadian system, which can be considered open and uses a point system. If a person can accumulate seventy points according to the Canadian point scheme, he or she can self-petition.

Therefore, to become a U.S. permanent resident you must first find a category for which you are eligible. This book is organized to assist that search. Part 1 will help you understand terms, immigration cases, and the first steps before applying for anything. Part 2 contains the various green card eligibility categories. They have been arranged starting with the most available visas or those that are easiest to apply for. In other words, if you are not certain which visa you might qualify for, you could look at the chapters in order until you see one that might apply to you.

While the various categories might seem confusing, there are basically four ways through which the vast majority will qualify for a green card: through their family, their job, as asylees or refugees, or through the diversity visa lottery. The other categories are fairly restrictive and will only apply to a limited number of qualified people. But it never hurts to consider each of them.

The majority of filings are in the family-based categories. These applications may be attempted without outside assistance. The only exception is for adopted children. However, there are certain eligibility categories for which one reading this book should not attempt to apply on their own. The employment-based categories require familiarity with technical requirements well beyond the scope of this book and therefore the adjustment process has not been described in detail.

Part 3 of the book contains background information regarding the green card process. It may either be read through or used as a reference for the information contained in any eligibility chapter.

NOTE: *Throughout the book, there are references to various supporting documents. Many of these are explained in detail in Chapter 15 as opposed to explaining them each time they are mentioned.*

The glossary at the back of the book is designed to be a unique resource. Not only does it contain a complete definition for all immigration terms, but it also attempts to provide perspective of the term in the overall immigration scheme. Thus, the reader is hopefully brought up to speed in regards to that concept. While such generalizations will not always prove accurate, they are still useful as a starting point.

NOTE: *Any reference to a section of law refers to the Immigration and Nationality Act (INA).*

Appendix E contains actual INS forms for your use.

Anyone who wishes to comment on any aspect of this book can contact the author at:

Edwin Gania
Mark Thomas and Associates
11 S. LaSalle Street
Suite 2800
Chicago, IL 60603
312-236-3163
edgania@cs.com

SECTION 1:

BEFORE BEGINNING THE IMMIGRATION PROCESS

Your Immigration Status

1

A good place to begin is to understand the different types of immigration status, and then, understand your own. Every person in the U.S. has an immigration status. It is one of the following:

1. **U.S. citizen.** This is a person who was born in the U.S., naturalized or born abroad to U.S. citizen parents. These are only persons in this list who are not subject to deportation proceedings.

2. **lawful permanent resident (LPR).** This is a green card holder who is eligible to reside permanently in the U.S. and apply for naturalization.

3. **asylee/refugee.** A person who was either granted asylum in the U.S. or who entered the U.S. as a refugee and has not yet been granted permanent residence.

4. **temporary resident.** This is one who applied through the 1986 amnesty program and was "legalized" but has not yet applied for a green card. Fewer and fewer people are in this category.

5. **nonimmigrant.** A nonimmigrant is one who has come to the U.S. temporarily on a valid nonimmigrant visa for a specific purpose, such as to study, work, or invest.

6. ***temporary protected status.*** These people have obtained status as a citizen of a country that Congress has designated to receive protected status on account of armed conflict, natural disaster or other extraordinary circumstance. They are in a position to possibly benefit from U.S. legislation allowing permanent residence.

7. ***out of status.*** This is one who initially lawfully entered on a nonimmigrant visa but the visa has expired or its terms violated.

8. ***undocumented alien.*** This is a person who has entered the U.S. without documentation, such as across the Mexican or Canadian border, or on a false passport.

This book is intended to assist those in categories 3 through 8 gain permanent residence status in the U.S. The primary focus of this book is on applying for adjustment in the U.S. as opposed to applying for permanent residence at an embassy or consulate in a foreign country. While the eligibility requirements are the same and some parts of the process are identical, the information in this book is not sufficiently detailed to be a guide to the entire process of applying abroad.

NOTE: *All of the above terms are explained in more detail where relevant in the text or in the glossary at the back of the book. Also, many of the documents you need to support your petitions are described in Chapter 15.*

UNDERSTANDING IMMIGRATION TERMS AND CASES

Immigration law is already complex without the use of numerous difficult terms. While you will never need to know most terms, there are several terms that are widely used in the immigration field. It is helpful to learn these right from the beginning and to also understand where the INS will be deciding on your application.

IMPORTANT TERMS TO KNOW

IMMIGRANT VISAS

The first important term is the difference between an immigrant and nonimmigrant visa. An *immigrant visa* is really just another name for a *green card*. A person issued an immigrant visa is said to have *adjusted* (upgraded) status from a non-immigrant to that of a lawful permanent resident. This book will cover only this process.

NOTE: *At an embassy, one is said to be applying for an immigrant visa as well.*

NONIMMIGRANT VISAS

On the other hand, a *nonimmigrant visa* is every other type of temporary visa granting status to live in the U.S. for a certain fixed period of time. With few exceptions, nonimmigrant visas do not lead to a green card. There are almost as many types of nonimmigrant visas as there are letters of the English alphabet. The letter name of the visa reflects the section of the statute (law) that defines it.

The most common type of *nonimmigrant visa* is the tourist visa, B-1 or B-2 visa, or the student visa, F-1. One is said to *change status* when he or she applies for and is granted another type of nonimmigrant status, say from a tourist to a student visa. One is in status if the time period reflected on the I-94 card stapled into the passport at the time of entry into the U.S. has not yet expired.

PETITIONER AND
BENEFICIARY

A *petitioner* is one who applies for the benefit of a second person, the *beneficiary*. The petitioner is either a U.S. citizen, a green card holder, or a U.S. corporation. It is the beneficiary who will at some point be an applicant for adjustment of status.

NOTE: *Refer to the detailed glossary at the back of the book if you come across any term that you do not understand.*

SUPPORTING
DOCUMENTS

Throughout the book, you will notice that each petition or filing requires certain documents to help prove your case. Many of these forms are self-explanatory, such as a passport, or birth certificate. For those that are not self-explanatory, you may find Chapter 15 helpful. It explains many of the major supporting documents. Refer there whenever a document is mentioned in the text that you do not understand.

FILING A CASE: LOCAL INS OFFICE, SERVICE CENTER, OR EMBASSY

Before discussing the specific eligibility categories in Part 2 of this book, it will be helpful to provide some orientation as to where an application is filed.

There are three agencies of the federal government that handle immigration: the Departments of Justice, State, and Labor. The State Department runs the U.S. embassies and consulates in foreign countries where it issues immigrant and nonimmigrant visas that a person requires to enter the U.S. The Labor Department has a limited but important role only in the initial aspect of an *employment-based application*. (An historical note is that it was initially the Labor Department that issued green cards in the early 1900s. They made them green to reflect the fact that the card allowed one to work in the U.S. and therefore were the equivalent of money.)

INS OFFICES   Once a person is in the U.S., he is under the jurisdiction of the Justice Department which most likely means the Immigration and Naturalization Service. He might also be under the jurisdiction of the immigration court (EOIR) or the Board of Immigration Appeals (BIA).

There are three places where the INS may decide an adjustment application. These are your local INS district office located in each major city; one of the five INS service centers which is responsible for your state of residence; or, the embassy or consulate in your native country.

Those already in the U.S. will want to file their application and complete processing in the U.S. Those abroad will most likely file at their embassy. However, with law changes, it will be increasingly likely that a person will have no option except to leave the U.S. and attempt adjustment at their embassy. As you might expect, there are several problems associated with this option.

SERVICE CENTERS   For those in the U.S., adjustment applications are increasingly filed at an INS service center. In fact, the general rule is that most applications are now filed at the service centers. The only applications that are filed locally are the family-based adjustment of status cases. This is because every family-based application will definitely require an interview. All other adjustment cases are filed at the service center. If a case at the service center is thought to require an interview, the file is then transferred to the local INS office. If one's case is with the local INS office, he or she also files for a work permit and travel permission with the local office.

In case you have not heard of the service centers, they are relatively new processing centers. These centers are increasingly handling much of the paperwork and decisions of cases, particularly for cases that are not commonly interviewed or do not require contact with the applicant. They are located in remote areas and for the most part, do not have any public access, except for very busy telephone numbers. Nonetheless, the system appears to be a success. By their very removal from the public, they appear to be fair and uninfluenced by outside factors. The cases that require interviews, such as marriage cases, citizenship, or processing for work permits are handled by the local INS office.

One advantage of having your case at the service center is that it is easier to keep track of it. You can call the number at the bottom of the receipt notice, and punch in your case number. You should call late at night to avoid the busy signals during the day. An automated system will often give you important update information such as that an approval or Request for Evidence (RFE) was sent out. If need be, you can call back during the day to talk to an information officer. The number is often busy, but if you continually call in the early morning for ten minutes or so, you can usually get through. The information officers are often helpful in clearing up a bureaucratic problem with the application.

LOCAL OFFICE
Cases at the local office can be difficult to track. If your application is lost or drags on, information is hard to come by.

WEBSITE
Recently, the INS has developed a website, which states where each form is filed and the filing fee. It is important to get the most up to date information because there are constant changes to forms, filing fees, and place of filing that you will need to be aware of.

EMBASSY CONSULATE
You also have the option of obtaining permanent residence at the embassy or consulate in your native country. An application at an embassy is decided by a *consular officer* as opposed to an immigration officer in the states. However, under the new laws passed in 1996, there are severe restrictions on leaving the U.S. to process your case at the embassy. If one is out of status more than 180 days starting from April 1, 1997, then he or she is barred for three years after leaving the U.S. If you are out of status more than one year starting from April 1, 1997, then you are barred for 10 years from obtaining any immigration benefit. (This means either an immigrant or nonimmigrant visa.)

There is a *waiver* possible to avoid the harsh effects of the three or ten year bar. However, this waiver is difficult to obtain in normal circumstances. Moreover, this waiver is only available to those who have a U.S. citizen or lawful permanent resident parent or spouse. But that is just the beginning. It must be demonstrated that there would be an extreme hardship to that qualifying relative if the alien is not allowed to enter the U.S. There is more on this in Chapter 11.

CHANGING IMMIGRATION LAWS 3

Immigration laws change often. As immigrants generally do not have special interest groups on their side, they are subject to the unrestricted whim of Congress whenever political advantage can be had. While it is popular to blame the INS for its harsh treatment of aliens, it must be kept in mind that the INS is only carrying out the laws as enacted by Congress and signed by the President. In fact, it would be an illegal act if a particular immigration officer did not carry out federal law and instead thought, well, this person should get a green card anyway because he or she really deserves it.

The U.S. is certainly in a period of restrictive immigration laws. Immigration laws underwent a drastic revision in 1996 in response to the tragic bombing of the federal building in Oklahoma City on April 22, 1995. In the days that followed, many believed that the bombing was the work of a Middle East terrorist, even though the bombing turned out to be the work of an American Nonetheless, Congress vowed to pass restrictive legislation affecting criminal aliens, if not all aliens.

The new statute in 1996 severely affected criminal aliens. Then, in July 1996, Congress enacted another highly restrictive legislation affecting aliens more generally. These laws targeted and wiped out critical avenues for immigration benefits.

Section 245(i) and the LIFE Act

The biggest impact may have been the demise of Section 245(i)of the Immigration and Nationality Act (INA). Under it, a person could have overstayed their nonimmigrant visa or he or she could have entered the U.S. without inspection by an immigration officer, (that is, snuck into the country). They benefited greatly from Section 245(i) because it allowed these applicants for adjustment to pay a $1000 fine and adjust status in the U.S.

Prior to the terrorist events of September 11, 2001, it appeared as though there was support to ease immigration law. President Bush had even referred to a type of amnesty, at least for Mexicans. However, the fact that the tragic events of September 11 were caused by illegal aliens, may set immigration reform back for years to come. See Chapter 23 for a more detailed discussion.

As a compromise, Congress passed the LIFE Act which allowed those out of status to apply for a green card if they had filed an alien petition prior to April 30, 2001, and were physically present in the U.S. on December 20, 2000.

At the time of publication of this book, an extension is being discussed in Congress to allow immigrants to be eligible under Section 245(i) if the family relationship existed prior to August 15, 2001, or a labor certification was filed prior to that date.

NOTE: *The previous law had been that if someone was the beneficiary of an I-130 petition or a labor certification application filed prior to January 18, 1998, then the beneficiary was section 245(i) eligible.*

SECTION 2:

PERMANENT RESIDENCE
ELIGIBILITY CATEGORIES

FAMILY-BASED PETITIONS

Family-based petitions are probably the largest group of permanent residence petitions. They encompass immediate relatives, widows, fiancés, and various others called *preference categories*. These categories will be discussed later in this chapter. Furthermore, there are even some family-based petitions that allow an immigrant to have *temporary status* prior to obtaining permanent residence. They, too, will be discussed later in this chapter.

Because this category of family-based petitions is so large, this chapter will naturally include a lot of information. Do not let this overwhelm you. If you fall into one of the family-based petitions, you need only concern yourself with the information pertaining to that particular status.

MINOR CHILDREN AND PARENTS OF U.S. CITIZENS—IMMEDIATE RELATIVES

An *immediate relative* is actually well named. They are relatives who may immediately file for a green card, which gives you permanent residence (also called an immigrant visa). U.S. citizens may apply for the following family members for which there is no wait for a visa number:

- parents;

- minor children; or,

- spouse (discussed in the next part of this chapter).

The parent, spouse, or minor child of a U.S. citizen is an immediate relative. This means several things. Most importantly, it means there is no wait for a visa number, since Congress has placed no limitation on the number of immediate relatives who may enter the U.S. each year. For other relatives, those in *preference categories*, there is a set number that can come to the U.S. each year. (This has resulted in a waiting list and is discussed later in this chapter.)

QUALIFYING AS
A MINOR CHILD

The following are important points regarding a U.S. citizen parent who is applying for a minor child:

- The children being applied for must be under the age of 21. (If they are 21 or over, they fall into a *preference category* as described later in this chapter.)

- The minor children must be unmarried. (If they are married, they also fall into a *preference category*.)

- Any children of minor, unmarried children may be included.

- The parent may apply for stepchildren if the parent's marriage took place before the step child turned 18.

- A parent may apply for adopted children if the adoption took place before the adopted child turned 16 and the parent and child have lived together for at least two years.

The first task is to gather the required supporting documents that you need to file along with the petition. The *petitioner* (in this case, the parent) must provide a document to prove his or her U.S. citizenship. An acceptable document is one of the following:

- birth certificate, if born in U.S.;

- naturalization certificate;

- certificate of citizenship; or,

- U.S. passport identification page.

The petitioner must also supply some documents about the beneficiary (in this case, the minor child).

The required documents are different depending on which parent applies. If the mother is petitioning, she must provide the child's birth certificate showing the names of both the child and the mother. If the father or stepparent is petitioning, he (or she) must provide the child's birth certificate showing the name of the child and that of both parents, and the marriage certificate. Documentation of legal termination (such as a divorce) of any previous marriages is required.

Finally, if any name on a supporting document has changed, a legal document proving the name change is required, such as:

- a marriage certificate;

- an adoption decree; or,

- a court order.

Provide only photocopies of all documents. The originals will be brought to the interview as discussed later in Chapter 17. All birth and marriage certificates must have been issued by (or registered with) the proper civil authority in the foreign country. If a document is not in English, it must be submitted along with a certified English translation (see page 138). If any document is unavailable, see Chapter 15 for more information. (All forms and documents are discussed in detail in Chapters 14 and 15.)

QUALIFYING AS A PARENT

The following are important points to remember where a U.S. citizen applies for his or her parents:

- the U.S. citizen child must be 21 years of age or over;

- a separate I-130 petition must be filed for each parent;

- a petition for the parents does not include the minor children of the parents, that is, the brothers or sisters of the petitioner. (The siblings fall into a preference category—see page 24); and,

- the U.S. citizen may apply for a stepparent (that is, someone who is married to his or her natural parent).

The petitioner (in this case, the adult child applying for his or her parents) must provide a document to prove his or her own U.S. citizenship. An acceptable document is one of the following:

- birth certificate, if born in U.S.;

- naturalization certificate;

- certificate of citizenship; or,

- U.S. passport identification page.

The petitioner must also supply some documents about the beneficiary (in this case, the parent or parents seeking to immigrate to the U.S.). The required documents differ, depending on which parent the petitioner is applying for. When applying for a mother, the petitioner must provide a copy of the petitioner's birth certificate showing his or her name and that of his or her mother. When applying for a father, the petitioner must provide a copy of the petitioner's birth certificate showing his or her name and that of *both* parents, and a copy of his or her parents' marriage certificate. Documentation of legal termination (such as a divorce) of any previous marriages is always required.

Finally, if any name on a supporting document has changed, a legal document proving the name change is required, such as:

- a marriage certificate;

- an adoption decree; or,

- a court order.

Provide only photocopies of all documents. The originals will be brought to the interview as discussed in Chapter 17. All birth and marriage certificates must have been issued by (or registered with) the proper civil authority in the foreign country. If a document is not in English, it must be submitted along with a certified English translation (see page 138). And, if any document is unavailable, see Chapter 15 for more information. (Again, all forms and documents are discussed in detail in Chapters 14 and 15.)

SPOUSES OF U.S. CITIZENS (OTHER IMMEDIATE RELATIVES)

The prevailing wisdom at the INS is that a high percentage of marriage cases are fraudulent. Even those that have a legitimate case often have to fight for respect from the INS because of the false cases. Estimates as to the amount of fraud vary, but the expectation is that half of the 80,000 or so marriage cases filed annually might be false.

Nonetheless, very few cases are actually denied. If the INS is unsure, they will send the file to investigations or delay the case at the examinations section. They know that time is on their side. The longer they delay, the more likely the suspect couple will separate or divorce.

NOTE: *If you are still married to a spouse overseas or cannot get a copy of a foreign divorce decree, it is very easy to simply get divorced in the U.S. In most states, it is a very short and inexpensive process to get divorced if the spouse resides outside the state. While this type of divorce serves only to dissolve the marriage and the court has no authority to order alimony, division of property or child support, it is sufficient as a divorce for any immigration or other purpose.*

See page 14 under the minor children and parents section for a list of supporting documents the U.S. citizen must have to establish his or her citizenship. A marriage certificate is required to establish that the petitioner is in fact legally married to the beneficiary spouse. This certificate must establish that both the husband and wife were present at the ceremony.

The documents on page 18 are required in every case. In some cases, other documents must be provided. If either the husband or wife was previously married, then a divorce decree must also be submitted. If any name has been changed from one of the supporting documents, then documentation as to this change must be provided through the documents on page 18.

The most important supporting documents are to establish that the marriage is *bona fide*, that is, it was entered into for love and affection rather than for a green card. The list contained on the next page contains examples of useful supporting documents for proving a bonafide marriage. The more of these documents that are obtained, the quicker and easier the case will be granted.

Again, provide only photocopies of all documents. The originals will be brought to the interview as discussed in Chapter 17. All official certificates must have been issued by (or registered with) the proper civil authority in the foreign country. If a document is not in English it must be submitted along with a certified English translation (see page 138). And, if any document is unavailable, see page 138 for more information.

PROVIDING A
BONA FIDE
MARRIAGE

The critical aspect of a marriage case is to prove that the marriage was entered into for love and affection rather than a green card. In order to do so, the following should be demonstrated:

- joint obligations for housing and living expenses;

- joint management of finances;

- joint ownership of property; and;

- evidence that the couple hold themselves out as married.

The following documents are also useful to prove that a marriage is bona fide:

- birth certificates of children born of the marriage;

- joint income tax returns;

- joint bank account;

- wedding pictures;

- photos that show both of you together with family or friends;

- evidence of vacations taken together such as airline tickets, photos, bills;

- joint apartment lease or letter from parent or letter from landlord that have been living together;

- joint property deed or mortgage;
- if the spouse has taken the married name, any document showing married name such as Social Security card, driver's license, state I.D. card, credit cards, club cards etc;
- joint auto title or registration;
- joint car insurance;
- letter from current or former employer of one spouse showing a change in records to reflect new marital status;
- letter from current or former employer of one spouse showing spouse was designated as person to be notified in event of accident, sickness or emergency;
- health insurance plans naming spouse as member or beneficiary;
- life insurance policy naming spouse as member or beneficiary;
- letters (and envelopes if possible), birthday or holiday cards;
- telephone bills or any proof of correspondence between couple;
- utilities in joint names: phone, gas, electric, cable;
- joint credit cards or department store cards;
- receipts, invoices or installment contracts for major purchases made together such as car, furniture, television, VCR, stereo, refrigerator, washer, dryer showing date, address, and name of one or both spouses;
- religious marriage certificate if there was a church wedding;
- receipt for wedding reception;
- receipt for purchase of wedding rings;
- mail received at house (or old address now being forwarded);
- correspondence, invitations, or cards sent to the couple;
- day care or school records showing spouse as parent or guardian;
- medical or dental records; or,
- affidavits from family or friends.

This is a fairly comprehensive list meant only to offer suggestions. By no means would (or should) any couple come to an INS interview with all or even most of the above items. For example, if one has a wedding album showing a large reception attended by family and friends, then that alone and an apartment lease might suffice. However, if a couple has a wide age difference, or is of clearly different ethnic, religious, or language backgrounds, then more pieces of evidence are required.

SPECIAL INTERVIEW QUESTIONS

A special wrinkle is presented at an interview for a marriage-based case and should be discussed now so that you are prepared. If the INS officer is unsure whether the marriage is bona fide, then he may ask personal questions of the couple. The officer may or may not separate the couple and then compare answers. The following is a list of typical questions:

- What time did you and spouse wake up?

- Who cooks which meals?

- What meal was eaten for breakfast today or dinner last night?

- Where do your in-laws live and what is the address?

- What are the names of your spouse's brothers and sisters?

- What is the date of your spouse's birth and the names of his or her parents?

- Why did you come to U.S. in the first place?

- Who invited you?

- Where did you meet your spouse?

- Who proposed and after dating for how long?

- What did you do last valentine's day?

- What was the last gift you received from your spouse?

- How did you get to the interview?

- Did you sleep together before marriage? If so, how often?

- Do you know your spouse's family, their names, where they live, and when his or her parents passed away?

- What school do your step-children attend?

- Where does your spouse work?

- How many bedrooms or rooms are in your apartment?

- What type of stove is in the kitchen (gas or electric)?

- Describe the headboard on your bed, curtains in the room, the dresser, other furniture, and color of the carpet?

- Does the alien spouse talk to his or her in-laws?

- How much is rent, expenses, salaries, and who pays the bills?

- Why did you marry the other person?

NOTE: *While the above are typical questions, each officer has his or her own way of questioning.*

BREAKING UP   At least half of all marriages end in divorce. It is likely that for recent immigrants the percentage might be higher. It is difficult enough to maintain a relationship, without adding on all of the problems of adjusting to a new culture, being without status, or even likely being in a lower income bracket. Plus, it is disheartening to consider how a U.S. citizen spouse will use his or her leverage over the immigration status of the other.

The legal standard to be granted permanent residence is whether the marriage was bona fide *at the time it was entered into*. It is not the state of the marriage by the time of the interview, except to the extent that this indicates whether the marriage was initially bona fide. While the INS tends to ignore this distinction, an immigration judge will not.

So what if your marriage falls apart before the interview? Unfortunately, the only answer is to fix the relationship. If that requires marriage counseling, then do it. That constitutes good evidence of a bona fide relationship.

CONDITIONAL
PERMANENT
RESIDENCE AND
REMOVING
CONDITIONS

If at the time of the *adjustment of status* (becoming a permanent resident) the marriage was less than two years old, then the alien becomes a *conditional resident*. The classification is CR1 (if processed at an embassy) or CR6 (if processed in the U.S.). This status expires within two years. If the marriage has been in existence for more than two years at the time of the interview, then a permanent green card is issued.

The purpose of the two-year temporary resident status is so that the INS has another opportunity to determine whether the marriage was in fact bona fide. (The conditional resident must file form I-751 to remove conditions within the ninety-day period prior to the expiration date on the conditional green card, which is discussed in Chapter 14.)

If you miss the two-year deadline, then you have to show exceptional circumstances for late filing. The exceptional circumstances should be supported with documentation. For example, if you were travelling outside the U.S. around the deadline, show proof of travel. If the deadline is missed, you will have to re-file the original adjustment packet, discussed in Chapter 14. However, this time permanent status will be granted (as IR1 or IR6).

ADOPTED CHILDREN (IMMEDIATE RELATIVES)

If a child is under the age of 16 and cannot qualify for permanent residence through his or her own family, adoption by a U.S. citizen or green card holder might be an excellent means for the child to obtain permanent residence—even if both parents of the child are still alive. For example, a U.S. citizen or permanent resident over the age of 21 can apply for his or her niece, nephew, grandchild, or even a child not related to them.

NOTE: *This process would only provide status for the child and not for his or her natural parents. Even when the child turns 21 and is a U.S. citizen, he would not be able to apply for his or her natural parents.*

Because of the technicalities involved with qualifying through an adoption, this book cannot provide details about the specific process and required applications. The child has to be eligible to be adopted according to the laws of the particular state or foreign country. To proceed with such a case, the person will need to consult with an immigration attorney or organization who is familiar with adoptions. However, this discussion will help to identify children who would benefit from the adoption process.

The adopted child would become an immediate relative to the adopting U.S. citizen, meaning there is no wait for a visa. Adoption may also work for a lawful permanent resident parent, although there would be an approximately five year wait for a visa. This long wait is alleviated somewhat by the option of obtaining lawful status through a "V" visa filing after the I-130 petition has been pending more than three years, which is discussed later in this chapter.

The main hurdle to overcome in an adoption case is the requirement that the child have lived with the U.S. citizen adopted parent for two years before filing the I-130 alien relative petition. These two years may be either in the native country or in the U.S. If the U.S. citizen adoptive parent lives in the U.S. and the child is in the other native country, then the two year residence requirement may be difficult to satisfy. In this event, it may be necessary for the child to enter the U.S. on a type of *nonimmigrant visa*, such as a student or tourist visa.

ILLEGAL ENTRY   A child that enters the U.S. illegally (across a border without documentation) may not qualify for permanent residence in the U.S. unless they are Section 245(i) eligible. (see Chapter 5.) However, after he or she accumulates two years of residence with the adopted parents, he or she may return to the native country and apply there for an immigrant visa. If he or she is under the age of 17, he or she does not accumulate unlawful presence in the U.S. and so there is no bar on returning. It is likely that during the period of stay in the U.S., there would be an *amnesty* allowing adjustment of status. (See Chapter 9.)

NOTE: *Orphan petitions are treated under different rules. Cases involving orphans are too complex for any person unfamiliar with the process. Orphan petitions require an analysis of state laws and also laws of the foreign country where the child is from. INS must perform a home study. Get the assistance of an immigration attorney or the non-profit organization involved.*

PREFERENCE CATEGORIES

In addition to the immediate visa categories mentioned already, U.S. citizens may also apply for the following relatives—together called the *preference categories*. Each category is assigned an INS preference visa category number with the second preference having two parts (2A and 2B). There is, however, a waiting period for a visa number:

- a single child 21 years of age or over—adult child (first preference);

- a married child of any age (third preference); and,

- a brother or sister of any age (fourth preference).

If a parent only has a green card and is not a U.S. citizen, then he or she may only apply the following relatives:

- a spouse and single child under the age of 21 (preference 2A); and,

- a single child 21 years of age or over (preference 2B).

Unlike an immediate family visa category, the preference visa categories are *backlogged*. One must consult the *visa chart* published by the Department of State to determine when to file the adjustment application.

It is extremely important to understand the visa chart as published monthly by the Department of State in order to know when to apply for adjustment of status. The chart tells those who have already filed the alien relative petition (I-130 petition) when they may file for adjustment of status (on form I-485).

The Department of State publishes an updated visa chart each month. This chart reflects the waiting times for each of the preference visas. The priority date is the date reflected on the I-130 approval notice. It is the date on which you filed the I-130. For the preference visas, you may only apply for adjustment once a petition becomes current, ie. a visa becomes available as reflected in the State Department chart. A petition is *current* when the date the particular preference category moves past the priority date on the I-130 petition.

In order to check the visa chart for the status of the petition, one must be familiar with the visa categories. They are again as follows:

First preference: Unmarried, adult sons and daughters of U.S. citizens. (An adult is one who is 21 years of age or older.)

Second preference: Spouses of lawful permanent residents (category 2A) and the unmarried sons and daughters (of any age) of lawful permanent residents and their unmarried children (category 2B).

Third preference: Married sons and daughters of U.S. citizens, their spouses and unmarried minor children.

Fourth preference: Brothers and sisters of adult U.S. citizens, their spouses and unmarried minor children.

Remember, this chart applies only to preference visas. Those in an immediate category may apply for adjustment at any time. The chart looks confusing, but it is not really that complicated. The following steps will help you to easily use the chart, especially for the first time:

1. Get a current version of the monthly visa chart. You can either find it on the Internet at:

http://www.travel.state.gov/visa_bulletin.html

or else call 202-663-1541. It is sometimes easier to call the recorded message and immediately the dates like those on the sample chart will be read off in the same order as on the sample chart.

2. Know which preference visa category you fall into. This table contains only a short description of each category. The preference category is also contained on your approval notice. If you need further assistance, you should refer back to see which chapter in Section 2 applies to you.

3. Check your I-130 approval notice for your *priority date.* This will normally be the date that you filed the I-130 petition and is often found in one of the boxes in the upper left corner or on the right side of an older approval notice.

4. Find the applicable cut-off date corresponding to your preference category and country. Only one of the three country columns on the right will apply to you.

5. Compare your priority date to the reported cut-off date. If your priority date is earlier than the cut-off date, you will have to wait before filing the adjustment application. If your priority date has passed the cut-off date, then you may go ahead and file for adjustment of status.

6. Do not despair if there appears to be a long wait based on your priority date and the cut-off date. Cut-off dates can move backwards and forwards rapidly. However, over the past several years, the 3rd and 4th preference categories have typically progressed less than one month for each calender month. Unavailable categories generally become available again after October 1 of each year, which is the start of the government fiscal year and a fresh allocation of visa numbers.

Cut-off Dates

FAMILY PREFERENCE CATEGORIES	ALL COUNTRIES EXCEPT MEXICO AND PHILIPPINES	MEXICO	PHILIPPINES
1st single child 21 or over of a U.S. citizen	01 JUL 96	Unavailable	01 NOV 89
2A spouse or single child under 21 of a permanent resident	15 MAY 97	15 DEC 94	15 APR 97
2B single child 21 or over of a permanent resident	08 DEC 93	Unavailable	08 DEC 93
3rd married child of a U.S. citizen	08 AUG 96	15 JUL 92	01 JUL 89
4th brother or sister of an adult U.S. citizen	01 JUL 90	08 APR 90	01 AUG 81

NOTE: *In contrast to the above chart, all employment categories are now current and have been so for the past couple of years.*

You must wait until the date passes. It cannot just be in the same month. The INS officer will check at the interview that the visa was actually current at the time the petition was filed. If it was not current, the application will be denied although they can allow a new application to be filed and paid for on the same day.

Recently, there has been a problem with the visa numbers in preference categories. These numbers have progressed only one month in the past year. The cause of this backup is that the INS is processing an unusual number of cases to clear up the long backlog of adjustment applications pending at the local INS offices.

FIRST PREFERENCE

The single adult children of the U.S. citizen petitioner must be unmarried. If they are married, they fall into the third preference category, which requires starting the waiting period over. Any minor children of the unmarried adult child may be included. Furthermore, the petitioner may apply for stepchildren if the parent's marriage took place before the stepchild turned 18. Prove citizenship and the parent-child relationship with the same documents listed for immediate relatives previously in this chapter.

SECOND PREFERENCE— SPOUSES (2A)

Permanent residents may apply for a spouse, under the same guidelines as a U.S. citizen spouse. (see page 17.) The difference is that there is a wait of approximately four or five years for a visa number. However, if the permanent resident spouse *naturalizes* (becomes a U.S. citizen), then the alien spouse may apply immediately for permanent residence. The permanent resident spouse will need a copy of the green card in place of proof of U.S. citizenship. Otherwise the required documents are the same as for a U.S. citizen spouse earlier in this chapter.

SECOND PREFERENCE— UNMARRIED CHILDREN (2B)

The following are important points regarding lawful permanent resident petitioners who are applying for an unmarried child (of any age):

- The children of permanent U.S. residents must be unmarried. If they are married, they can only be applied for by a U.S. citizen parents.

- Any children of the unmarried child may be included.

- The permanent resident parent may apply for stepchildren if the parent's marriage took place before the children turned 18.

- The permanent resident parent may apply for adopted children if the adoption took place before the child turned 16 and the parent and child have lived together for at least two years.

The same documents are required here as for immediate relatives listed earlier in this chapter. However, a copy of the parent's green card replaces proof of U.S. citizenship here.

THIRD
PREFERENCE

The U.S. citizen petitioner who is applying for a married adult child may include the spouse of the adult child in the petition. The single unmarried children of the adult children being applied for may be included as well. Such children must adjust status (become a citizen) prior to turning age 21 or they will be excluded from the petition.

The U.S. citizen must establish his or her citizenship by one of the documents indicated on page 14. The birth certificate of the adult child must be filed to establish the qualifying relationship. This birth certificate must show the name of the parent who is filing the petition. If the father is petitioning, then his marriage certificate must also be provided. Finally, if any name on a supporting document has changed, a legal document to evidence the name change is required, such as a marriage certificate, adoption certificate, or a court order.

FOURTH
PREFERENCE

A quick glance at the visa chart on page 26, reveals that the fourth preference (siblings of U.S. citizens) petitions will take many years to become current. However, experience has shown that some do not file a petition on the theory that it would take too long. Time has a way of flying by. Plus, benefits may accrue by simply being the beneficiary of a petition filed before a certain date. Since it is an easy and inexpensive petition to file, it must be filed in all circumstances as soon as possible.

The following are important points regarding the U.S. citizen petitioner who is applying for a brother or sister:

- the U.S. citizen petitioner must be 21 years of age or over;

- the spouse of the adult sibling may be included; and,

- the single unmarried children of the adult sibling may be included. Such children must adjust status prior to turning 21 years or be excluded from the petition.

DEATH OR ILLNESS OF PETITIONER

If the petitioner is deceased prior to filing the adjustment, consult with an immigration attorney to determine whether you have any options. If the petitioner becomes ill while the adjustment application is pending, notify the local INS office and request that the interview be scheduled as soon as possible. Include a letter from the physician and other evidence of the medical condition.

SELF-PETITIONS

There are two main family-based categories where a person can petition to immigrate to the U.S. for themselves. One way is as a widow or widower of a deceased U.S. citizen. A second way is as an abused spouse of a U.S. citizen.

WIDOWS OR WIDOWERS An individual may obtain permanent residence through a deceased U.S. citizen spouse if:

- the alien spouse was married for at least two years to a U.S. citizen;

- the U.S. citizen was a citizen for at least two years at the time of death;

- the petition is filed within two years of the death of the U.S. citizen spouse;

- the alien spouse was not legally separated from the U.S. citizen spouse at the time of death; and,

- the alien spouse has not remarried.

The minor unmarried children of the widow or widower may also obtain status.

ABUSED SPOUSE   An individual may obtain permanent residence through a U.S. citizen spouse if:

- the alien spouse is married or was divorced within the past two years to a U.S. citizen;

- the alien spouse is a person of good moral character;

- the alien spouse has resided with the U.S. citizen spouse;

- the marriage was entered into in good faith; and,

- the alien spouse (or his or her minor child) was battered or the subject of extreme cruelty.

The rules recently changed for *former* spouses of abusive U.S. citizens or lawful permanent residents. It used to be that one was *ineligible* to self-petition if the abused spouse was *not* legally married to U.S. citizen or legal permanent resident spouse on the day the petition was filed. Now a petition may still be filed if the divorce took place during the two year period immediately *preceding* the filing of the self-petition. It must also be shown that the divorce was connected to the battery or extreme mental cruelty, although this may already be proven by the other evidence. However, the divorce judgment need not specifically state that the divorce was caused by domestic violence.

NONIMMIGRANT VISAS 5

If you are in the U.S. on a *nonimmigrant visa*, it is critical that you remain in valid status. This will preserve your right to obtain permanent residence or change status to another nonimmigrant visa classification.

Those seeking to become a permanent resident in the future will normally need to be in a valid status to do so unless they fall within one of two exceptions. These are if the person is Section 245(i) eligible, or if they are eligible to adjust through an immediate family visa.

SECTION 245(I)

Those that are 245(i) eligible are those that have an I-130 filed on their behalf prior to April 30, 2001, during the mini amnesty period. Such a person also must have been present in the U.S. on December 20, 2000. Or, if the I-130 was filed before January 18, 1998, then the person is 245(i) eligible whether or not they were present in the U.S. on December 20, 2000.

Immediate Family

The other exception is if the person is the beneficiary of an immediate family visa petition such as:

- marriage to a U.S. citizen;

- parent of a U.S. citizen; or,

- minor unmarried child of a U.S. citizen.

These people must have made a lawful entry into the U.S. and not have worked without authorization in the U.S. However, the INS currently does not appear to be enforcing this last provision in many cases.

Travel outside the U.S.

The other important aspect of maintaining nonimmigrant status is the right to travel outside the U.S. during the time you wait for the adjustment interview. If you were out of status more than six months at the time you file an application for adjustment of status, then you will not qualify for *advance parole* on account of unlawful presence. Thus, you may not travel outside the U.S. until your status is adjusted. While the backlog for adjustment interviews have decreased substantially in recent months, one's case can still drag on for various reasons after the interview.

Keep a copy of both sides of each I-94 and turn in to the airline whether they ask for it or not. Ask at the gate whether the airline will be collecting the I-94s or not. If the airline is not collecting the I-94s then it is possible to go to the embassy and hand it in. The other option is to keep a copy of the airline ticket and perhaps proof that you actually arrived in the foreign country. When applying for a new visa, you can show it to the consulate that you honored your last visa by leaving in time. Also, if applying for an immigrant visa at an embassy, it might be useful to show you returned to the U.S. and were not *unlawfully present*, which may bar the immigrant visa.

TYPES OF NONIMMIGRANT VISAS

Most non-immigrants enter as one of the following:

- tourists;

- businesses;

- treaty investors or traders;

- entertainers or athletes; or,

- intra-company managers.

Following is a fairly complete list of the nonimmigrant categories. The rest of this chapter, however, will only detail the family-based ones. (The rest are beyond the scope of this book.) The non-immigrant categories are:

A-1, A-2, A-3: foreign government employees (such as diplomats and officials) and their families, servants, and private employees;

B-1, B-2: business visitors (to attend conferences, trade shows etc.) who are not employed in the U.S. and tourists visiting for pleasure (obtaining medical treatment, conventions, incidental school attendance);

C-1, C-2, C-3: aliens in transit through the U.S. or en route to the United Nations;

D-1, D-2: foreign crew members of ship and aircraft;

E-1, E-2: aliens entering the U.S. to engage in trade or investment pursuant to a bilateral treaty between the U.S. and their country of nationality. This classification authorizes employment in the U.S. to manage the trade or investment enterprise.;

F-1, F-2: foreign students authorized to study in the U.S. Limited work authorization available during and after completion of the course of study;

G-1, G-5: employees of international organizations and their families/servants;

H-1, H-2, H-3, H-4: certain qualified temporary workers, trainees and their families. The H-1B category is accorded to individuals employed in a specialty occupation and is one of the most important nonimmigrant categories for employers wishing to hire a foreign national in a professional or highly technical position;

I: media representatives;

J-1, J-2: exchange visitors and their families. Allows nonimmigrants to enter the U.S. for purposes of engaging in lecturing, research, study, observation or training. Most individuals in J status are subject to a requirement that they return to their home country for at least two years upon completion of the J program. Waivers of this requirement are available in some circumstances;

K-1, K-2, K-3, K-4: fiancés of a U.S. citizen and their minor children; or spouses of U.S. citizens with I-130 pending and their minor children;

L-1, L-2: intracompany transferees who are managers, executives and employees with specialized knowledge of international corporations to the U.S.;

M-1, M-2: vocational students and their families;

N: family members of G-4 special immigrants;

O-1, O-2, O-3: aliens of extraordinary ability in the sciences, arts, education, business or athletics and accompanying family members. Must be at the top of their field to qualify although lower standard for artists and entertainers (must have achieved prominence);

P-1, P-2, P-3: athletic teams and entertainment groups who are recognized internationally;

Q: international cultural exchange aliens;

R-1, R-2: ,ministers, religious workers and their families;

S-5, S-6: also called "Snitch visa". Promised frequently but awarded sparingly in the U.S. to individuals who assist with a criminal investigation;

TN: Canadian and Mexican citizens qualified as temporary workers under NAFTA; and

V Visa: the spouse and minor children of an LPR whose I-130 petition was filed more than three years prior. See Chapter 14.

In addition to the above specific criteria, there are requirements that are common to many nonimmigrant visas, such as that the applicant not be an *intending immigrant* (that is, the person intends to return to their native country before expiration of the visa).

V VISA

The *V visa* is an important new nonimmigrant classification. It applies to those beneficiaries who are in the family-based second preference (F2A) category. That is, it applies to the spouses and minor unmarried children of legal permanent residents only.

This new classification was created by the LIFE Act in December 2000. To qualify, the alien must be the beneficiary of an immigrant visa I-130 petition that has been pending with the INS for more than three years or has been approved, but more than three years have passed since its filing. Since the wait for a visa number in the F2A category is six years and longer for citizens of Mexico, this is an important new benefit. *V visa* status allows the recipient to obtain *work authorization* and *advance parole* discussed in Chapter 14.

This visa allows such individuals to enter the U.S. from abroad or to acquire lawful status in the U.S. no matter what their status is or how they entered the U.S. (See Chapter 14 for procedure and forms for this visa.)

V VISA
ELIGIBILITY
AND BENEFITS

To be eligible for V visa status, the alien must not be inadmissible under section 212(a) of the INS Code with certain exceptions. For example, he or she might be barred by a criminal record, unlawful presence, etc.. A V visa applicant also needs to be aware that obtaining V visa status does not ensure that he or she qualifies for a green card.

A person in V visa status may travel outside the U.S. without advance parole. However, to re-enter the U.S., he or she will be required to obtain a V visa at an embassy or consulate. While it appears that the applicant may be admissible to the U.S. by the unusual exceptions to section

212(a) in the LIFE Act, a consular officer may still have the discretion to deny the V visa. Anyone other than a V Visa applicant who applies for a nonimmigrant or immigrant visa after having entered the U.S. without inspection and accruing unlawful presence would simply be denied.

If an alien is in immigration proceedings, then the V visa will be particularly helpful. If the case is before the Immigration Judge or the Board of Immigration Appeals, then the alien should request that the proceedings be administratively closed. If an alien has a motion pending with the Board of Immigration Appeals (BIA), such as a motion to reopen, then he or she should request that the motion be continued indefinitely.

However, a person who has a final order of deportation or removal, needs to first get the order reopened. This is a technical process for which an immigration lawyer must be consulted.

V VISA
STATUS ENDS

V visa status ends when one of the following occurs:
- the I-130 petition is denied, withdrawn, or revoked;
- the alien's application for adjustment of status visa is denied;
- the alien's application for an immigrant visa is denied;
- a spouse becomes divorced (minor child remains in status);
- a minor child turns 21 or marries; or,
- the legal permanent resident petitioner naturalizes.

K-1 VISA

A U.S. citizen may apply to bring his or her fiancé into the U.S. through an embassy or consulate. The fiancé enters on a K-1 visa. (The fiancé's minor unmarried children under the age of 21 enter in K-2 status.)

The U.S. citizen must establish his or her citizenship by one of the documents indicated on page 14. The petitioner then should draft a statement as to the history of the marriage.

In some cases, other documents must be provided. For example, if a person was previously married, then a divorce decree must also be submitted. If any name has been changed from one of the supporting documents, then documentation as to this change must be provided.

The most important supporting documents are to establish that the engagement is *bona fide*. That is, show that it was entered into for love and affection rather than for U.S. immigration status. The list on page 18 contains examples of useful supporting documents. The more of these documents that are obtained, the quicker and easier the case will be granted.

K-1 Benefits and Eligibility A K-1 status person may go to the local INS office and immediately obtain a work permit card. Also entering the U.S. on K-1 status, the beneficiary must marry the U.S. citizen petitioner within three months. After marriage, a *onestop application* is filed with the local INS office. (see Chapter 14.)

There are harsh consequences if the intended marriage does not take place. If the beneficiary does not marry the petitioner within 90 days and pursue adjustment of status on that basis, he or she may not pursue adjustment of status by any other avenue. Even Section 245(i), which helps applicants who enter illegally, does not assist the K-1 fiancé who does not marry. The only possible exception is to apply for *asylum* within one year of entry. (see Chapter 9.)

K-3 and K-4 Visas

The K-3 and K-4 visas are new nonimmigrant classifications to speed the entry of spouses and minor unmarried children of U.S. citizens into the U.S. These visas came into being with the LIFE Act, along with the V visa. One applies for the K-3 visa in place of applying for an immigrant visa at an embassy.

EMPLOYMENT-BASED PETITIONS

An employment-based visa application can be a long and arduous process, particularly where a *labor certification* is required. A labor certification means that after a supervised recruitment period, a state employment agency certifies that there is no U.S. worker who can assume the job offered to the alien. If a labor certification is required, then the case may require an additional six months to one year (or more) depending on locality. Normally, an attorney *will be required* to process an employment-based application.

With the demise of Section 245(i) described in Chapter 3, an individual must be *in status* (ie. on an unexpired nonimmigrant) at the time the application for adjustment of status is filed. There are a couple of exceptions. If before April 30, 2001, an individual filed a labor certification application or was the beneficiary of an immediate relative petition, then he or she may apply for adjustment if he or she was physically present in the U.S. on December 20, 2000. Otherwise, if the labor certification or an I-130 petition was filed before January 18, 1998, then he or she may also adjust.

FIRST PREFERENCE: EXTRAORDINARY ABILITY

This category is comparable to the nonimmigrant O and P visas. These include aliens of extraordinary ability in the sciences, arts, education, business or athletics and accompanying family members. In the case of P visa holders, athletic teams and entertainment groups that are recognized internationally are included.

Federal regulations define *extraordinary ability* as a level of expertise indicating that the individual is one of a small percentage who have risen to the very top of a particular field in the sciences, arts, education, business, and athletics. Such a person will have received national or international acclaim.

The extraordinary ability category is a very difficult standard to meet. For example, only the top players in the major professional sports leagues would qualify. A wide variety of artists, such as those in the culinary and visual arts, may qualify with a slightly lower standard of having achieved "prominence".

Further, this category does not necessarily require a job offer, but most applications will likely need one or at least correspondence with prospective employers. There is no labor certification required. The petition may be filed by a prospective employer or by the alien himself. As these petitions are difficult to document and are not easily approved by the service center, the assistance of an attorney will be necessary.

OUTSTANDING PROFESSOR OR RESEARCHER

Generally, this category is available to professors and researchers with a demonstrated record of excellence in the field and who have been offered a tenure-track position with a U.S. institution of higher education, a similar position at a research institution, or an established research division of a corporation. This category does not require a labor certification.

MULTINATIONAL EXECUTIVES AND MANAGERS

This category is intended to facilitate the transfer of key managerial and executive personnel within a multinational corporation. This classification is generally available to an individual who has been employed abroad in a managerial or executive capacity by a branch, subsidiary, affiliate or parent of a U.S. company for at least one year and who is being transferred to the U.S. company. Such persons may be in the U.S. on an L-1A visa. This category does not require a labor certification.

SECOND PREFERENCE: EXCEPTIONAL ABILITY

This classification is available to individuals demonstrating exceptional ability in the sciences, arts, or business. Federal regulations define *exceptional ability* as a degree of expertise significantly above that ordinarily encountered in the sciences, arts, or business. A *labor certification* and a *job offer* are required unless they are waived by approval of a national interest waiver.

PROFESSIONALS WITH ADVANCED DEGREES

Qualification in this category requires demonstration that the beneficiary holds an advanced degree in the field and that the position offered to the beneficiary requires an individual with an advanced degree. A labor certification and a job offer are required unless they are waived by approval of a national interest waiver.

THIRD PREFERENCE: SKILLED WORKERS

This is the most common category in which employment-based applications are made. This category requires a job offer and a labor certification. It includes entry-level professionals with a Bachelor's degree and skilled workers in occupations that require at least two years experience, training, or education.

FOURTH PREFERENCE: UNSKILLED WORKERS

This group includes unskilled workers in occupations that require less than two years of experience, training, and education. Since it is subject to severe limitations on annual availability, it is generally regarded as a *distinct category*. Often, there is a significant backlog in this category, and this classification does require a labor certification.

SHORTAGE OCCUPATIONS

At the present time, only two occupations—physical therapists and registered nurses—have been designated by the Department of Labor as *shortage occupations*. These are called *Schedule A* occupations since that is how they are named in the Department of Labor regulations. The benefit of such a designation is that a labor certification is not required.

HOW TO FILE A LABOR CERTIFICATION

A labor certification is a requirement for most employment-based adjustment applications. It is an actual recruitment of U.S. workers, under the supervision of the Department of Labor and a State Employment Security Agency (SESA) in order to establish that there is no U.S. worker who is ready, willing, able, and qualified to take the position offered to an alien.

There are two tracks to a labor certification—the normal slow-track application (discussed in the next section) and the new fast-track *reduction in recruitment process (RIR)*.

RIR   The newer *RIR* was developed to reduce the substantial backlog that had developed at many state offices. The RIR track can reduce the first stage of processing to several months instead of a year or more, depending on the office involved. RIR is used where the company has already attempted to recruit a worker for the specific job without success. There is no need for a supervised recruitment by the SESA (discussed in the next section.)

To qualify for an RIR, a company must have already attempted to recruit a qualified worker and found that it was unable to do so. Then along with the normal labor certification applications, it will submit a report as to recruitment, along with copies of all evidence of recruitment. It will ask that the application be decided on without a supervised recruitment through the Department of Labor.

Sufficient recruitment. What constitutes *sufficient recruitment* may vary slightly by region. Typically it is as follows:

- one print advertisement in a newspaper of general circulation or relevant journal, plus,

- enough other activities to show evidence that a pattern of recruitment has been completed to adequately test the labor market for the given occupation.

The following recruitment efforts will be useful:

- job order with the state workforce agency;

- internal company recruitment activities;

- company and commercial Internet web page ads;

- community, college, or other job fairs;

- private employment agency; or,

- additional print advertisements.

In addition to considering the above evidence, the Department of Labor may consider its own experience with such cases and obtain general job market information as well.

NORMAL TRACK   If the RIR is not a feasible option, then the labor certification cannot be avoided. A labor certification is normally a three-step process. A labor certification may be approved where there is no U.S. worker who can do a certain job. There is a wide variety of jobs that can fit into this category, such as nanny, ethnic chef, or even software engineer.

Basically, the labor certification process is in some ways a "game" played between the applicant and local state agency as to the job description. The employer wants to make the job description fit the alien's credentials as closely as possible, while the SESA attempts to force a broader definition in order to include more U.S. workers.

RELIGIOUS WORKERS

The religious worker is *really* one of the employment-based categories, but is separated here since the documentation required is unique. It is available to certain qualified ministers and religious workers coming to the U.S. to practice their vocation. A labor certification is not required.

The religious worker program has been extended by Congress through September 30, 2003. Despite the substantial fraud in this category, Congress appears likely to keep extending the duration of this program.

ELIGIBILITY   The nonimmigrant R-1 visa for religious workers has different eligibility requirements than those required for the immigrant visa. For this nonimmigrant visa, one merely has to show that they were a member of the church organization for two years and have an offer of employment from the church. As for most nonimmigrant visas, one must demonstrate that he or she will return to their native country at the end of the visa period.

The requirements for the immigrant visa are more strict. The regulations are contained in 9 FAM 42.32(d)(1). Any person, including an alien, can file a petition for another alien who for the past two years has been a member of a religious denomination that has been a bona fide nonprofit, religious organization in the U.S. This person must also have been carrying on the vocation, professional work, or other work described below, continuously for the past two years, and seeks to enter the U.S. to work solely as one of the following:

- as a minister of that denomination;

- in a professional capacity in a religious vocation or occupation for that organization; or,

- in a religious vocation or occupation for the organization or its nonprofit affiliate.

The religious worker must have a full-time job offer by the religious organization. Along with the offer, there must be a demonstration that the alien's services are needed by the organization in the U.S. Such a demonstration requires an analysis of the staff size, congregation size, specific duties, prior experience of the alien, and prior staffing of a particular position. The organization must also demonstrate that it has sufficient funds to pay the salary.

INVESTORS 7

This category is actually a fifth preference under employment-based petitions. However, it deserves separate treatment for the purposes of this book because it has different qualifications.

QUALIFICATIONS

An alien investing a specified amount of capital *at risk* in a commercial enterprise may be eligible in this category. The enterprise must generate full-time employment for U.S. workers and permanent residence is granted conditionally.

The following criteria must be met for a new commercial enterprise:

- the investor will be engaged in a managerial or policy-making capacity;

- the investor must invest or be actively in the process of investing at least $1 million in the enterprise, or $500,000 if the investment is in a rural area or high unemployment area;

- the enterprise must benefit the U.S. economy and create full-time employment for at least ten U.S. citizen workers not related to the investor;

- the capital must have been obtained through a lawful means; and,

- the investment must be made in a new commercial enterprise (such as a new business), purchase and restructuring of an existing business, or expansion of a business so as to result in a 40% increase in net worth or number of employees.

It is important to realize that the entire investment need not be made at the outset. However, it usually must be made by the end of the two-year conditional period except if unusual circumstances exist.

Multiple investors may pool their money into an investment as long as each investor meets the above requirements. Investment funds may come from any legal source, including gifts and divorce settlements.

Investor petitions are highly technical and also involve substantial sums of money. Given these factors, one should definitely not proceed with such a petition without expert assistance.

GREEN CARD DIVERSITY LOTTERY 8

Once a year, normally in October, the Department of State holds a *green card diversity lottery* with 50,000 green cards up for grabs. This lottery has provided major relief to hundreds of thousands of immigrants.

The idea behind this give-away is to create diversity by offering green cards to people in countries that do not normally immigrate to the U.S. in large numbers. Therefore, those from countries that send more than 50,000 immigrants to the U.S. in the previous year are prevented from applying. In 2001, the barred countries were: Mexico, Canada, United Kingdom, India, Pakistan, South Korea, Philippines, Colombia, Dominican Republic, El Salvador, Haiti, and Jamaica.

The problem with the lottery is that it has became hugely popular in recent years. Something like 12 million applications were received last year. Considering that 100,000 acceptance letters are sent out and a couple of million applications are thrown out for not following instructions, the odds of winning are approximately 1 in 100. If a person is married and both file a separate application, the odds are cut in half to 1 in 50. If one were to file applications over a five year period, then the odds might drop to 1 in 20 over that time.

Since there is no fee to file the application and it is an easy application to complete, it is well worth doing each year. The most difficult part of the process might be to get the timing right. The thirty day window for the application changes slightly but recently has been starting in early October of each year. An application must be properly filed and received within the thirty day application period.

QUALIFICATIONS

Other than not being from one of the excluded countries, you easily *qualify* by being a high school graduate. If you have more than two years work experience within the past five years in an occupation or trade that requires at least two years of training or experience to perform, you also qualify. One also needs to meet all of the normal requirements for a green card such as having a valid affidavit of support. Both spouses may submit an application, and include any unmarried children under the age of 21.

The lottery application must be completed and received at the Department of State during the thirty day period set for the year. The application cannot be sent by an express service. It must be received by the Department of State by regular mail. If the mail in your country is not reliable, by all means use an address in the U.S. that is reliable. You may need to place a "c/o" line on the address to ensure proper delivery.

The application must be carefully completed and all instructions carefully followed. Any application not completed according to the instructions will be discarded. Be sure to do the following:

- include each member of the family in the application;
- personally sign the application, as the signature will be compared to that on the green card application;
- use correct photos: 2" x 2" with the person directly facing camera;
- tape (not staple) photos of each family member to the application; and,
- write sender and return address information on the envelope correctly.

In approximately April of the next year, winners begin to be notified. Although there are only approximately 50,000 visas (including dependents) available each year, the State Department mails out approximately 100,000 acceptance letters each year. The timing of visa processing for diversity visa winners coincides with the government fiscal year which starts on October 1 and ends on September 30 of each year. The visa numbers become available on October 1st and then expire on September 30 of the next year. Any person who has not *adjusted* by September 30, will simply not become a permanent resident, including derivative family members who are overseas. The visa numbers cease to exit after September 30 with no exceptions whatsoever.

Every year, there are people who did not complete their case by September 30 and are left out. Their only option is to sue the INS in federal court. But these cases are difficult to win. The INS is more careful now than it used to be about explaining the processing deadlines.

Since there are more diversity visa winners than visa numbers, a shortage of visa numbers may develop—especially towards the end of the government fiscal year. In August and September, the diversity visa numbers start to become scarce. While a single individual can probably always scrounge up a number, a family of five may not.

Acceptance letters are sent over several months period of time. Any lottery applicant who has not received a letter by June of the next year, will probably not be selected.

It is possible to qualify for permanent residence through a grant of *asylum*. One whose asylum application is granted, whether by the asylum office or by an immigration judge (IJ), is called an *asylee*. After one year in asylee status, that individual may apply for a green card. It will actually take a number of years thereafter to receive the green card due to the four year backlog in visa numbers for asylees.

REFUGEES

You may have heard of the term *refugee*. The use of this term is somewhat confusing. In common usage, a refugee is one was has had to escape their native country for whatever reason, usually war or natural disaster. In the immigration sense, a refugee is one who is granted specific status allowing that person to enter the U.S. and apply for adjustment after one year's residence in the U.S.

The legal definition of refugee according to the United Nations is one who has a "well-founded fear of persecution" and therefore cannot return to their country of citizenship. The persecution must be on account of one of five grounds:

- political opinion;
- race;

- religion;

- gender; or,

- social group.

An applicant for asylum must meet the same legal standard. The next section explains these concepts a little more.

Refugee Status versus Asylum

If one is outside the U.S., then one applies for refugee status at one of the several refugee processing centers. Asylum, on the other hand, is for one who is able to enter the U.S. either on a type of visa—such as a tourist or work visa, enter illegally through Canada or Mexico, or with a false passport.

There are numerous advantages to applying for asylum in the U.S. rather than refugee status abroad. The first advantage is no limit on the number of asylum cases that may be granted in the U.S. The limitation does come in when the *asylee* applies for a green card. However, one is allowed to live and work in the U.S. during this time as well as travel abroad, so the hardship is reduced. The problem for those applying for refugee status is there are relatively few visa numbers allowed per year—approximately 50,000. Even these numbers are fewer than it seems, since there are restrictions by region. This means that there may be a longer wait for a number, even if the case is granted.

The other principal advantage is that it is easier to get the case approved in the U.S. Consular officers at an embassy are not the easiest people to convince as to the genuineness of any case. (Neither are the asylum officers in the U.S.) However, the advantage is that a case that is not granted by the asylum office but rather is referred to the Immigration Court allows a second (and a better) opportunity to the asylum applicant to prove his or her case. The hearing process is about as fair a process that can be provided to an alien.

Those applying for asylum are often concerned about the effect their manner of entry will have on their application. While one generally does not earn points for making any type of unlawful entry, it is generally understood that one fleeing persecution will enter the U.S. in any possible way if their lives or well-being is at stake.

Those that enter the U.S. on a work visa, such as an H-1B, are sometimes viewed more suspiciously. It is more important to be able to explain the type of entry you made and why it was necessary than to enter in any particular way.

The post September 11 climate appears to have chilled the Asylum Office. The Chicago Asylum Office reports that their approval rate prior to September 11, 2001, was 33%. Six months after, the approval rate had dropped to 18%. It has since recovered to its normal levels. There are also fewer applications being filed on account of the one-year filing deadline.

QUALIFICATION

What exactly is meant by a "well-founded fear of persecution"? Numerous cases from the Board of Immigration Appeals have grappled with this question. A well-founded fear is broken down into two components. It means one whose claim is *subjectively genuine* and *objectively reasonable*. In the end, the Board has said that if there is a 10% chance of actual persecution happening in the native country, then asylum should be granted.

The conditions in certain countries render their citizens most likely to be granted asylum. The former Soviet block countries certainly dominated the asylum top ten charts before the break-up of the Soviet Union. Today, countries such as China, Iraq, Iran, and Ethiopia are probably the easiest countries to be granted asylum from. There are, however, many countries where repressive regimes and persecution are a way of life.

Of course, the present approval rate of the asylum offices, which is roughly 33%, does not give one much hope. However, one's chances before the immigration court, in most cities, are substantially greater. Chicago, in particular, has very principled and fair immigration judges who seek to find reasons why a case should be granted. This is in contrast to the asylum office, where the officers are really looking to find reasons why the case should be denied.

If you have a real case where you did have problems with the authorities in your country or with groups the government is unwilling or unable to control on account of one of the five protected grounds, then you have a good chance. The more documentation you have, the better your chance.

Documentation that is useful is anything that will prove any part of your claim:

- photos;

- medical records;

- police records; and,

- newspaper articles that mention you, your family or relatives.

You must go to the State Department human rights section and print out the *Country Report* for your country and at least be familiar with it.

The *Profile of Asylum Claims* and *Country Conditions* could also be referred to. It is much harder to find a copy. Plus, it was last printed in 1997. However, it is authoritative with the immigration court. If it is not helpful, do not include it in evidence. But if you are lucky enough to have it support your claim, it could be entered and the pertinent sections highlighted.

Check out the websites in Appendix C under human rights organizations. Find reports and articles that help your claim. Search for other supporting documents on the Internet. Your public library might help you do a search on Lexis Nexis™, which is a database containing all legal articles of the leading newspapers, journals and news wires around the world. You can search using words that might appear in a article. The information is out there, you just have to find it.

BENEFITS OF APPLYING FOR ASYLUM

OBTAINING
WORK
AUTHORIZATION

A major benefit of an asylum case is that the applicant becomes eligible for a work permit five months after the application is filed. While an application for asylum is pending, the applicant may apply for work authorization. There is no filing fee for the first application.

However, to discourage asylum filings to only obtain work authorization, the first application for work authorization may only be filed 150 days after the asylum application itself is filed. And this is if there have not been any delays in the process caused by the alien.

Congress has mandated that an asylum applicant have both his asylum interview and his hearing before the immigration judge within six months after filing. This is a tough haul just to get work authorization. It has proven effective in decreasing the number of frivolous applications and reducing the burden on the system.

See Chapter 13 to apply for work authorization five months after filing the asylum application.

DELAYING
DEPORTATION

If one is placed into proceedings, even a weak asylum case may be helpful simply as a means to delay deportation. It will take perhaps one year for the individual hearing date, two or more years for an appeal to the BIA, and then another year for the appeal to one of the federal circuit courts.

During the four year period, the alien can hope that a family-based or employment-based petition becomes approved. If the asylum case is still pending with any court, then *a motion to remand* may be filed, which will bring the case back to the immigration judge for a decision on the adjustment application. Finally, one can always hope that in the meantime an *amnesty* or other immigration benefit will be enacted by Congress.

STOPPING ACCRUAL OF UNLAWFUL PRESENCE

An alien begins to *accrue unlawful presence* once their nonimmigrant visa expires or once they enter the U.S. without inspection. Accrual of six months of unlawful presence will prevent that person from re-entering the U.S. for three years. One year of unlawful presence serves as a ten-year bar. These bars go into effect only if the person departs the U.S. and then seeks to re-enter.

One of the several exceptions to accruing unlawful presence is if the alien has pending a *bona fide* asylum application. It does not matter whether the application is eventually denied. The fact that it is "pending" stops the accrual of unlawful presence.

APPLYING FOR FAMILY MEMBERS

One who within the past two years was granted asylum or who was admitted to the U.S. as a refugee may apply for a family member. Only the principal individual who was granted asylum or refugee status may apply for family members.

Such a person may apply for his or her spouse or unmarried child under 21 years of age. He or she must follow these rules:

- He or she may apply for a family member whether in U.S. or not.

- The relationship must have existed on the date of asylum approval or the date the applicant was admitted to the U.S. as a refugee and continues to exist as such at the time of filing.

- Both husband and wife must have been physically present at the marriage ceremony.

- A child may be only conceived on the date of asylum approval or admission to U.S. as refugee.

- An applicant may apply for stepchildren.

- An applicant may apply for adopted child. (Submit adoption decree and proof of two years residence with child.)

- Persons granted *derivative status* may not apply for their family members.

APPLYING FOR PERMANENT RESIDENCE

One year after the grant of asylum, an asylee may apply for adjustment of status. All asylee-based adjustment applications are filed at the Nebraska Service Center in Lincoln, Nebraska.

There is currently a long wait for visa numbers. As Congress has ordered that only 10,000 people may adjust status each year on account of being granted asylum (including dependent family members) there is a long waiting period. The priority date for a visa is the date of filing.

NOTE: *The grant of adjustment will be slightly backdated from the actual date the case is processed.*

REFUGEE FILING

The filing for a refugee application is very similar as for an asylee application. Refugees may also apply for adjustment one year after their entry. There is no filing fee for the refugee adjustment application or for fingerprints. The affidavit of support form is not required.

NOTE: *The official date of adjustment of status is backdated to the date of original entry into the U.S.*

AMNESTIES 10

Amnesties are not a frequent occurance in the U.S. as they are fraught with numerous problems. For one thing, they cause a tremendous burden on the system in terms of a huge number of applications in a very short period of time. The system is already running at capacity and subject to huge backlogs.

Another problem is fraud. An amnesty usually means persons qualify by proving residency in the U.S. prior to a certain distant date. With the availability of computers and laser printers, it is too easy to falsify documents.

Amnesties also reward those who have violated immigration laws and not those who are waiting patiently in their home country for a visa number.

It used to be thought that the amnesty might solve the problem of illegal immigrants. However, it is now realized that it only *exacerbates* illegal immigration by encouraging future illegal aliens.

RECENT "AMNESTY"

The LIFE Act passed on December 20, 2000, is referred to by some as a mini-amnesty. It allowed those who were the beneficiary of an I-130 petition or who filed a labor certification by April 30, 2001, to be eligible to adjust status in the future on that petition or any other petition for which they might be eligible. It does not matter if the petition is later approved or not, so long as it was approvable when filed. The applicant needs to preserve proof that he was present in the U.S. on the day that the statute was passed, December 20, 2000.

Congress appears about to pass an extension of Section 245(i) that may not prove helpful to many people. It requires that the family relationship take place prior to August 15, 2001. For a marriage case, this means the marriage had to have taken place by that time. This will be disheartening to many couples who would have married had they known there might be a deadline. Some states recognize a common law marriage. In these states, it may be possible to claim an earlier official marriage date by qualifying through the *common law marriage* criteria.

NOTE: *You must talk to a domestic relations attorney to determine if you can qualify through this common law marriage criteria.*

"Late Amnesty" Class Members

Approximately 400,000 *late amnesty* class members had a deadline of May 31, 2002, to file an application for adjustment of status. These are individuals who claim to have resided in the U.S. before 1982, but were improperly denied an opportunity by the INS to file for the 1986 amnesty announced by President Reagan by the amnesty's 1988 deadline because they had traveled abroad. These individuals later registered because of one of the three class action lawsuits filed against the Department of Justice. Many class members have been living in "immigration limbo" with work authorization since 1990. The LIFE Act gave class members one last chance to file for a green card if they can prove they entered the U.S. prior to 1982 and resided continuously in the U.S. through May 1988.

NOTE: *Because the deadline to file has past, any further discussion as of this writing is beyond the scope of this book.*

CANCELLATION OF REMOVAL: 10 YEARS IN THE U.S.

One may qualify for permanent residence if he or she has lived in the U.S. for the past ten years and meet other criteria. This type of relief is only available to those who are in *removal proceedings* before the immigration court. This can be frustrating to someone who feels he or she has a strong case and want to be placed in proceedings. Ironically, those that wish to be placed in proceedings will not receive the cooperation of the INS.

As described earlier, removal proceedings are initiated when the INS serves a document called a *Notice to Appear*. This document lists certain factual allegations and what are called the *grounds of removability*. These are the sections of the Immigration and Nationality Act that make you removable. Often, the ground is simply overstaying your nonimmigrant visa or entering the U.S. without inspection.

QUALIFICATION

To qualify for cancellation of removal, one must demonstrate the following grounds to an immigration judge:

1. ten years presence in the U.S. prior to the service of the *Notice to Appear*;

2. you have been a person of good moral character throughout this period;

3. you have not been convicted of a criminal offense in sections 212(a)(2), 237(a)(2) or 237(a)(3) of the INA (Immigration and

Nationality Act). These are a long list of crimes including multiple misdemeanor offenses such as retail theft, drug possession and the majority of felony offenses; and,

4. removal would result in exceptional and extremely unusual hardship to a U.S. citizen or lawful permanent resident spouse, parent, or child.

These cases are very difficult to win. Some immigration judges may only grant three out of every fifty cancellation cases. (In each of those cases, there is sometimes a U.S. citizen child who had a birth defect requiring treatment or therapy only available in the U.S.)

LIVING
CONTINUOUSLY
IN THE U.S.

The first part of the case is to prove you entered the U.S. at least ten years ago and lived continuously in the U.S. You may have left the U.S., but for no more than three months at a time or six months in total. It can be difficult to prove continuous presence in the U.S. if one does not have a social security number and cannot get accounts in his or her name. Also, many people do not keep records going back ten years especially when they might be moving frequently.

HARDSHIP

The fourth ground in particular, *exceptional and extremely unusual hardship*, is what the case will be fought over. As you can imagine, it is very difficult to establish an exceptional and extremely unusual hardship.

These are the factors that courts look at to prove hardship:
- age of the qualifying family member;
- family ties in the U.S. and abroad;
- length of residency in the U.S.;
- conditions of health requiring treatment in the U.S.;
- economic hardship;
- acculturation; and,
- balance of the equities.

Essentially, those that create a life for themselves in the U.S. by marrying, having children, or starting a business, are the ones who are more likely to win this case. Those that were cautious, and waited to have status will not have as much ammunition in trying to prove a cancellation case.

To demonstrate continuous physical presence provide:
- leases;
- mortgages or property deeds;
- utility bills;
- licenses;
- purchase receipts or letters from companies;
- correspondence;
- documentation issued by governmental or other authority;
- birth records;
- hospital or medical records;
- church records;
- school records;
- employment records;
- letter from employer;
- W-2 forms;
- tax returns;
- bank records;
- personal checks with cancellation stamps;
- credit card statements;
- INS documents such as work permits; or,
- insurance policies.

To demonstrate good moral character provide:
- police records from each jurisdiction where you resided in the past ten years;
- affidavits of two U.S. citizen persons attesting to good character;
- an affidavit or letter from your current employer; or,
- evidence of tax payments.

To prove hardship provide:
- an affidavit of an expert witness;

- medical records, where relevant;

- school records of children;

- records of participation in community organizations or a church (or letter from minister or officer of organization);

- records of volunteer work; or,

- if self-employed, records showing the number of people employed.

To prove when you entered the U.S. provide:
- a passport with entry stamp;

- form I-94 (arrival-departure record);

- nonimmigrant visa issued;

- form I-20 (certificate of eligibility for student status); or,

- form IAP-66 (certificate of eligibility for exchange visitor status).

Other useful documents are court conviction records and proof of child support payments.

Who Obtains Residence

Bear in mind, as difficult as this case is, only the applicant will obtain permanent residence. The applicant's spouse and foreign born children, unless they are in proceedings themselves, will not also obtain status from the judge. They will have to be applied for by the legal permanent resident, which may take about five years, and that is if the beneficiaries are eligible to adjust under Section 245(i).

BATTERED
SPOUSE OR
CHILD

There is a special rule that applies to a battered spouse or child. The immigration judge may grant cancellation of removal if a person has been battered or subjected to extreme cruelty in the U.S. by a spouse or parent who is a U.S. citizen or lawful permanent resident, has been present in the U.S. for at least three years, and the person is of *good moral character*.

MISCELLANEOUS CATEGORIES 12

These categories stand on their own and usually have unique circumstances. It is beyond the scope of this book to give any detail on how to file for them. An attorney should be consulted for assistance.

U.S. CITIZEN GRANDPARENT: TRANSMITTED CITIZENSHIP

If someone has a grandparent who is a U.S. citizen, then that person may be able to obtain citizenship through the parent who may unknowingly be a U.S. citizen. These laws, contained in Section 301 of the INA, are complex and vary with the date of birth of the parent.

NOTE: *Consult an immigration attorney to confirm a particular situation.*

PRIVATE BILLS

A *private bill* is an option of final and last resort. It involves having a member of Congress sponsor an individual to become a permanent resident. Or, more realistically, remove a bar to permanent residence such as a criminal record. A private bill is one that affects only one individual or a small group of people. (A *public bill* affects the public generally.)

In a recent session of Congress, fourteen private bills were introduced and two passed. It is not a realistic option in most cases. However, with a combination of the right contacts, facts, and marketing ability, it is worth a try.

A private bill must be approved by the House Judiciary Committee's Subcommittee on Immigration, and Claims and by the Senate Judiciary Committee's Immigration Subcommittee before going to each respective chamber for a *floor vote*. Clearly, the passage of a private bill is long and difficult road at best.

The House subcommittee has recently put together a very helpful guide to the private bill process at:

http://www.house.gov/judiciary/privimm.pdf.

This guide describes the criteria used by the subcommittee in considering a bill. The Senate also published a set of rules in 1993 which are not available on the Internet but can be ordered at:

www.senate.gov.

CUBANS

Any native or citizen of Cuba who was admitted or paroled into the U.S. after 1958 may apply for adjustment of status. He or she must have been physically present in the U.S. for one year.

S "SNITCH" VISA

The S visa category allows for those that assist the INS in an investigation to be given nonimmigrant status. They can then later apply for adjustment of status. While this visa is often promised by agents of the INS, it is rarely delivered on. The S visa is also known as the *snitch* visa.

NOTE: *Any promise to be petitioned for by an INS officer should be put in writing.*

T AND U VISAS

The new T and U nonimmigrant visa categories are for victims of smuggling or people-trafficking and who can show they would suffer extreme hardship if removed from the U.S. After three years in this status, such a person may apply for adjustment of status.

REGISTRY

The *registry* is rarely used anymore. Nonetheless, anyone residing in the U.S. since before 1972 may be admitted as permanent resident if he or she can show good moral character. However, this provision would only seem to apply to those that missed the 1986 amnesty.

Section 3:

The Permanent Residence Application Process

Work and Travel While Adjustment is Pending

13

Two important interim benefits are available to those who have an adjustment of status application pending. These are to obtain work authorization and obtain permission to reenter the U.S. after travel outside the U.S.

Work Permit

An adjustment or asylum applicant may apply for a work permit while his or her application is pending. A *work permit* allows an alien to be lawfully employed to the same extent as a U.S. citizen. In fact, it is a violation of federal law for an employer to discriminate against an individual because they only have a work permit instead of a green card or a naturalization certificate.

An asylum applicant may file for a work permit if their asylum application has been pending more than 150 days. However, if the asylum applicant has requested a continuance from either the asylum office or the immigration court during the 150 day period, they may not qualify until the "clock" starts again and 150 days are accumulated.

LOCAL INS
OFFICE FILING

Whether the work permit is applied for at the local INS office or a service center depends on the basis for the work permit. For family-based or diversity visa-based adjustment applications, the work permit application is filed at a local INS office. For these applications, a complete filing consists simply of the following three items:

- Form I-765;

- filing fee of $120; and,

- a copy of the adjustment receipt notice.

The procedure for filing a work permit at a local INS office varies. In most cities, the application is mailed rather than filed in person. Sometime after filing, a scheduling notice will be mailed to the applicant. A state-issued identification card or passport and the original receipt notice for the underlying adjustment application should be brought to the work permit appointment.

SERVICE CENTER
FILING

For the following categories, the work permit application is mailed to the appropriate service center:

- employment-based adjustment applications;

- investor based adjustment applications;

- asylees or asylee based adjustment applications; and,

- refugees or refugee based adjustment applications.

Employment and investor-based work permit applications are mailed to the service center having jurisdiction over the particular state. On the other hand, all asylee and refugee-based work permit applications are filed at the Nebraska Service Center. There is no filing fee for the initial asylee or refugee based work permit application.

For the above categories, a work permit application consists of the I-765 form and several supporting documents. The following list contains all supporting documents to include with the work permit application:

- Form I-765;

- filing fee of $120;

- 2 green card style photos;

- a copy of adjustment receipt notice or status of asylum application (eg. interview notice, court notice);

- a clear copy of a current work permit showing picture; and,

- a clear copy of a state issued drivers license or I.D. or identification page of passport showing picture.

PROCESSING   Regardless of where the work permit application is filed, the INS is supposed to process it within 90 days. In the meantime, an individual with a receipt notice for a work permit application and a social security number, is immediately authorized to work during this 90-day period.

If the work permit is not received within 90 days, regulations permit an individual to obtain a temporary work document at their local INS office. Such persons should walk into their local office with their original work permit filing receipt notice or cancelled check and a letter from their employer stating they require immediate proof of work eligibility.

OBTAINING A SOCIAL SECURITY NUMBER

In addition to a work permit, one must also have a social security number to be employed. The Social Security Administration, which is entirely separate from the INS, issues social security numbers.

An alien with an adjustment application pending is entitled to a social security number once he or she obtains a work permit. This card takes approximately one week to arrive in the mail. The card will be marked "Not valid for work except with INS authorization". After adjustment of status to a permanent resident, a new card may be obtained without this designation.

TRAVEL PERMISSION: ADVANCE PAROLE

In order to depart the U.S. during the time an adjustment application is pending, one must first obtain prior permission of the INS. This document is called *advance parole*. Upon re-entry into the U.S., one presents this document in order to re-enter the U.S. and resume the adjustment of status application.

In the past, there were restrictions that there be a personal emergency or business reasons to necessitate the granting of advance parole. Currently, any valid reason to travel is sufficient. The only restriction to obtaining advance parole, is that one not have accumulated more than six months of unlawful presence in the U.S. prior to filing the adjustment application. *Unlawful presence* is time spent *out of status* after April 1, 1997.

NOTE: *Even if one obtains advance parole and re-enters the U.S. after the unlawful presence, they could be prevented at the interview from obtaining permanent residence status.*

The following is a fully documented application for advance parole (permission to travel or reenter U.S.):

- Form I-131;

- filing fee of $110;

- 2 green card style photos;

- copy of drivers license or state I.D. or identification page of passport;

- Form I-485 receipt and a copy of the receipt letter;

- Form I-94 arrival-departure document;

- proof of current status in the U.S.:

  - Form I-797 approval notice indicating current status;

  - passport of last entry;

  - Form I-20 if here on the F-1 visa;

  - Form IAP-66 for a J-1 visa;

  - previous advance parole documents; and,
- supporting letter such as medical emergency, wedding invitation, airline tickets, or itinerary.

To find out more about some of the support and documentation required, read Chapter 14. Many are explained there.

NOTE: *If one has a student visa marked "duration of status" (D/S), he or she does not acquire unlawful presence until an INS officer or Immigration Judge finds a status violation. Therefore, such persons are eligible for advance parole when applying for adjustment.*

REQUIRED FORMS AND INSTRUCTIONS 14

Each category of immigrants (and nonimmigrants) has its own specific required forms and documents. Carefully read the section in this chapter that applies to you to get you started with the proper requirements.

IMMEDIATE RELATIVES

You may file the I-130 alien relative petition with a local INS office *along with* the I-485 adjustment of status application, if the relative is already in the U.S. and eligible to adjust in the U.S. Filing these together is called a *onestop application*. The different purposes of the I-130 petition and I-485 form are important to understand. The I-130 petition establishes the petitioner's relationship to the alien relative. It is not an application for a green card by itself, but is the first step. The I-485 form, on the other hand, is filed by the alien relative on his own behalf and relates only to his own eligibility for permanent residence.

Those alien relatives, such as married children, who fall into a preference category will first file only the I-130 petition with a service center. After they receive a visa number, they will file the I-485 adjustment application along with the I-130 approval notice with the local INS office. These procedures will be explained in detail later in this chapter.

ONESTOP
ADJUSTMENT

A onestop adjustment of status application packet consists of numerous forms and supporting documents. However, the required forms and documents vary slightly by case. The following outline is a useful checklist of all of the possible forms and documents. A more detailed explanation follows the outline.

The following are required for filing the onestop adjustment:

- Form I-130 alien relative petition and supporting documents or approval notice;

- filing fee of $130;

- Form I-485 adjustment application (see page 81 for instructions for filling it in);

- filing fee depends on age (see chart in Appendix D);

- fingerprint fee of $50;

- Form G-325A biographic information for applicant (see page 84 for more information on this form); and,

- 2 green card style photos.

The following are also mandatory items. You should either file these initially, which is preferable, or bring them to the interview:

- Form I-485 Supplement OR proof of legal entry such as copies of visa page in passport, I-94s and relevant approval notices or copy of Canadian citizenship;

- a copy of applicant's birth certificate and translation;

- Form I-693 medical form and vaccination sheet in sealed envelope;

- Form I-864 affidavit of support with documentation; and,

- a job letter.

The following may be required in some cases:

- proof of eligibility under Section 245(i);

- physical presence in the U.S. on December 20, 2000;

- Form I-601 waiver of inadmissibility and supporting documents;

- cable request for overseas dependents;

- marriage certificate;

- divorce decrees or termination of previous marriages;

- birth certificates of beneficiary's children; and,

- documents related to convictions or other special circumstances.

How to file. To properly file the onestop application, follow these suggestions:

- Make a copy of all documents and keep them in a safe place.

- Write the name and "A" number or date of birth in pencil on the back of the photos.

- Attach a money order or cashier's check made out to "INS".

- Make sure the name of the applicant is on check.

- If the case requires special processing, such as expedited processing, place a colored sheet of paper on top of the application and state clearly the reason.

- Confirm the correct address. It is not the same address as the INS office. There is typically a specific post office box for an adjustment application. While an application sent to the local address might be forwarded, this is a risky proposition.

- If a deadline needs to be met, file using express mail through the U.S. Post Office. They deliver to post office boxes unlike Federal Express. If no deadline is involved, file using regular mail.

- Any address changes must be sent by certified mail, return receipt requested, since such requests may not be processed by the INS and will result in a closed case.

I-130 PETITION   An I-130 petition filing requires the following:

- Form I-130 (see instructions next);

- filing fee of $130;

- Form G-325A for husband;

- Form G-325A for wife;

- 1 green card style photo for both husband and wife;

- proof of petitioner's U.S. citizenship (birth certificate, if born in U.S.; naturalization certificate; certificate of citizenship; or, U.S. passport identification page);

- marriage certificate if the father is the petitioner;

- documentation of legal termination of any previous marriages; and,

- documentation as to a name change on a supporting document (marriage certificate; adoption decree; or, court order).

The above listing consists of the entire I-130 packet that will be filed with the local INS office. The I-130 form itself must be carefully completed. Fill it in as follows:

☞ Part A. Relationship: Fill in the correct category of the alien relative being applied for. If the wrong box is checked, the approval notice may reflect the wrong relationship.

☞ Part B. Information about you. This means the petitioner and his or her personal information. Enter your name as it is currently being used. If a different name is on an official document such as the naturalization certificate or birth certificate, enter this name in response to Question 7. Also include in Question 7, all other names used, such as married or maiden names.

☞ Question 10 asks for the alien registration number. It may be found on the naturalization certificate just below the certificate number or on the green card if the petitioner is a permanent resident.

☛ Question 13 may be a little confusing. A petitioner who obtained U.S. citizenship through naturalization will check the "Naturalization" box and enter the certificate number, and date and place of issue. The "Parents" box is used for those who have a citizenship certificate rather than a naturalization certificate. Such persons were never permanent residents but were later determined to be U.S. citizens at birth.

☛ Part C. Information about your alien relative. This means the person being applied for and his or her personal information. If the alien relative is abroad, enter his or her mailing address as opposed to physical address.

☛ Questions 9 and 10 ask for social security and alien registration numbers. Aliens may not have either number in which case these questions should be marked "N/A".

☛ Question 13 asks whether the alien relative is presently in the U.S. If so, Question 14 seeks the status of the relative upon entry. Typically, this will be as B-2 visitor or F-1 student. If the relative entered illegally across the border, then the correct answer is EWI. The I-94 number is found on the white I-94 card issued at the point of entry. If this card is lost, so indicate.

☛ Question 15 asks for employment information. Be careful. Working without INS authorization may prevent future adjustment of status.

☛ Question 16 asks whether the relative is in proceedings. If the answer is yes, the service center will ask for documents concerning the type and outcome of the proceedings.

☛ Question 16 also asks that the spouse or children of the alien relative be listed. It is particularly important that any children of the relative be listed especially if they will also be seeking permanent residence status.

☞ Question 21 should be answered carefully. If a person has any intent of filing in the U.S., then mark the second box. If the first box is marked, the file will be transferred to an embassy or consulate who will continue processing the case. They will look to cancel the visa petition if the beneficiary does not continue with permanent residence processing within one year. Marking the second box will allow the beneficiary to wait as long as necessary in the U.S. before applying. For example, a person may have to wait for an extension of Section 245(i) before applying. (One can always apply later at the embassy by filing form I-824 with the appropriate service center, although this may cause a delay of several months.)

☞ Part D. Other Information. Question 1 asks whether other I-130 petitions are being filed for other relatives at this time. For example, are both parents or more than one child being applied for. If so, write down their names and relationship.

☞ Question 2 asks whether the petitioner has previously filed for any other relative. If so, write in the information. For example, you might put down: "John Smith; son; filed on 3/15/1990 at Nebraska Service Center; petition was approved on 10/15/1990."

☞ Finally, the petitioning relative signs where indicated on the bottom of the second page.

NOTE: *The other required form is the G-325A biographic information form. Both the husband and wife complete this form.*

After the I-130 petition is complete and the above documents assembled, refer to page 78 for a description of how and where to file the I-130 petition.

If the I-130 was filed before April 30, 2001 without the I-485, then, the applicant is still eligible to file for adjustment. However, he or she will then have to file the I-485 Supplement and pay the $1000 fee. Fill in the Supplement as follows:

☞ Part 1. Information about applicant: This means the applicant and his or her personal information. Fill in all required information as on the I-485 application.

☞ Part 2. Basis for Eligibility: For each question, check the appropriate answer and follow specific instructions. For question 1, refer to part 2 of the I-485 form. In response to question 4, those that entered the U.S. illegally will check the box beside "without inspection". Those that entered on a tourist visa will mark the last box and write in "B-2" on the space provided. (This form is to be filed and paid for only if specifically instructed to do so at the end of page two of the form.)

☞ Part 3. Signature. The applicant signs where indicated.

I-485   The other important form is the I-485. This is the actual adjustment of status application. See page 105 for additional information on adjusting status. It should be carefully completed as follows:

☞ Part 1. Information about you: This means the applicant and his or her personal information. Fill in all required information. Many applicants may not have a social security number or alien registration number in which case respond to these questions "N/A".

The I-94 number is found on the white I-94 card issued at the point of entry. If this card is lost, so indicate. If the alien crossed the border illegally, mark "N/A".

☞ The last questions asks for the current status of the applicant. Typically, this will be as B-2 visitor or F-1 student. If the relative entered illegally across the border, then the correct response is EWI. If the person has overstayed a visa, write in "B-2 overstay".

☞ Part 2. Application Type: Check the box that applies to the type of case. For example, if the applicant is being applied for by an immediate relative check box a. If the applicant was selected in the diversity visa lottery, check box h. and write in "Diversity Visa Selection 2003".

☛ Part 3. Processing Information: Enter the specific background information requested. If the applicant did not make a lawful entry, there is no I-94, border inspection or visa. Therefore, enter "N/A" in response to these questions.

☛ Section B asks for the names of all relatives. The applicant should fill in the names of any spouse and all children regardless of status.

☛ Section C asks for the names of organizations of which the applicant has been a member. Military service in the U.S. or in a foreign country is probably most important and should be listed. Asylum applicants should also maintain consistency with their asylum claim.

☛ Page 3 has a list of questions that must be answered "yes" or "no". If any box is marked "yes", it may be necessary to consult with an attorney.

The most important of these is question 1 regarding the applicant's criminal record. If the applicant has ever been arrested, let alone charged or convicted, it must be disclosed here. Check the "yes" box and write in something like "Arrested 2/20/02 in Chicago, Illinois for retail theft; charge dismissed by Circuit Court of Cook County on 4/15/01."

☛ Part 4. Signature. The applicant signs where indicated.

The filing fee is either $255 if the applicant is 14 years of age over and $160 if under. Likewise, those 14 or over require fingerprints and will pay the $50 fingerprint fee. A completed G-325A form is required for all applicants 14 years of age or over.

Include two green card style photos no matter what the applicant's age.

This list describes the minimum documents required for filing the adjustment packet. The remaining items may be brought to the adjustment interview or filed with the initial packet.

Where to file. Now that the I-130 is completed and the correct supporting documents obtained (see Chapter 15), it can be filed. The question now is where to file it. If the parent or child seeking to immigrate is eligible to adjust in the U.S. as mentioned earlier, then file the I-130 along with the I-485 at the local INS office.

The following persons will file the I-130 with a service center, rather than the local INS office:

- preference category relatives;
- immediate relatives residing outside the U.S.;
- immediate relatives in the U.S. but ineligible to apply for adjustment; or,
- immediate relatives who are in deportation proceedings.

Be sure to make a copy of the petition and supporting documents and keep them in a safe place. Also attach the correct filing fee of $130 as a money order or cashier's check made out to "INS". Make sure the name of the petitioner is on the check and confirm the correct address of the service center.

NOTE: *There is typically a specific post office box for an I-130 petition. If you are close to a deadline, use express mail to the street address of the service center and place the P.O. Box on label.*

Once the petition is approved, it will be sent to the National Visa Center who will hold the file until a visa number is available. They will then forward the file to the appropriate embassy or consulate.

NOTE: *Most often, the I-130 and I-485 are filed simultaneously in what is called a* onestop *application.*

SPOUSES

A U.S. citizen may apply for an alien spouse for whom there is no wait for a visa number. The first stage is the I-130 petition which depending on certain circumstances may or may not be filed with the adjustment of status packet. This first section deals with preparing the I-130 petition.

An I-130 petition filing requires the items listed on page 78. The items listed consist of the entire I-130 packet that will be filed. The I-130 form itself must be carefully completed. Page 78 contains detailed instructions on how to do so.

G 325A   The other required form is the G-325A biographic information form. This form is completed by both the husband and wife.

The documents listed in Chapter 4 for proving a *bona fide marriage* do not need to be filed with the I-130 petition if the I-130 is filed locally. They may be gathered while the application is pending and brought to the interview. However, if the I-130 is to be filed with a service center, there hopefully will not be an interview. In that instance only should you gather sufficient evidence and file it with the I-130 petition.

If both spouses are not at the interview, the application will be denied. It is better to ask that the interview be rescheduled to allow time to work out the problem. This should be done well before the interview in writing. Any rescheduling letter must be sent by certified mail with a return receipt. Then if the case is closed out by the INS, you will have proof of mailing.

If the U.S. citizen spouse dies before the interview, then it may be possible to self-petition. There is a requirement that the marriage have lasted longer than two years prior to the death of the spouse. (The I-360 should be filed first with the service center, but this is beyond the scope of this book.) See Chapters 4 and 17 for more information about the interview.

Where to file. File the I-130 petition and the G325A form with a service center or a local INS office.

CONDITIONAL
PERMANENT
RESIDENT AND
REMOVING
CONDITIONS

The following documents are filed if the alien spouse is a conditional resident as described in Chapter 4:

- Form I-751;

- filing fee of $145;

- 2 green card style photos;

- copy of conditional green card;

- joint tax returns;

- apartment lease or joint deed;

- substantial evidence as to bona fide marriage—see page 18; and,

- court dispositions if arrested after conditional adjustment.

I-751

The conditional resident must file form I-751 to remove conditions within the 90 day period prior to the expiration date on the conditional green card.

The following constitutes a complete I-751 filing:

- Form I-751;

- filing fee of $145;

- two green card style photos;

- a copy of the conditional green card;

- joint tax returns;

- an apartment lease or joint deed;

- substantial evidence as to a bona fide marriage—see page 18; and,

- any court dispositions if arrested after conditional adjustment.

The filing fee of $145, in the form of a money order, should be attached to the completed I-751 form, along with two green card style photos. On the back of the photos the person's name and number should be written in pencil or with a felt pen. A photocopy of the green card must be submitted. The most important part of the filing is the evidence that the marriage was bona fide. As many of the documents listed on page 18 should be attached to establish beyond any doubt that the marriage is real.

If sufficient documents to prove a bona fide marriage are submitted, then the petition will be approved by the service center. Otherwise, the petition will be forwarded to the local INS office for an interview.

Where to file. The I-751 packet is filed with the service center responsible for your jurisdiction. You will receive a receipt notice within several weeks, which will serve to extend your permanent residence status and provide evidence of employment authorization.

Even though the conditional green card stamp in your passport may have expired, you do not need to get a renewal stamp placed in your passport. You may simply travel on your now expired conditional green card, your passport, and the original receipt notice.

NOTE: *If you get divorced after being granted adjustment but before filing the I-751, there is no deadline for filing the I-751. However, your file will certainly be transferred to the local INS office for interview.*

Grounds for filing. There are two grounds for filing the I-751. The first is that the marriage was entered into in good faith and the second is extreme hardship. However, it is apparently very rare to proceed on the second standard only. The INS officer may not even know how to proceed. Be prepared to show that this second standard exists if you wish to rely upon it.

In this instance, it is important to carefully prepare for the interview. You will need fairly extensive documentation of the bona fide marriage. These cases are scrutinized carefully by the INS. It is not unusual for the officer to call the former spouse to get his or her side of the story. This is problematic because the former spouse may resent that the alien received status through them.

The interview. Hopefully, the case will be approved at the interview. If the case is approved, the officer should stamp your passport at the interview.

If the case is not approved at the interview, a Request For Evidence (RFE) will be issued asking that certain documents be submitted within a time period. Sometimes the RFE is used to prevent making a decision at the interview.

Care must be taken at the interview to ensure prompt handling of the case by the officer. Here are some tips to help you protect yourself:

- get the name of the officer;

- tell the officer how long it will take to submit documents;

- ask how long it will take after submission of the documents to obtain a decision. Even though they may not stick to it, it is helpful to be able to say to the officer later or to the supervisor what time frame was promised;

- if the documents cannot be obtained, ask what will happen to the case;

- ask the officer how to follow up if you do not hear after 30 or 60 days (get their phone number and extension);

- if you think you have supplied enough information and the officer is not specific about why the case is not being approved, ask to see the supervisor; and,

- take detailed notes after the interview as to what was asked and what the answer was.

NOTE: *If your I-751 application is pending, and it has been at least two years nine months since becoming a lawful permanent resident, you may still file a citizenship application. The INS will schedule your interview with an officer who is familiar with adjudicating both citizenship and the I-751 petitions. At the time of the interview on the N-400, bring your U.S. citizen spouse and all necessary documents in order to complete the I-751 interview.*

If it is denied, the I-751 application is reviewable in immigration court by an immigration judge. There may be a substantial delay before being placed in proceedings. Many INS offices have a large room full of files to be processed for immigration court. However, once in court, the judge will review the entire application and take testimony from the alien and any witnesses. In many ways, it may be a much fairer proceeding than the interview at the INS. As in any proceeding before the immigration court, it will require the services of an immigration attorney.

FAMILY-BASED PREFERENCE CATEGORIES

If the relative being applied for is in a *preference visa category*, then the I-130 is first filed with the appropriate service center, the necessary time period waited (see below), then the I-485 is filed at the local INS office. A copy of the I-130 approval notice will be included with the I-485 filing.

FIRST
PREFERENCE

The required documents for the *first preference* are similar to those for immediate relatives:

- Form I-130 alien relative petition;

- filing fee of $130;

- proof of petitioner's U.S. citizenship(birth certificate if born in the U.S; naturalization certificate; certificate of citizenship; or, U.S. passport identification page.);

- birth certificate of the adult child showing the name of the petitioner and child. If the father is the petitioner, his marriage certificate;

- legal termination of any previous marriage of father, if he is the petitioner; and,

- evidence of legal name change, if necessary (marriage certificate; adoption decree; or,court order).

The above listing consists of the entire I-130 packet that will be filed. The I-130 petition must be completed (see page 78). It then must be supported by several documents. First, the U.S. citizen must establish his or her citizenship by one of the documents indicated above. The birth certificate of the adult child must be filed to establish the qualifying relationship. This birth certificate must show the name of the parent who is filing the petition. If the father is petitioning, then the father's marriage certificate must also be provided. Finally, if any name on a supporting document has changed, a legal document to evidence the name change is required.

Page 78 contains detailed instructions on completing the I-130 petition. This form should be carefully filled out and signed. After the I-130 petition is filled in and the above documents assembled, refer to page 78 for a description of how and where to file the I-130 petition packet.

SECOND PREFERENCE

The required documents for the *second preference* include the I-130 petition. The I-130 petition is prepared in a similar fashion as described previously for a U.S. citizen spouse (see page 78).

The I-130 petition is filed with a service center, as are preference petitions. See page 78 for detailed instructions on completing the I-130 petition. This form should be carefully filled out and signed.

After the I-130 petition is filled in and the above documents assembled, refer to page 78 for a description of how and where to file the I-130 petition packet. Be sure you have all documents listed in Chapter 4 included in the packet.

THIRD PREFERENCE

The required documents for the *third preference* are listed on page 78. Detailed instructions on completing the I-130 petition are also found on that page. This form should be carefully filled out and signed.

After the I-130 petition is filled in and the documents assembled, refer to page 78 for a description of how and where to file the I-130 petition packet.

FOURTH
PREFERENCE

A similar I-130 packet that is filled for the other three preferences must be filed for the fourth preference:

● Form I-130 alien relative petition;

● filing fee of $130;

● proof of petitioner's U.S. citizenship (birth certificate, if born in U.S.; naturalization certificate; certificate of citizenship; or, U.S. passport identification page.);

● birth certificate of petitioner and of brother or sister showing names of both parents;

● birth certificate of brother or sister showing names of both parents. If they have different mothers, the supply a marriage certificate of father to both mothers and also legal termination of any previous of the fathers' previous marriages; and,

● evidence of legal name change, if necessary (marriage certificate; adoption decree; or, court order).

The I-130 petition must be completed (see page 78). It then must be supported by several documents described in the above outline. First, the U.S. citizen sibling must establish their citizenship by one of the documents indicated. The birth certificate of the U.S. citizen petitioner and that of the brother or sister must be filed to establish the qualifying relationship to an identical parent. These birth certificates must show that the siblings have the mother or father in common. If only the father is in common, then the marriage certificates of the father to both mothers is also required. Finally, if any name on a supporting document has changed, a legal document to evidence the name change is required. See page 78 for detailed instructions on filling in the I-130 petition.

After the I-130 petition is filled in and the above documents assembled, refer to the next section for a description of how and where to file the I-130 petition packet.

How to file. Persons filing for the preference categories file the I-130 with the service center. Ensure that you have the I-130 petition complete. Attach the filing fee of $130 in a money order. Do not forget to include the supporting documents as described earlier depending on which preference category the relationship between the petitioner and beneficiary belongs.

Remember to provide only photocopies of all documents. The originals will be brought to the interview as discussed in Chapter 17. All birth and marriage certificates must have been issued by or registered with the proper civil authority in the foreign country. If a document is not in English it must be submitted along with a certified English translation (see page 138). (If any document is unavailable, see page 138 for more information.)

Other points to follow in filing the I-130 petition:

- Make a copy of the petition and supporting documents and keep them in safe place.

- Attach a money order or cashier's check in the amount of $130 made out to "INS".

- Make sure the name of the petitioner is on the check.

- Confirm the correct address of the service center. There is typically a specific post office box for an I-130 petition. (If a deadline needs to be met, file using express mail to the street address of the service center and place the P.O. Box on label.)

Check Appendix B for the service center address for your state.

These petitions may take an extended period of time to be decided on since there are long waits for visa numbers in most preference categories. The service center will send a request for evidence if further information is required to approve the case. Once the petition is approved, it will be sent to the National Visa Center who will hold the file until a visa number is available. They will then forward the file to the appropriate embassy or consulate.

WIDOWS AND WIDOWERS

A filing for a widow or widower consists of the following:

- Form I-360;

- filing fee of $130;

- U.S. citizenship of spouse;

- marriage certificate;

- death certificate of U.S. citizen spouse;

- divorce judgements or marriage terminations as applicable for either spouse;

- birth certificates of children of alien; and,

- evidence as to validity of relationship (may be required).

These petitions are filed with the appropriate service center. See the documents list contained in Chapter 4 and begin to gather evidence that the relationship was bona fide. This evidence may be required if the case is interviewed. The I-360 can be obtained from the INS website at:

www.ins.gov/forms.

Instructions for this form are also there.

Once the I-360 is approved, an adjustment application may be filed with the local INS office.

ABUSED SPOUSES

Abused spouse self-petitions are filed with the Vermont Service Center and include:

- Form I-360;

- filing fee of $130;

- U.S. citizenship or LPR status of spouse;

- marriage certificate;

- evidence that the alien resided with spouse;

- evidence that the marriage was entered into in good faith;

- evidence of the abuse of the alien spouse:

  - medical reports;

  - police reports;

  - affidavits;

  - order of protection;

  - photos;

- evidence of good moral character;

- affidavits, police certificates;

- divorce judgements or marriage terminations as applicable for either spouse;

- Birth certificates of the children of the alien.

Once the I-360 is approved by the Vermont Service Center, the individual then files for adjustment of status with the local office. (See the next chapter.) An affidavit of support form is not required for an abused spouse or child adjustment application.

NOTE: *You must read the section on page 132 entitled "Filing the Adjustment of Status Application" for the rest of the procedure to immigrate to the U.S.*

NONIMMIGRANT VISAS

See Chapter 5 for a detailed explanation of which visa you may qualify for here.

PROCEDURE   The procedures for obtaining a nonimmigrant visa varies with the type of visa. If the person is in the U.S., one must be in status on a valid non-expired visa to extend or change status. The I-94 will be marked with the date of expiration for the visa regardless of the date of expiration on the visa stamped in the passport. Then an application is made on the I-539 form to either extend or change status.

A common scenario is to enter the U.S. as a tourist and then attempt to change status to that of a student. This application is not as easy as simply registering at a school to be a full-time student. The problem is the issue of *intent*. The INS will want to be satisfied that the person in fact came to the U.S. to be a temporary visitor and to return to their country of origin and did not come to the U.S. with the real intent of enrolling as a student. Therefore, it will be necessary to explain why the person came to the U.S. strictly to be a visitor and why there was a change of plan to become a student once in the U.S. The procedure is to enter the U.S. as a nonimmigrant may be either a two or three step process depending on the type of visa.

For some petitions, it may be necessary to file a petition first with the service center in the U.S., which has jurisdiction over the petitioner or sponsoring company. For example, the H, L and E visas require an approved petition from a service center. The service center will transmit the file to the designated consulate upon its being approved.

Then, the applicant will processed through the consulate or embassy to obtain the visa. In some cases, the application is filed directly at the consulate. For example, tourist visas, student visas, and religious worker visas are directly filed with the consulate.

Third, the visa is given a final lookover by the inspections officer at the place of entry. They have the right to deny entry on the visa if they suspect the terms of the visa may be violated. This is much less likely to happen where a petition was approved first by a service center and then by an embassy. (It is the B visa which tends to come under closer scrutiny at the place of entry.)

V VISA
PACKET—
SPOUSE AND
MINOR
CHILDREN OF
PERMANENT
RESIDENTS

The following are required to get a V visa:
- Form I-539 application to change nonimmigrant status;
- filing fee of $140;
- fingerprint fee of $50 for each person 14 or over;
- Form I-539 Supplement A for dependent children;

- a copy of the I-130 receipt or approval notice, or correspondence to and from Service Center regarding petition filed before December 20, 2000;

- a marriage certificate (if I-130 pending);

- birth certificates with English translations of dependent children showing names of parents, if applicable;

- Form I-693 medical examination (vaccination supplement not required) for the applicant and each dependent on Form I-539 Supplement A;

- Form I-765 work permit;

- filing fee of $120;

- signature card;

- 2 green card style photos; and,

- Form I-601 waiver (if necessary).

Form I-539. The above listing consists of the entire packet that will be filed. First, the I-539 form should be carefully filled out as follows:

☞ Part 1. Information about you: This means the applicant and his or her personal information. Fill in all required information. Many applicants may not have a social security number or alien registration number in which case respond to these questions "N/A."

The I-94 number is found on the white I-94 card issued at the point of entry. If this card is lost, so indicate. If the alien crossed the border illegally, mark "N/A."

The last questions asks for the current status of the applicant. Typically, this will be as B-2 visitor or F-1 student. If the relative entered illegally across the border, then the correct response is EWI. If the person has overstayed a visa, write in "B-2 overstay."

☞ Part 2. Application Type: Check the box that applies to the type of case. For example, if the applicant is being applied for by an immediate relative check box a. If the applicant was selected in the diversity visa lottery, check box h. and write in "Diversity Visa Selection 2003."

☞ Part 3. Processing Information: Enter the specific background information requested. If the applicant did not make a lawful entry, there is no I-94, border inspection or visa. Therefore, enter "N/A" in response to these questions.

☞ Part 4. Signature. The applicant signs where indicated.

The I-539 must then be supported by the several documents described in the above list. If the beneficiary has minor unmarried children, then Supplement A must be completed with the names of the children. An I-130 approval or receipt notice must be submitted showing proof of an I-130 petition filed prior to December 20, 2000. If the I-130 petition is not yet approved, then a marriage certificate is required. Finally, the birth certificates of the dependent children and the medical examination form for each dependent must be submitted.

Work authorization. Most V visa applicants will also want to file for work authorization. This application may be made with the initial filing or whenever employment is sought. To file for work authorization, complete the I-765 application. Fill in the personal information requested on this form. In response to Question 16, simply mark "V visa applicant." A separate fee of $120 is required along with 2 green card photos.

Criminal record. If there is a criminal record causing inadmissibility (see Chapter 16), a waiver on Form I-601 must be filed. The assistance of an attorney may be necessary.

Filing. The application is mailed to:

U.S. Immigration & Naturalization Service
P.O. Box 7216
Chicago, IL 60680-7216

These petitions will be forwarded to the Missouri Service Center for processing.

NOTE: *Dependent children are included on the principal's I-539 application, but you must pay a $50 fingerprint fee if they are 14 years of age or older.*

Work Permit and Adjustment. Those entering the U.S. on V visa may apply for a work permit card by mail with the Missouri Service Center. Supply the following to do so:

- Form I-765;

- filing fee of $120;

- a copy of the V visa in passport or copy of I-94;

- a signature card; and,

- 2 green card style photos.

The V visa recipient will apply for adjustment with their local INS office once the I-130 petition is current.

K-1 Visa Packet— Fiancés

The first step is approval of the fiancé visa petition with the service center in the petitioner's jurisdiction. The following documents need to be filed:

- Form I-129F;

- filing fee of $110;

- Form G-325A for petitioner;

- Form G-325A for beneficiary;

- the petitioner's naturalization certificate or birth certificate;

- the petitioner's statement as to the history of the relationship;

- evidence of the relationship;

- phone bill showing calls to the beneficiary;

- photos of vacation together;

- a copy of airline tickets showing recent meetings;

- copies of letters, cards, or e-mails sent between the couple;

- evidence of gifts;

- any other document that verifies validity of relationship; and,

- photo of the petitioner and beneficiary.

The above listing consists of the entire packet that will be filed. Each is required in every case. The I-129F form itself must be carefully completed. This form is similar to the I-130 form. Consult the I-130 instruction on page 78.

The other required form is the G-325A biographic information form. This form is completed by both the the U.S. citizen and the fiancé.

Then, the I-129F petition must be supported by several documents.

Embassy Requirements. After approval of the I-129F, the service center will transmit the file to the designated embassy or consulate. It may take a month or more for the file to be transmitted. The consulate will issue a notice for an interview.

The documents required for the embassy to complete processing are:
- DS-156 application form;

- a passport valid six months beyond the date of intended entry into the U.S. (K-4 maybe included in K-3's passport);

- documents to prove the relationship is bona fide;

- birth certificates;

- local police certificates;

- court records;

- divorce decrees or death certificates for any previous marriage;

- IV medical exam minus vaccinations on form DS-2053; and,

- three color green card style photographs.

NOTE: *No affidavit of support is required but you may be questioned to ensure you will not become a public burden.*

K-3 AND K-4 VISAS—SPOUSE AND MINOR CHILDREN OF U.S. CITIZENS

The first step to a K-3 visa is ensuring that an I-130 packet, discussed on page 78, was filed previously with the service center that has jurisdiction over the U.S. citizen petitioner. However, the I-130 only has to be *pending*. Any minor children of the U.S. citizen spouse may be included on the spouse's I-130. (See page 78 for information on filing an immediate relative I-130 petition.)

Then the U.S. citizen petitioner must also file a second petition, the I-129F, with the Missouri Service Center. This petition must be approved by the INS before the alien can continue processing for the K visa at an embassy. The I-129F again will include the petitioner's stepchildren.

The I-129F Packet. The following constitutes the I-129F filing:

- Form I-129F;
- filing fee of $110;
- G-325A for beneficiary;
- two green card style photos;
- I-130 receipt notice or approval notice or other proof of a pending or approved petition;
- petitioner's naturalization certificate or birth certificate; and,
- a copy of a marriage certificate (if I-130 pending).

The above listing consists of the entire packet that will be filed. The I-129F form itself must be carefully completed. This form is similar to the I-130 form. Consult the I-130 instructions on page 78.

The other required form is the G-325A biographic information form. This form is completed by beneficiary. Also include two green card style photos.

An I-130 receipt or approval notice must be attached to the I-129F form. The U.S. citizen must establish their citizenship by one of the documents indicated on page 14. If the I-130 petition is pending, a marriage certificate is required.

All I-129 documents are mailed to:

U.S. Immigration & Naturalization Service
P.O. Box 7218
Chicago, IL 60680-7218

These petitions will be forwarded to the Missouri Service Center for processing. Once the petition is approved, the Missouri Service Center will forward the paper case file to the National Visa Center. The National Visa Center will scan the I-129F petition and perform a criminal records check. The National Visa Center will then e-mail the case to the embassy in the country of marriage or to the spouse's country of residence if married in the U.S.

The embassy will then send the beneficiary a letter describing the documents required for K-3 and K-4 issuance:

- DS-156 application form;

- a passport valid six months beyond the date of intended entry (K-4 may be included in K-3's passport);

- documents to prove the relationship is bona fide;

- birth certificates;

- local police certificates;

- court records;

- divorce decrees or death certificates for any previous marriage;

- IV medical exam minus vaccinations on form DS-2053; and,

- three color green card style photographs.

NOTE: *No affidavit of support is required but you may be questioned to ensure you will not become a public burden.*

Once in the U.S., the K-3 or K-4 status person may apply for a work permit with the Missouri Service Center by submitting the following:

- Form I-765;

- filing fee of $120;

- a copy of K visa in passport or copy of I-94;

- a signature card; and,

- two green card style photos.

The K-3 or K-4 recipient may then file an adjustment packet with their local INS office. If the I-130 petition is not approved, approval may be waited for or a duplicate petition may be filed. Attach the I-130 receipt notice as proof of payment.

LABOR CERTIFICATION FILING

Refer to Chapter 6 for any details you need on Reduction in Recruitment (RIR) and State Employment Security Agency (SESA). This section pertains to filings for both.

FILING AN RIR   The following consists of an RIR filing:
- ETA 750A—two duplicate originals;

- ETA 750B—two duplicate originals; and,

  - a cover letter summarizing:
  - the background of company;
  - the offered position;
  - the alien's credentials;
  - recruitment efforts;
  - results of recruitment efforts;
  - a copy of advertisements;
  - a job posting; and,
  - prevailing wage determination.

There is no filing fee.

The above is the entire RIR packet that is filed with the local state employment security office. First, complete the ETA 750A and B forms.

See the next section for detailed information on completing these forms. They are filed in *duplicate originals*, that is, two copies each with an original signature. Also required is a detailed cover letter on the employer's letterhead summarizing the points listed above. Other documents that must be included are a copy of all advertisements placed, other evidence of recruitment, a job posting and proof as to the prevailing wage determination. The offered wage must be at least 95% of the prevailing wage in the particular jurisdiction.

If the recruitment is found to be inadequate, then the application simply reverts to a normal slow-track application with a priority date according to its filing. The application will then be scheduled for supervised recruitment on the same schedule as if it were originally filed as a slow-track application.

If the application is approved, it is forwarded to the Department of Labor for review and certification. The vast majority of the time, an application approved by the SESA will be rubber stamped by the Department of Labor.

REGULAR
TRACK LABOR
CERTIFICATION

In a normal labor certification case, there has not been any prior recruitment. A filing is made with: Form ETA 750A, and Form ETA 750B. There is no filing fee

Completing ETA forms. The employer completes the ETA 750A as follows.

- ☞ Enter the name and address of the alien and employer where indicated on page 1 of the form.

- ☞ Enter the type of business activity, job title and work hours.

- ☞ The rate of pay in response to question 12 must be within 95% of the prevailing wage for the job. The prevailing wage can be found on the Department of Labor website (see Appendix C).

- ☞ Then for questions 13, 14 and 15 describe the job and education, training and experience necessary. This is the critical part of the labor certification application and must be answered carefully. A detailed job description must be provided. List all aspects of the proposed job. Then list the background requirements for the job. That is, whether a college degree is required and if so, in what field.

☞ Special requirements sought in question 16 might include a specific language skill or training such as computer language.

☞ The employer then signs on page 2 where indicated.

The prospective employee completes the ETA 750B form by filling in the resume-type information requested. The employee through his education, training, and experience must meet the criteria for the

Filing with the SESA. These forms are filed in duplicate with the local SESA. The ETA forms must be printed so that they are double-sided and both copies must contain original signatures.

After the application is filed, a receipt notice will be sent. Then the application sits in the backlog. Unfortunately, there has developed a substantial backlog in many states at the SESA stage. An application may be pending a year or more without any action. To check the backlog in a particular area go to:

http://workforcesecurity.doleta.gov/foreign/times.asp.

Processing. The SESA will begin processing of the application with one of two types of action. If there are mistakes in the application, it will return both copies of the application and indicate where revisions need to be made. Often, it determines that the prevailing wage is too low for the job description and experience required.

Then, it will send a *recruitment notice* indicating that the supervised recruitment period should begin. An advertisement must then be placed as soon as possible. Sometimes the notice will suggest which newspaper. If not, then it should be placed in a general circulation paper. Most often, the ad must be placed for three consecutive days. It should be bourne in mind that for many papers the Sunday supplement is the most popular resource for would-be job applicants. There is no requirement that the ad be placed on this day. The page containing the ad and date of publication should be taken from the paper each day for later submission with the report of recruitment.

Any applicant that appears to be qualified must be sent a certified letter asking that they appear for an interview. At the end of the recruitment, a final report of recruitment is due. This report will include copies of the ads, internal job postings and resumes. It will be necessary to state a valid business reason why each applicant is not qualified for the position.

The SESA will make a decision on the application. If the application is approved, it is forwarded to the Department of Labor for review and certification. As with the RIR, the vast majority of the time, an application approved by the SESA will be rubber stamped by the Department of Labor.

FILING FORM
I-140

Upon approval of the labor certification, the I-140 Form may be filed with the appropriate service center along with:

- a filing fee of $135;

- approved labor certification (or ETA 750, Parts A and B with proof qualifies as a Schedule A shortage occupation or approved national interest waiver);

- employer's letter;

- proof of employer's ability to pay the wage;

- documentation to prove eligibility for a preference category; and,

- documentation to prove that the alien satisfies educational, training, and, experience requirements of the ETA 750 Part A.

The purpose of the I-140 petition is to prove eligibility for the particular preference category that the alien satisfies all requirements, and that the employer has the ability to pay the required wage.

Along with the I-140 form, several documents need to be attached as set forth on page 104. These are the original approved labor certification obtained from the Department of Labor. An employer's letter on the company letterhead should be prepared renewing the employee's job offer at the required salary. Finally, documentation as to the alien's education and credentials to prove he or she meets with the educational, training and experience requirements of the particular position. (For example, school transcripts and diplomas, or training certificates should be included.)

The above packet can then be filed with the appropriate service center. (See Appendix B for the correct address.)

I-140 petitions are now typically decided on by the service center within a couple of months. The service center will send a request for evidence if further information is required to approve the case. Once the I-140 is approved, the beneficiary may apply for adjustment of status.

FILING FOR ADJUSTMENT OF STATUS

After the I-140 petition is approved, the applicant may apply for adjustment of status. Unlike an adjustment filing with a local INS office where only certain forms and documents are initially required, a complete adjustment packet for an employment-based case should be filed with the service center. In this way, the chances of the case being referred back to a local INS office for interview are reduced.

NOTE: *Transfer of the file to the local INS office will cause a substantial delay and heartache.*

The adjustment filing consists of numerous forms and supporting documents. The following outline is a useful checklist of all of the possible forms and documents. A more detailed explanation follows the outline.

The following packet should be filed with the service center:
- Form I-485 adjustment of status form;

- filing fee of $255;

- fingerprint fee of $50;

- Form I-140 approval notice;

- two green card style photos;

- Form G-325A biographic information sheet;

- Form I-485 Supplement OR proof of legal entry into the U.S. and maintenance of status:

  - copies of the visa page in your passport;

  - I-94s and relevant approval notices;

  - a copy of Canadian citizenship (if any);

- Form I-693 medical examination form and vaccination supplement completed by physician in a sealed envelope;

- recent job letter confirming job offer;

- applicant's birth certificate;

- marriage certificate;

- cable request for overseas dependents;

- documents related to convictions;

- Form I-601 waiver of inadmissibility (if required) with supporting documents; and,

- Form I-864 affidavit of support only if a relative owns more than 5% of petitioning company.

If you are filing under the LIFE Act you need to additionally provide proof of physical presence on December 20, 2000. (This is not necessary for dependents.) Also, if this labor certification was filed after April 30, 2001, proof of prior I-130 or labor certification filing must be shown.

WORK AUTHORIZATION

If you want to work as soon as possible, you must file the following for work authorization:

- Form I-765 work permit;

- filing fee of $120;

- two green card style photos; and,

- a copy of state issued I.D.

TRAVEL PERMISSION

To travel in the meantime, file:

- Form I-131 travel permission (if eligible);

- filing fee of $110;

- two green card style photos and,

- a clear copy of an identity document.

The principal form is the I-485 adjustment of status form. It should be carefully completed. See page 81 for detailed instructions. The filing fee is $255 if the applicant is 14 years of age over, and $160 if under 14 years of age. Likewise, those 14 or over require fingerprints and will pay the $50 fingerprint fee. A completed G-325A form is required for all applicants 14 years of age or over as well. Every applicant requires two green card style photos to be included.

Eligibility. The next aspect which is critical to the permanent residence process, is *eligibility.* If the applicant is in valid non-immigrant status at the time of the filing of the application, then they are eligible to file for adjustment. If the applicant is out of status, then they must qualify under Section 245(i) (see Chapter 15 for a detailed discussion). Basically, if the labor certification was filed before April 30, 2001, then the applicant is eligible to file for adjustment. However, they will then have to file the I-485 Supplement and pay the $1000 fee (see page 81 for instructions).

The medical examination form (Chapter 15) must be filed. Employment- based adjustment applicants do not typically require the affidavit of support (Chapter 15) since a job offer is pending. Only if a relative owns more than 5% of the petitioning company is the affidavit of support required to be filed by that relative. However, a current job letter stating that the position is offered to the alien at the required salary must be submitted.

If there is any *condition of inadmissibility* (see Chapter 16), such as for criminal record or entry on a false passport, the I-601 waiver must be filed and fee paid. For any criminal record, original certified records of disposition must be obtained from the clerk of the court and included with the filing.

Since you will not be at an interview to fill in the missing holes and provide documents, these filings should be as complete as possible. If you wish to make the examiner's job easier than prepare a supplemental letter addressing the following:

- If the I-485 supplement is not being filed, document your entire nonimmigrant history: submit a road map for the entire time you have been in the U.S. and not just since the most recent entry. Include all available documentation such as copies of I-94s, passport visas, I-797 approval notices, I-20s, IAP-66s, etc.

- Clarify that you have not worked without authorization (at all times—including during any nonimmigrant stays) and support it with copies of work permits, I-797 approval notices, passport visas, and the like.

- Provide complete documentation for dependent applications to establish a relationship to the principal alien (a birth certificate and if the principal applicant is the father, a copy of the marriage certificate. If applicable, provide evidence of termination of any prior marriages).

- Submit a copy of the local INS office's current list of civil surgeons and highlight the name of the doctor who conducted the exam. You should remind your doctor that the form will be reviewed for eligibility. Therefore, the doctor should print his name clearly and be sure it is complete including TB tests and vaccinations.

- Submit any history of appearing in immigration court, including documents such as a final order.

- If there are many documents, you can place tabs (for service centers use the tabs along the bottom of the page, not along the sides).

Receipt notice. Several weeks after filing, a *receipt notice* will be received. This receipt contains your case number and should be safely kept. Depending on the backlog, the application will be decided in due course. If any information is missing or documentation incomplete, then a Request for Evidence (RFE) may be issued. You will then have an 84-day period to provide the required information.

NOTE: *This is a very strict deadline. Any response should be returned to the INS by overnight mail so that proof of mailing is available should the INS claim it was never received.*

You have generally one chance to comply with the RFE, so be sure you have enclosed all of the information. If some information is not available provide a detailed explanation as to why.

The adjustment process varies by service center. You will need to go the service center web site to confirm the processing time before taking additional action.

If the processing time is past the time indicated on the receipt notice, wait an additional week or two. If nothing happens, you should call the number at the bottom of the receipt notice. It is possible to call the service center late at night when the phone lines are free. Eventually, you will be asked to punch in your case number including the three-letter service center designation as a number. For example, "LIN" for the Lincoln service center is "546" on the keypad.

You might get useful recorded information about your case. For example, the recording might say that an approval notice or request for evidence was sent.

Processing Problems and Denial. To clear up processing problems, it is possible to call the service center and speak with an information officer. This is not an officer who will be adjudicating the application. The information officer will not have access to the file and may only have the same information that is in the automated system.

A case will not be denied without allowing an opportunity to remedy the problem. You may reapply if the grounds for denial can be overcome. You will, however, need to be in status to do so unless the petition is *grandfathered* under Section 245(i).

If the case is granted, an *approval notice* will be mailed to the applicant. The applicant will be required to appear at their local INS office for ADIT processing.

INTERVIEW The majority of applications filed with a service center will not be interviewed. They may be interviewed if:

- the applicant's identity, legal status, admissibility and/or qualifications are questionable;

- the applicant fails to admit arrests or convictions and the service center learns through a fingerprint check;

- the applicant admits a conviction for one or more crimes involving moral turpitude (CIMT) and an I-601 waiver is required;

- the applicant entered the U.S. without inspection;

- the applicant is not presently employed by the petitioner; or,

- the application was selected as part of a random sample for purposes of quality assurance.

If the case requires an interview, the applicant will receive a transfer notice indicating that the file has been transferred to the local INS office. An interview should be scheduled in accordance with its filing date with the service center and not the date of the transfer to the local office. All further inquiries should be directed to the local office.

It would now be an excellent time to seek the advice of an immigration attorney to review the file, if one has not been previously consulted. It will be critical to identify the problem area and provide documentation to remedy it. See Chapter 17 for more information on the interview process.

LOTTERY

A diversity winner may apply in the U.S. or abroad at an embassy. It does not matter if the selection letter is received at an address in the U.S. or abroad, one may apply for a green card wherever they are eligible or it is more convenient.

If one is applying through the embassy, then carefully follow the directions contained in the acceptance packet. Recently, the process and the forms have changed for processing a diversity visa application. The packet must be carefully reviewed and complied with. One of the forms is to be completed and returned immediately to the new processing center in Kentucky. From there, the State Department will send the immigrant visa processing packet to the address indicated. The procedure will vary with the particular embassy.

If the diversity winner is in the U.S., he will need to be in a valid non-immigrant status (with certain exceptions). If a person is out of status and wishes to apply in the U.S., he or she must be eligible under Immigration law. (Section 245(i).) The criteria for eligibility in the U.S. is the same as for anyone applying for adjustment in any other category.

The following is an outline of the necessary adjustment packet to be filed with the local INS office:

- Form I-485 adjustment application (see page 81 for instructions
- filing fee, which depends on age (see chart in Appendix D);
- fingerprint fee of $50;
- a copy of the diversity visa acceptance letter from the State Department;
- Form G-325A biographic information for the applicant;
- two green card style photos.

The following are also mandatory items. You can either file them initially, which is preferable, or bring them to the interview:

- Form I-485 Supplement OR proof of legal entry into the U.S., such as copies of the visa page in your passport, I-94s and relevant approval notices or a copy of Canadian citizenship;
- a copy of the applicant's birth certificate and translation;

- proof of high school graduation or two years work experience in trade requiring two years experience;

- Form I-693 medical form and vaccination sheet in a sealed envelope;

- Form I-134 affidavit of support with documentation; and,

- a job letter.

The following is required in some cases:
- proof of eligibility under section 245(i);

- physical presence in the U.S. on December 20, 2000;

- Form I-601 waiver of inadmissibility and supporting documents;

- cable request for overseas dependents;

- marriage certificate;

- divorce decrees or proof of termination of previous marriages;

- birth certificates of beneficiary's children; and,

- documents related to criminal convictions or other special circumstances.

The principal form is the I-485. This is the actual adjustment of status application. It should be carefully completed. See page 81 for detailed instructions. The filing fee is $255 if the applicant is 14 years of age over and $160 if under age 14. Likewise, those 14 or over require fingerprints and will pay the $50 fingerprint fee.

A completed G-325A form is required for all applicants 14 years of age or over. Every applicant requires two green card style photos to be included as well.

This list describes the minimum documents required for filing the adjustment packet. The remaining items may be brought to the adjustment interview or filed initially.

ELIGIBILITY The next aspect that is critical to the permanent residence process is *eligibility*. If the applicant is in a valid non-immigrant status at the time of the filing of the application, then he or she is eligible to file for adjustment. If the applicant is out of status, then he or she must qualify under Section 245(i) (see Chapter 5 for a detailed discussion). Basically, if the I-130 was filed before April 30, 2001, then, the applicant is eligible to file for adjustment. However, he or she will then have to file the I-485 Supplement and pay the $1000 fee (see page 81 for instructions).

The medical examination form (Chapter 15) and affidavit of support (Chapter 15) must be filed. This is the short I-134 form which requires only one year's of tax returns or a job offer. If there is any condition of inadmissibility (see Chapter 16), such as for criminal record or entry on a false passport, the I-601 waiver must be filed and fee paid. For any criminal record, original certified records of disposition must be obtained from the clerk of the court and included with the filing.

To properly file the adjustment application, follow these suggestions:

- Make a copy of all documents and keep them in a safe place.

- Write name and "A" number or date of birth in pencil on back of photos

- Attach a money order or cashier's check made out to "INS" in the amount of the correct filing fee

- Make sure name of applicant is on check

- Confirm the correct address. It is not the same address as the INS office. There is typically a specific post office box for an adjustment application. While an application sent to the local address might be forwarded, this is a risky proposition

- Send any address changes by certified mail return receipt requested since such requests may not be processed by the INS resulting in a closed case

The timing of the filing is very important in a diversity visa case. If an applicant is seeking to adjust status in the U.S., then it is critical to wait until after October 1 to file the adjustment application. It may be hard to wait 6 months from when the acceptance letter is received to apply for adjustment, particularly where there is a race against time to complete the processing and obtain a first-come-first-served visa number. But an adjustment application filed before October 1 must actually be denied since there is no visa number in existence. If the INS is not considerate enough to mail the application back, they could deny the application and then process the file for immigration court.

It is also critically important to mark the outside of the mailing envelope: "Urgent - Diversity visa filing". The same should be marked on a colored piece of paper on top of the application packet. Since the backlog at many INS offices is about a year, there is not time for the application to go through the normal application track. It must be treated as an expedited application so that it is completed on time.

WHAT TO
EXPECT

As with any adjustment filing, a *receipt notice* should be received in the mail within several weeks. Then, a *fingerprint notice* will be received. The fingerprints should be taken as soon as possible.

Next is the wait for an *interview notice*. In some jurisdictions, the interview may be delayed until there is actually a visa number. It may be somewhat confusing that there should be a wait for a diversity visa number when the applicant has already won the lottery and is racing to complete processing by the end of the government fiscal year.

While 50,000 diversity visas are made available each year, there may still be a wait, depending on one's selection number. If someone has a selection number in the low thousands, it is likely current right off the bat. A number over 5,000 for Europe or Africa may not become current for several months. Those with a selection number over 10,000 may be waiting until the summer for a visa number. Check the visa bulletin on the Department of State's website for the cut-off number. It used to be risky to even file an adjustment application for which there was no number. Now the policy is to accept the filing, and hold it until a visa number becomes available.

THE INTERVIEW

In many jurisdictions, the adjustment interview is scheduled for January whether or not there is a visa number. It is critical that all remaining documents and applications be brought to the interview. If the case is not completed, then it will be extremely difficult to follow-up with the officer later. Ask the officer how to follow-up on the case. The best scenario is that the officer holds on to your file and maintains responsibility for it. Be sure to ask the officer for his or her name and phone number so that you may contact them. Ask the officer when it will be appropriate to follow-up.

I-551 STAMP

The U.S. based adjustment applicant will want the I-551 stamp in his or her passport as proof that the case is approved. It is somewhat risky to rely upon the officer or supervisor saying the case is approved.

NOTE: *If one has dependents waiting to process overseas, then bear in mind that they must not only complete processing at the embassy but they must also actually enter the U.S. prior to September 30.*

ASYLUM

There is now a one-year deadline to file for asylum from your last arrival in the U.S. If you were in the U.S. longer than one year, and then left, and re-entered, then time starts from the date of re-entry. Also, if you are in status say on a student visa, then you may apply for asylum as long as you are in valid status, even if that is more than one year.

There are exceptions to this rule, such for minor children or if there are changed conditions in your country.

There are two steps to an asylum application. It is first filed with the appropriate service center on form I-589 with all necessary documentation:

- Form I-589 accurately completed;

- two green card style photos for each family member;

- supplemental detailed statement as to problems;

- copies of all identification documents, marriage certificate, birth certificates of all applicants;

- any documentation such as news articles or reports as to the problem; and,

- affidavits from witnesses.

NOTE: *There is no filing fee.*

The service center then sends the file to one of the nine asylum offices for interview. With the decreasing numbers of asylum applications, the interview will occur approximately six weeks after filing.

ASYLUM OFFICE INTERVIEW

Your application will first be interviewed by an asylum officer. Unfortunately, with any system involving humans, the end result may depend on who the officer is. This really holds true in a close case, which many applications are.

NOTE: *If you want to get a background on the asylum interview process, there is an excellent documentary called Well-Founded Fear, which analyzes the asylum process including the interview.*

These days the asylum office gives an answer on an application fairly quickly. It used to be that many asylum cases would drag on for months or years. After 10 days for those who are out of status, you will go to the asylum office to pick up the result, which may be either a grant of asylum or referral.

The reason why a case is *referred* will not be detailed. In a few sentences, it will simply say that the applicant did not meet the standard for asylum. That is, he or she did not demonstrate a *well-founded fear of persecution*.

It almost does not matter what is written on the referral notice except if it says that there is a finding of a lack of credibility. Essentially, this means the applicant was thought to be dishonest with regards to his or her testimony before the asylum officer. This may catch the eye of the Immigration Judgeor the trial attorney during the court.

If the applicant is in status, the procedure is substantially different. He will not be asked to pick up a decision but rather will be mailed either an *approval letter* or a *Notice of Intent to Deny*.

The latter consists of a detailed summary of your testimony and the precise reasons why your case is intended to be denied. The applicant will then have 16 days to respond to this notice and provide detailed reasons and documentation to overcome the denial. This opportunity is provided for those in status, because they will not have a chance to contest the decision in immigration court. (Since they are in status, they cannot be placed into deportation proceedings.)

In the end, if the case is referred, bear in mind that the best opportunity still lies ahead. As previously discussed, one's chances of winning an asylum case are much better in immigration court.

ASYLUM OFFICE QUESTION SHEET

This guideline provided to asylum officers demonstrates the types of questions that will be addressed in an asylum interview.

ASYLUM DECISION MAKING FORMAT

I. Who is the Applicant?

- Name? Date of birth? Place of birth? Last habitual residence?

- What was the Date and Manner of Applicants entry into U.S.?

- Time spent and countries transited en route to the U.S.?

- Family Members: In the U.S.? Still in the country of origin?

II. Why did the Applicant leave his or her country of origin? [Claim]
- Does the Applicant fear returning home? If so, why?

- What—specifically (summarize in assessment)—does he or she fear?

- Who does the Applicant fear will do these things?

- Why was the past harm done, or future harm feared?

- Has anything—specifically (summarize in assessment)—yet been done to the Applicant [eg., threats, harm, beating, arrest, detention]?

- If so, What? When? Where? How? Why? Who?

- Has anything—specifically (summarize in assessment)—yet been done to someone the Applicant knows/knows of [eg. threats, harm, beating, arrest, detention]? If so, What? When? Where? How?

- Is there a reasonable "nexus" between the harm experienced by that someone else and the Applicant?

III. Is the Applicant's testimony credible?
- Is the evidence (direct or circumstantial) and/or testimony detailed and specific?

- Is the evidence and/or testimony consistent?

- Is the evidence/testimony plausible in light of Country Conditions?

- Does any specific Country Conditions info specifically refute claim?

continued

IV. Is the Applicant a refugee? [Analysis]

- Is the harm experienced/feared "persecution" or does it "rise to the level of persecution's over time (cumulatively; in the totality of the circumstances)?

- Is the Applicant singled out, or similarly situated?

- Is the claim based on past persecution or future?

- If past, does the preponderance of evidence establish what country conditions have changed such that a fear of future harm is not a reasonable possibility?

- Chen Analysis If so, has the Applicant presented compelling reasons why he or she should not return on account of the atrocious and severe character of his/her past persecution?

- If future, is the fear well-founded [use Mogharrabi/Acosta]?

- Is the fear reasonable, country-wide, or localized?

- Is the [feared] persecutor the government, or someone the government is unable or unwilling to control?

- Is the harm linked to "on account of" one of the five protected grounds of the statute? If so, which one?

- Is the Applicant willing to return to his or her country?

V. Are there any bars?

- Mandatory: Persecution of others? Firm resettlement?

- Multiple nationality? Conviction for particularly serious crime in U.S. National security danger?

- Discretionary: Commission of crime outside the U.S.? Avoidance of overseas refugee processing? Fraudulent entry into U.S. [in connection with flight from harm/fear of harm]? Filed within one year of entry?

VI. Decision. [Conclusion on eligibility]

IMMIGRATION
COURT AND
APPEALS

The procedure before the immigration judge is really a deportation proceeding. At the first brief master hearing, once the alien concedes that he is deportable, then the immigration judge will ask what relief he or she is seeking from the court. The alien should state that he or she is seeking to renew the asylum application. At the master hearing, the asylum applicant must decline to designate a country of deportation.

The immigration judge will then set an individual hearing date at which time the applicant may again attempt to prove his asylum case. It is a brand new hearing with an opportunity to submit evidence, testimony, and witnesses before the court.

Expert witness. It is highly recommended for all but the most obvious cases to have an expert witness brought in to assist with proving the case. Given the stakes involved for an asylum case before the immigration judge, it is necessary to pull out all the stops. It is the last realistic opportunity to win the case.

An asylum case is decided by the ability to convince the immigration judge as to the country's conditions as they relate to that particular applicant. An expert witness puts the INS attorney on the defensive in trying to disprove his or her testimony which is very difficult to do. This is a dangerous path for the trial attorney if he or she tries to confront the expert. It may end up merely giving the expert another opportunity to put across his or her point of view and discuss the basis for that opinion. In any event, it never hurts to have an expert. In a close case, it will certainly tip the balance in the alien's favor.

Further, one simply never knows what point an immigration judge will get stuck on with regard to your case. An expert can assist the court with any unique question arising from the case and provide critical background information. The expert is also useful in providing reports and articles that corroborate the case.

(See Chapter 19 for more detail on appearing in immigration court.)

THE GRANT OF ASYLUM

If the asylum application is approved by the asylum office, then the initial grant letter will indicate that it is a temporary grant pending a background check. This is almost always just a formality. There should be a final approval approximately a month later if there is no hitch in the fingerprint and bureaucratic process. A grant of asylum by the immigration judge constitutes a final grant.

Asylee status is an indefinite status since it has no set expiration. However, it can be determined by the Asylum Office that asylees from a certain country no longer require asylum if conditions in that country improve dramatically. For example, the thousands of Iraqis granted asylum in this country may not require asylum if Saddam Hussein and the Baath Party are removed as that country's government. (To my knowledge, there has been no extensive attempt to revoke asylee status recently. Nonetheless, it is a good idea to apply for adjustment at the first available opportunity, which is one year from the grant.)

An asylee must apply for work authorization through the Nebraska Service Center each year. It is a good idea to apply about two months in advance.

Travel. In order to re-enter the U.S., the applicant must obtain travel permission from the INS. Such travel permission can take two forms. First, travel authorization may be had through the Nebraska Service Center in the form of a *refugee travel permit.* This permit is a small white book that can substitute for a passport. It also allows re-entry to the U.S. within one year. It typically takes about two to three months to obtain this travel permit from the INS.

If one needs to travel on short notice, they can apply for *advance parole* on form I-131 with their local office. Different offices have different procedures to obtain such parole. This filing is also made on form I-131.

- Form I-131
- filing fee of $110;
- two green card style photos;

- a letter stating reason for travel;

- proof of identity, such as a driver's license or passport asylum approval; and,

- a copy of the I-94.

You can expect to spend a number of hours at the INS in order to obtain the advance parole. Unlike, the travel document, you will require a passport to travel. The grant of advance parole appears to be limited to 60 days when obtained at the local INS office. Thus, if one has time, it is much easier to apply through the Nebraska Service Center.

An asylee may not travel back to his or her home country under any circumstances. (Green card holders usually cannot travel back to their home country either.)

Asylees and refugees are entitled to receive certain benefits through the Office of Refugee Resettlement, which administers various federal and state programs. These programs include cash and medical assistance, employment preparation, job placement, and English language training. Call 800-354-0365 or go to the website:

http://www/acf.dhhs.gov/programs/orr.

For assistance with a job search and training, call 877-US2-JOBS or go to:

http://www.servicelocator.org.

FAMILY   A person granted asylum may apply for their immediate family members within two years of being granted. The application is as follows:
- Form I-730;

- evidence of asylee or refugee status; and,

- a clear photo of the family member.

NOTE: *There is no filing fee.*

If petitioning for a spouse, also include:
- a marriage certificate; and

- legal termination of any previous marriages.

If the mother is petitioning for a child, also include a birth certificate of the child showing the names of both child and mother.

If a father is petitioning for a child, also include a birth certificate of the child showing the names of both child and father.

If married to child's mother, also include marriage certificate and legal termination of previous marriages of father and mother.

If not married to child's mother, also include evidence child was legitimated by civil authorities.

If not legitimated, also include evidence that a bona fide parent-child relationship exists, ie. have emotional and financial ties to child and have shown genuine concern and interest in the child's support, education and general welfare. Such evidence may be:

- money order receipts or canceled checks showing financial support of child
- IRS returns showing child claimed as dependent;
- medical or other records showing child as dependent;
- school records for child;
- correspondence with child;
- affidavits of those knowledgeable about relationship; or,
- evidence of legal name change of beneficiary, if necessary.

The above application is filed with the Nebraska Service Center. If the person is in the U.S, once approved he or she may file for a work permit. One year after approval, he or she can file for permanent residence. Those abroad must go to an embassy or consulate and receive a visa to enter the U.S.

PERMANENT RESIDENCE

The following comprises an application for an asylee-based adjustment of status application:

- Form I-485 adjustment application (see page 81 for instructions)
- a filing fee of $255;

- fingerprint fee of $50;

- Form G-325A biographic information sheet for applicant;

- Form I-693 medical and vaccination form completed by physician and put in a sealed envelope;

- proof of asylee status: (asylum grant letter or immigration court order);

- copies of all pages of the passport and I-94s;

- applicant's birth certificate;

- 2 green card style photos for adjustment;

- documents related to criminal convictions, if applicable; and,

- Form I-602 waiver of inadmissibility (if required) with supporting documents.

Optional benefits can be applied for, such as a work permit or travel permission. (see Chapter 13)

Form I-765 work permit:
- filing fee of $120;

- two green card style photos;

- copy of state issued I.D. or passport; and,

- asylum grant letter or immigration court decision;

Form I-131 refugee travel document/advance parole (if eligible):
- filing fee of $110;

- two green card style photos;

- copy of state issued I.D. or passport; and,

- asylum grant letter or immigration court decision.

FORM I-485   The principal form is the I-485. This is the actual adjustment of status application. It should be carefully completed. See page 81 for detailed instructions. The filing fee is either $255 if the applicant is 14 years of age or over and $160 if under 14. Likewise, those 14 or over require fingerprints and must pay the $50 fingerprint fee.

FORM G-325A   A completed G-325A form is required for all applicants 14 years of age or over. Every applicant requires two green card style photos to be included. The medical examination form and vaccination supplement must be obtained (Chapter 15).

FORM I-864   There is no requirement for the I-864 affidavit of support, which normally accompanies an adjustment application. Further, the INS has stated that refugees and asylees can use any public benefits, including cash welfare, health care, food programs, and other non-cash programs without hurting their chances of obtaining permanent residence.

FORM I-602   If there is any condition of inadmissibility for a criminal record only, the I-602 waiver must be filed and fee paid (see Chapter 16). For any criminal record including arrests, original certified records of disposition must be obtained from the clerk of the court and included with the adjustment packet.

ADJUSTMENT APPLICATION   To properly file the adjustment application, follow these suggestions:

- Make a copy of all documents and keep them in safe place.

- Write your name and "A" number or date of birth in pencil on the back of photos.

- Attach the correct filing fee: a money order or cashier's check made out to "INS" can be used for all of the fees.

- Make sure the name of the applicant is on the check.

- Confirm the correct address for the service center.

- Send any address changes by certified mail return receipt requested, since such requests may not be processed by the INS resulting in a closed case

The applicant will receive a receipt notice a few weeks after filing. While, the receipt notice may state the adjudication period as a reasonably short period of time, the current wait for adjudication does go back several years. Since there are no visa numbers for several years, there is no rush for the Nebraska Service Center to adjudicate the application.

The applicant will need to be fingerprinted prior to completion of the case. As fingerprints expire after fifteen months, the applicant is then in race against time to get the case closed out before the prints expire.

NOTE: *The official date of adjustment of status will be backdated to one year before adjustment was granted.*

RELIGIOUS WORKERS

The following is an outline of the complete packet to be filed with the appropriate service center for religious workers:

- Form I-360;

- filing fee of $130;

- a detailed letter from an authorized official of the religious organization establishing that the proposed services and the alien qualify for the benefit;

- a detailed letter from the authorized official of the religious organization attesting to the alien's membership in the religious denomination and explaining, in detail, the person's religious work and all employment during the past 2 years and the proposed employment;

- a copy of the applicant's religious training or ordination certificate; and,

- evidence establishing that the religious organization, and any affiliate that will employ the person, is a bona fide, nonprofit, religious organization in the U.S. and is exempt from taxation under Section 501(c)(3) of the Internal Revenue Code.

I-360 PETITION The purpose of the I-360 petition is to prove eligibility as a religious worker. Along with the I-360 petition, the several documents just listed need to be attached in support of it. Specifically, an authorized official of the church must explain in detail the need for the alien's services and the qualifying credentials of the alien. A copy of the alien's religious training must be provided. Finally, a Section 501(c)(3) letter must be attached to prove the religious organization is a tax exempt and non-profit one.

(The above packet can then be filed with the appropriate service center. See Appendix B for the correct address.)

ADJUSTMENT

Once the I-360 petition is approved, an adjustment application may be filed with the local INS office. This application may be filed in the same manner as for a family-based one except that an approved I-360 petition is substituted for the I-130 petition. Also, no affidavit of support is required with this adjustment packet.

While the adjustment filing does not require an affidavit of support, there may be a *public charge* problem on account of the low salaries paid to religious workers. The religious worker will be required to demonstrate that he is employed with the religious organization in a full-time capacity and will not need financial support.

A religious worker with an adjustment application pending is eligible to apply for work authorization. However, it may be considered a red flag to the INS officer if the applicant is employed in a non-religious field.

INVESTORS

All investor petitions are filed with either the Texas or California service centers. Those in the jurisdiction of the Nebraska Service Center will file their petition with the California Service Center while those who would normally file with the Vermont Service Center will file with the Texas Service Center.

An investor visa application is normally too complex to handle without the assistance of an immigration attorney. But it is useful to know what type of documentation is required. A filing for an investor visa might look as follows:

- Form I-526 Immigrant Petition by Alien Entrepreneur;
- filing fee of $400;
- letter summarizing eligibility;
- supporting documentation:
  - establishment of business (i.e. articles of incorporation);
  - partnership agreement, joint venture agreement, lease, or proof of ownership of property;
  - establishment in a rural or high unemployment area;
  - proof of investment (i.e. bank statements, assets or property transfer, loan or mortgages or other borrowing secured by assets of investor, certified financial reports);
  - capital obtained through lawful means (i.e. tax returns, evidence of source of capital);
  - employment creation (i.e. tax records, form I-9);
  - investor involvement in management (i.e. statement of position title, description of duties);
  - certificate evidencing authority to do business in a state or municipality; and,
  - business plan evidencing job creation.

The above outline describes the initial filing for an investor visa. The principal form is the I-526 petition. This form requests standard biographic and immigration status information about the investor and basic information about the corporation. The major part of the application is to prepare a detailed cover letter describing the business venture and to specifically address each of the specific criteria set forth above. Documentation as to each of the criteria must be included.

To reduce the risk of denial of the visa on a sizeable financial investment, an *escrow account* may be used so that the funds are committed to the enterprise only if the visa is approved and are returned to the investor if it is denied. The escrow agreement must state that the required initial capital contribution is actually committed to the new commercial enterprise immediately and *irrevocably* upon approval of the petition. The escrow agreement must *unequivocally* release the funds into the operations of the enterprise upon approval of the petition. These documents must be prepared carefully to meet the technical requirements of the INS.

If the service center requires additional information it will send a request for evidence. It may also send the file to the local district office for interview.

Once the I-526 petition is approved, then the individual and his or her spouse and children may apply for conditional permanent residence. (See Chapter 4.) The process for adjustment is the same as for a family-based petitions except that an approved I-526 rather than an I-130 petition is submitted. This adjustment application is filed with the local INS office.

CONDITIONAL
GRANT

The visa is initially granted on a conditional basis, similar to the conditional residence granted through marriage to a U.S. citizen. After two years, the investor must apply to remove the conditions by demonstrating that the investment was established and in continuous operation during the two-year period. The application to remove conditions is filed within the 90-day period prior to the expiration of the conditional green card.

An application to remove conditions is as follows:
- Form I-829;
- filing fee of $395;
- a copy of a conditional green card; and,
- supporting documentation:
  - establishment of enterprise (i.e. tax returns);
  - required amount of investment (i.e. audited financial statement);
  - proof that the investor sustained investments throughout conditional period;
  - bank statements;
  - invoices;
  - contracts;
  - business licenses;
  - corporate tax returns or quarterly tax statements;
  - payroll records; and,
  - I-9 forms.

The form I-829 should be completed and as many supporting documents as possible attached. It is necessary to prove the three points set out in the above outline, namely, that the enterprise was established, the required amount of investment was made, and the investment was sustained through the two-year conditional period.

The above application is filed with the same service center as the original I-526 petition.

Once form I-829 is approved and the conditions have been removed, the investment may be sold. It is advisable to wait until the green card actually arrives in the mail before doing so, however.

10 Years in the U.S.

At the master calendar hearing, the immigration judge will be asking what forms of relief you will be seeking in court if you have been in the U.S. for ten years. Once you or your attorney mention cancellation of removal, the immigration judge will instruct you as to the deadline and precise procedure to file the applications. You should listen carefully to the immigration judge and write down everything he or she says. The following are normally initially required:

- Form EOIR-42B;

- evidence of payment of $100 filing fee;

- fingerprint fee of $50;

- Form G325A (original to the INS attorney, copy to the court);

- certificate of service;

- proof of qualifying relative's immigration status; and,

- green card style photo.

The listing of documents in Chapter 11 is a complete list that may be used to prove a cancellation of removal case. The principal form to be completed is the EOIR-42B. It is a detailed seven-page form requesting seemingly every possible personal history item. Before this application is filed with the court, it must be paid for at the local INS office. The immigration court does not accept any filing fees. In order to pay for an application at the INS cashier and receive it back, you will need to complete a routing slip and place it on top of the application. After the application is filed, supporting documents will be due to the court fourteen days prior to the hearing date. Go through the list of documents and compile as many as possible for filing.

COURT RULES

Bear in mind that there are local rules that need to be complied with, particularly as they relate to the filing of documents. The immigration court will supply you with these rules. If you have an attorney, as you should in immigration court, he or she will be aware of them. But if you do not have an attorney you will need to read and understand the court rules.

Example: All documents must be two hole punched at the top and contain a table of contents. Most courts have a ten day or fourteen day rule which requires all documents be filed ten or fourteen days ahead of the court hearing. If they are not, the judge can deny their admission.

The original application and supporting documents are filed with the court after the fee is paid.

A copy of any document filed with the EOIR must be *served* upon the trial attorneys at their office, usually called the Office of District Counsel. All documents filed with the immigration court must include a *certificate of service*. The Immigration Court clerk can give you their address. It is imperative that you have the court clerk stamp your copy as proof of timely filing.

EVIDENCE

Since these removal cases are so difficult to win, it is essential that as much evidence be compiled and filed with the immigration court. However, take care to only include documents that are truly beneficial to your cases. Do not include documents for the sake of creating an impressively thick file. The documents should be organized in a way that aids understanding and impact.

The use of an expert witness is beneficial to assist in proving your case. The cases turn on the country conditions in the native country and an expert convincingly describing the conditions to the immigration judge. It is up to the trial attorneys to disprove an expert's testimony and this is very difficult for a lay person to do. This is a dangerous path for the trial attorney if he or she tries to confront the expert. It may end up merely giving the expert another opportunity to put across his or her point of view and discuss the basis for his or her position. In a close case having an expert will certainly tip the balance in your favor.

WHAT TO
EXPECT

These cases are difficult to win. The legal standard of *exceptional and extremely unusual hardship* is as difficult to prove as it is to contemplate. An immigration attorney will be required to assist with developing evidence and conducting the hearing. Chapter 19 deals in detail with handling a case before the immigration court.

If your case is granted, in order to receive a green card, you must complete ADIT processing through the local INS office. ADIT processing involves completion of the card that will be made into your green card by the service center. Until this happens, a person is not a permanent resident.

FILING THE ADJUSTMENT OF STATUS APPLICATION

After you file, you will receive a receipt notice with an original cash register receipt stapled to it. The notice and receipt should be safely stored. You will need the original receipt for when you obtain a work permit or advance parole or at the adjustment interview to prove the fees were paid.

If a receipt notice is not received after a prolonged period, say six weeks or more, check to see if the check was cashed by the INS. If it was, and more than 45 days has elapsed since it was cashed, make a clear copy of both sides of the cancelled check and mail to the INS with an inquiry letter. If the check has not been cashed, then wait an appropriate period and re-file the original packet. While it might be possible to make an inquiry through the INS it is much less time and trouble to simply refile, particularly if a copy was made of the application. But place a sheet of paper on time, notifying the INS that an application was previously filed on a certain date with no response.

In normal circumstances, if the I-765 application was filed with the onestop, you will receive a letter within a month or two from the INS notifying you that a work permit appointment has been scheduled. As the receipt letter indicates, you will require the original receipt letter and fee receipt when you show up for the work permit appointment. There is no interview for the work permit. The INS clerk will make certain that your case is pending and that you are the person who filed the case. Within one hour, hopefully, you will be your way with a work permit card.

If you do not already have a social security number, you may now apply for one with the work permit. Simply go to the nearest Social Security Administration office and apply for a number. Within one week, you will receive a card containing your new number in the mail.

As the date for your interview draws near, you will receive a notice to take fingerprints at an application support center. The purpose of the fingerprints is to check to see if they match a record on the FBI computer. This is now done electronically.

If you are not sure what is on your record, you can obtain a copy from the FBI in Washington, DC. You will need to bring a disposition for every arrest.

You will then wait for your interview to be rescheduled. The backlog for each INS office varies widely.

NOTE: *Now is the time to make certain you have all of the documents needed for the interview. (See Chapter 17 on preparing for the interview.)*

SUPPORTING DOCUMENTS 15

The previous chapters have discussed the specific *eligibility requirements* for each *eligibility category*. In this chapter, issues common to all adjustment filings will be explained, especially where supporting documents are concerned.

ELIGIBILITY TO ADJUST IN U.S.

An individual in the U.S. must be in valid nonimmigrant status in order to apply for adjustment with a couple of important exceptions:

1) If an individual is the beneficiary of any I-130 petition or labor certification filed before January 18, 1998, he or she may apply for adjustment on any available basis in the U.S. despite being out of status or even having entered the country illegally.

2) If an individual is the beneficiary of any I-130 petition or labor certification filed before April 30, 2001, and was physically present in the U.S. on December 20, 2000, then he or she may apply for adjustment on any available basis in the U.S. despite being out of status or even having entered the country illegally.

3) If an individual lawfully entered the U.S. on a nonimmigrant visa (other than a K-1 visa), he or she may apply for adjustment through an immediate relative petition despite overstaying the nonimmigrant visa as long as they have not worked without INS authorization.

Essentially, exceptions 1 and 2 listed on the previous page qualify an individual for adjustment under Section 245(i). This section lets an individual be out of status, or have violated status, and simply pay a $1000 penalty. In other words, someone might possess a valid, unexpired tourist visa but is working without INS permission. If this were discovered (and acted upon) by the INS officer, they would be barred from adjustment except under this new law.

While an individual who is ineligible for adjustment in the U.S. may theoretically return to their home country to apply through an embassy, this is not as easy now as it once was. Under the laws that went into effect in 1996, if you are out of status for more than 180 days starting from April 1, 1997, and depart the U.S., you are barred for three years from applying for any immigration benefit. If you are out of status more than one year from April 1, 1997, and depart the U.S. you are barred for ten years. There are two important exceptions to this provision. One is that you are not considered out of status if you are under the age of 18 or if you have had a bona fide asylum application pending with the INS.

There is a possible *waiver* for having been out of status but it is very difficult to have approved. It requires that you have a U.S. citizen or green card-holding parent or spouse and that you can show it would be an extreme hardship to them if you are unable to enter the U.S. *Extreme hardship* is difficult to show, particularly at one of the embassies. Simply showing the emotional difficulties of being separated from family members is NOT sufficient. You will need to provide evidence that your spouse or parent requires your assistance with a medical condition, financial support, or some major reason. You will need to document these conditions by their own detailed affidavit, or a letter from a doctor.

GREEN CARD STYLE PHOTOS

You need two photos. One photo will be used to make your green card. The other photo will stay in your file for identification purposes.

While the photos are called *green card style*, in fact they will be used for every immigration document you will seek to obtain, including a *naturalization certificate*.

There are certain requirements for these photos. If the studio does not recognize the term "green card style", then you should probably go someplace else to have the photo taken. Now, many places take such photos including print shops and drugstore chains. Avoid at all costs, the places nearest the INS office. They often charge as much as $30 for two photos that normally cost $7.

Whenever submitting a photo to the INS, write the name and "A" number on the back of each photo with a pencil or felt pen. The "A" *number* is the eight digit number assigned by the INS and appears on your work permit, and fingerprint and interview notices.

FINGERPRINTS

Before an applicant can adjust his or her status, he must have fingerprints taken so that the applicant's FBI criminal record can be accessed. For the vast majority of people, this is not a problem.

Not only must the prints be taken, but they must be valid at the time of the interview. That is, at the time of adjustment, the fingerprints must have been taken within fifteen months.

If you notice that your fingerprints have expired and you are still waiting for an interview or for your case to be processed, then you may want to write to your local INS office and ask that you be provided an *appointment letter for fingerprinting* (notice to appear for fingerprints at a specified place).

You will be asked in the letter to take fingerprints at the Application Support Centers (ASC) nearest you. If you happen to move and know of a center closer to you, you can simply go there with the original notice.

TRANSLATIONS

Every document in a foreign language requires an English translation. If you live in an area that has a large foreign-born population, then it may easy to find a place that will do translations at a reasonable cost. A birth certificate should not cost more than $10 or $15 to translate. If you do pay to get a translation, keep the original of the translation for your future use. The INS only needs a copy of the translation.

You may also translate your document yourself. An example is provided in Appendix E of how to format the translation and a certification form. It is good form to place the translation on top, followed by the certification form, and then, a copy of the document in the original language.

It is not as hard as it might seem to do a translation. Do not worry too much about translating the legalistic language found on many documents such as birth certificates. The most important part of the translation is the date and place of birth and the names of the parents.

UNAVAILABLE DOCUMENTS

If a birth, marriage, or death record is not available, then the following may substitute:
- church or baptismal record (a certificate issued by a church attesting to the birth or religious ceremony);

- school record (any record from a school showing the child's date of birth and names of parents);

- a census record showing name, date and place of birth; and,

- *affidavits* (sworn statements from two persons who were living at the time of the birth or marriage.) The affidavit should contain the affiant's name, address, date and place of birth, his or her relationship to the adjustment applicant, full information concerning event and how the affiant acquired the knowledge.

In order to substitute the above documents, a *certificate of non-availability* from the proper governmental authority in the native country may be required. Sometimes, it is possible to obtain such documents from the country's embassy in the U.S. However, these documents are not always accepted by the INS office. The immigration court is much more likely to use substitute records

MEDICAL EXAMINATION

The *medical examination* is a "check" that the applicant does not carry any communicable diseases. Such diseases that are tested for are HIV, tuberculosis, leprosy, sexually transmitted diseases, etc. One cannot enter the U.S. with an active, contagious disease except with a *waiver*, if available, such as for HIV or TB.

The medical examination must be obtained from a certified medical provider. Each city has its own list of medical clinics. This list is not presently available on the INS website. The list is most easily available from either the forms line or the local INS office. It is also possible to call 800-375-5283 and obtain the name of the nearest doctor by entering your zip code.

Call to get a quote. The immigration exam should cost approximately $70 not including vaccinations. It may also take up to a week for the lab tests to come back. If you are in a rush, then call around. Some clinics are much faster than others.

VACCINATIONS It is now a requirement that the applicant have received all appropriate vaccinations. If you have any type of vaccination record, you should bring it to your medical exam. It can save you from getting costly and perhaps unnecessary vaccinations. A full set of vaccinations can run several hundred dollars.

FILLING IN FORM COMPLETELY The biggest problem with the medical examination is that the form is not marked completely by the doctor. Remind the doctor to make certain all boxes are checked on form I-693 and on the vaccination form. The applicant should also double check his or her green receipt copy of the examination. Any X-rays received along with the sealed envelope are not submitted to the INS.

TIMING   The medical examination is valid for only one year. If the medical exam results are filed along with the adjustment application, then it is valid no matter when the interview is scheduled. If the medical is brought to the interview, it must have been taken within the past year. Therefore, one should wait until the adjustment interview is scheduled before taking the medical exam.

AFFIDAVIT OF SUPPORT

With the affidavit of support, the INS attempts to ensure that an intending immigrant has adequate financial support and is not likely to become a *public charge*. This is an area that frequently causes a delay or denial of an adjustment application. Needless to say, the I-864 is extremely important to the green card process and care must be taken to carefully prepare and document.

The INS ensures that the rules regarding affidavits of support are met. The two things to watch for here are that the income requirement is met and that all supporting documentation are submitted along with the forms.

By signing the affidavit of support form, the sponsor is undertaking an obligation that he will support the immigrant if necessary and will reimburse any government agency or private entity that provides the sponsored immigrants with federal, state, or local means-tested public benefits.

The INS is seeking to ensure that you do not become a public charge. Section 212(a)(4) states that anyone who is likely to become a public charge is inadmissible. If that is not enough, section 237(a)(5) says that any alien within five years of entry who becomes a public charge is deportable.

The income requirement may be one of the more difficult requirements to meet in completing an adjustment of status case. In order to obtain a green card, it must be demonstrated that you have sufficient income to not become a public charge.

The line had to be drawn somewhere in order to ensure this. It has been determined that an income of 125% over the poverty line is sufficient to adjust status. For 2002, the poverty guidelines are as follows:

SPONSORS 125% POVERTY LINE			
Household Size	48 States	Alaska	Hawaii
2	14,925	18,663	17,175
3	18,775	23,475	21,600
4	22,625	28,288	26,025
5	26,475	33,100	30,450
6	30,325	37,913	34,875
7	34,175	42,725	39,300
8	38,025	47,538	43,725
additional persons	+3,850 per person	+3,849 per person	+4,425 per person

These figures are revised approximately in April of each year.

NOTE: *Military members sponsoring their spouse or child only need to have 100% of the poverty line. Multiply the above 125% level figures by .75 to get back to the 100% level.*

Other requirements are that the sponsor be over 18 years of age, have a domicile in U.S., and be a U.S. citizen or lawful permanent resident.

INSUFFICIENT INCOME

First, look to assets to make up non-sufficient income. You must have cash assets worth five times the difference between the income requirement and your income. Attach a copy of a savings account, stocks, bond or certificates of deposit, life insurance cash value, or real estate. You must include evidence of liens, mortgages, and liabilities for the given asset. You may also add the assets and income of the immigrant being sponsored.

You may add the income of a household member that either lives with you or is listed as a dependent on your most recent tax return. That household member then executes I-864A. Add the income to the third page of the I-864.

JOINT SPONSOR

Or you may use a *joint sponsor.* A joint sponsor is any sponsor who is not the petitioner. It is better that the joint sponsor be a relative but anyone can qualify. In this event, both the petitioner and joint sponsor should submit a fully documented and *notarized* original I-864. The joint sponsor must submit proof of U.S. citizenship or lawful permanent resident status.

SUPPORTING
DOCUMENTS

The following documents are required to accompany an affidavit of support:

- Form I-864 (signed and notarized within past six months);

- Form I-864A supplement with notarized signatures (for household member, if necessary);

- last three year's federal tax returns including all schedules and all W-2 forms for each year;

- a job letter from the employer;

- proof of assets (if required to meet income requirement); and,

- proof of citizenship or LPR status for joint sponsor.

Tax returns. Each year's tax returns should be in correct order and stapled together. The W-2 forms are critically important and will be insisted upon by the INS officer.

NOTE: *An original signed and notarized I-864 and I-864A (if required) and one complete set of supporting documents much be submitted for each principal applicant. For other dependent family members, only a photocopy of the application is required but not copies of the supporting documents.*

You may substitute Letter 1722 (tax transcript) if you do not have the actual returns. To obtain the transcript, you will need to visit your IRS office.

If you did not have to file a tax return, then you are directed to attach a written explanation and a copy of the instructions from the Internal Revenue Service publication that shows you were not obligated to file. Check the first pages of the 1040 instructions booklet on who does not have to file:

http://www.irs.gov

If you have not filed a tax return you were supposed to file, then you should file a late return and pay the penalty. Those who live outside the U.S. must still file an annual return. If necessary, it is often easy to rectify the missing returns by simply filing late. The penalty is not as severe as you might think.

NOTE: *You cannot substitute state income tax returns. Copies of these are not required.*

JOB LETTER

If you cannot get a job letter, then you may substitute a pay stub. If you are self-employed, then prepare a letter on your business letterhead with a description of salary.

EXCEPTIONS

An exception to the requirement for the affidavit of support is that if you already have credit for 40 quarters of coverage under the Social Security Act.

THE SPONSOR

The sponsor needs to fully understand that he or she is legally responsible for financial support of the sponsored immigrant until becoming a U.S. citizen or can be credited with 40 hours of work.

NOTE: *A divorce does not terminate the financial obligations of the petitioner with regard to the INS.*

The sponsor may be asked to reimburse the government if the new lawful permanent resident receives a federal "means-tested public benefit". The majority of the aid programs such as SSI, food stamps, and medicare qualify as such benefits. If unsure, one may simply ask the benefit provider whether it is a means-tested public benefit.

ADDRESS
CHANGES

There is a requirement that address changes are filed with thirty days on form I-865. Strict fines are in place for failure to notify the INS as to an address change. However, it is doubtful that anyone will ever be asked to pay this fine.

PUBLIC CHARGE AND USE OF PUBLIC BENEFITS

An alien seeking adjustment of status is inadmissible if the individual is likely to be a public charge. The INS has moved to a *totality of the circumstances* test to make this determination. The office should consider factors such as the individual's age, health, family status, assets, resources, financial status, education, and skills.

An alien who has received certain public benefits may be determined to become a public charge. Such a person is inadmissible as a permanent resident. It can be difficult to determine which of the many assistance programs will render a person inadmissible.

In 1999, the Department of State and the INS issued guidance concerning this previously murky area. These regulations clarified which programs are to adversely impact an adjustment application.

The following programs may cause a public charge determination:
cash welfare such as Supplemental Security Income (SSI); cash Temporary Assistance for Needy Families (TANF); and, state general assistance.

The INS will not consider cash welfare received by an alien's children or other family members for family charge purposes, unless the cash welfare is the family's only means of support.

institutionalization for long-term care. This includes things like residing in a nursing home or mental health facility at government expense.

The following programs will *not* have an adverse impact:

health care benefits. This includes things like Medicaid, state Children's Health Insurance Program, or other health services unless Medicaid is used for long-term institutional care.

food programs. These are things like food stamps, WIC (Special Supplemental Nutrition Program for Women, Infants and Children), school meals, or other food assistance.

non-cash programs. These are public housing, child care, energy assistance, disaster relief, Head Start, job training, or counselling.

INADMISSIBILITY 16

All of these grounds of inadmissibility are contained in Section 212(a) of the Immigration and Nationality Act. For some of them, there may be a waiver available. Just because a waiver is available, does not mean it will be granted. It is critical to consult an immigration attorney to determine the appropriate course of action.

CRIMINAL CONVICTIONS

Section 212 of the Immigration and Nationality Act sets forth restrictions on who may obtain a green card. Those who have committed certain types of crimes are advised to check with an immigration lawyer as to their eligibility.

If an adjustment application fails because of a criminal record, then the person may find him or herself in removal proceedings without any relief possible in the immigration court. Filing such an application is a senseless endeavor.

The following will prevent a person from obtaining a green card:
- crime involving moral turpitude;
- multiple criminal convictions with aggregate sentence of five years;
- miscellaneous other crimes such as unlawful use of a firearm;

- controlled substance violation;
- controlled substance trafficking; or,
- aliens who have or are likely to have engaged in terrorist activity.

HEALTH CONDITIONS

Certain diseases may prevent you from obtaining permanent residence. These will be detected through the required medical examination. If it happens that you have such a disease, there may be a waiver available. Consult with an immigration attorney.

PUBLIC CHARGE

It is extremely important that the I-864 affidavit of support form be carefully completed and care taken to ensure that all financial requirements are met. This helps to ensure that no one will become a *public charge*, or financial drain for support on the government. See Chapter 14 for instructions and more information.

OUTSTANDING ORDER OF DEPORTATION OR REMOVAL

Apart from the above, anyone who has a deportation or removal order entered against them, is inadmissible. One may not apply for adjustment within five years of a final order of deportation or ten years after a final order of removal.

One can have a *deportation* order even if they never received notice of the court hearing. If there is any doubt as to whether such an order exists, they should call the immigration court status line and possibly follow up with the specific immigration court. It is better to find out sooner rather than be informed by the INS officer at the interview and possibly be taken into INS custody.

In some cases, it is possible to reopen the immigration proceedings. The other option is to file a *waiver* on Form I-212, if the applicant is eligible. However, even if the waiver is approved, the alien will be required to process for adjustment at an embassy abroad possibly causing a problem of unlawful presence in the U.S. The alien will really need to consult a attorney before proceeding with either of these options.

UNLAWFUL PRESENCE

Under section 212(a)(9), one may not adjust status if they have accumulated certain time in unlawful status. Especially at this time, the INS is sensitive to making sure an applicant has not been a member of any terrorist organization or convicted of any terrorist-sounding criminal charge.

If one was out of status in the U.S. for more than six months beginning April 1, 1997, and departs the U.S., he or she may not adjust status for three years. Similarly, if one accumulates one year of unlawful presence, they may not adjust status for ten years. Even if one is able to re-enter the U.S. after the unlawful presence, they could be barred at the interview.

A *waiver* exists for unlawful presence but it is difficult to obtain. One must have a U.S. citizen or LPR spouse or parent to qualify for the waiver. There must also be a demonstration of extreme hardship to that relative. These waivers are very difficult to obtain at an embassy. They are somewhat easier to obtain in the U.S. since the office can be face to face with the applicant and the qualifying relative. They might also be reviewable by an immigration judge.

NOTE: *If one has a student visa marked "duration of status" (D/S), they do not acquire unlawful presence until an INS officer or Immigration judge finds a status violation. Thus, such persons are much less likely to have acquired unlawful presence.*

OTHER IMMIGRATION VIOLATIONS

The following violations make an applicant inadmissible to the U.S. under 212(a)(6):

- present in U.S. without admission or parole (unless eligible under Section 245(i));

- failure to attend removal proceeding;

- fraud or willful representation;

- being a stowaway (that is, entered U.S. illegally by travelling on a commercial transportation such as a train, bus or boat where a fare should have been paid);

- alien smugglers;

- immigration document fraud; or,

- student visa abusers.

NOTE: *The alien should consult a attorney if one of the above conditions exists.*

THE INS INTERVIEW 17

After your forms are filed, you will most likely have to face the INS interview. This chapter will give you a good basis for what to expect and how to proceed.

EXPEDITING THE INTERVIEW

Making the interview happen quickly is generally difficult to do unless you fall into one of several circumstances:

- the petitioner is ill;
- the beneficiary will *age out* (that is, turns 21 years of age and loses eligibility under the petition);
- the case is a *diversity visa case* (which has a strict deadline of September 30 for completion or else the visa expires); or,
- some other verifiable emergency.

INS OFFICERS

While the public often has a stereotypical perception of what an INS officer is like, the reality is they differ very widely. A good starting point is to realize that many people attracted to a government job are those that like security and do not want to rock the boat. To be fair, the officers have to struggle with a difficult work environment, including interviewing fifteen or so cases each day.

On the other hand, there are some officers who may seem overly authoritative. If an officer strikes you as unnecessarily rude, it is appropriate to say so politely to the officer. If the behavior does not stop, then it should be reported to his or her supervisor. You should ask the officer the name of the direct supervisor. Ask for the supervisor to intervene at the interview or else ask to speak to the supervisor back at the reception desk. An officer does not want to frequently require the intervention of a supervisor at the interviews. Such a tendency may appear on their performance appraisals.

It is easy to feel that you are at the mercy of the officer. However, this is not completely true. An officer really does not have the necessary discretion to deny a case simply because they feel like it. There are too many regulations, memos, and supervisors floating around for that to be the case. They are in just as much fear of acting inappropriately as you are of having your case denied or delayed. Any adverse action has to be justified to the supervisor—particularly if you ask to speak to one to explain your side. The only revenge is really to delay processing of the case.

As the INS is increasingly becoming a high profile agency, it is attracting better qualified officers. The old guard is being replaced by officers who are better educated and more professional in demeanor.

BRIBERY

As an aside, the fact is that bribery is simply too hard to keep quiet. An officer accepting a bribe would be at the mercy of the alien to maintain secrecy. Needless to say, bribing an INS officer would be a great story for that alien, to be retold at parties, at the neighborhood bar and embellished to future generations. An officer would risk losing not only his or her job but his or her government pension. (Again, government employees are not risk-takers by definition.)

THE INTERVIEW DOCUMENTS

Your interview notice is your ticket inside the INS building, especially if your interview is in the morning. There may be a long line of people outside the building. If you have an interview, you do not have to wait in this line. You should go to the front of the line and show your appointment notice to the security guard who is letting people in the building. Once inside you will go through security.

The key to a successful interview is to be prepared with the correct documents and copies, if necessary. The following original documents should be brought to the interview even though copies may have been submitted with the application:

- drivers license or state I.D.passport;

- work permit;

- I-94 (if made legal entry);

- birth certificates;

- marriage certificate;

- approval notices;

- citizen certificates or green card;

- adjustment application receipt notice;

- Social Security card;

- original job letter on company letterhead; and,

- three years tax returns with W-2 forms for petitioner or sponsor.

You will need a copy of every document required in support of your application. Any document in a foreign language will require a properly certified English translation.

The petitioner is normally required at the interview. If the petitioner resides outside the U.S., arrangements can be made to have the petitioner report to his or her embassy or consulate in lieu of appearing at the interview. If the petitioner is ill or elderly, arrangements can be made.

Be sure that the INS file reflects your current address so that your green card does not get lost in the mail. You will want to bring your passport to the interview so that a green card stamp can be placed in it once the adjustment application is approved. If you do not have a passport, it is well worthwhile to make the effort to get one before the interview, both for identification purposes and to get the stamp placed in it. You may take an approval notice to the INS and have a stamp placed in it after the interview, but this may require waiting in line for several hours.

AFTERMATH

REQUEST FOR
EVIDENCE

At this time, the INS is not looking for cases to deny. It takes much longer to deny a case than to grant it. If you give them what their looking for, chances are you will muddle through.

These days, a decision should be made on the spot unless documents are missing. If your case is not approved at the interview, then you were probably issued a letter called a Request for Evidence (RFE). An RFE lists the documents required to complete the case and sets a time limit. This time limit is strict. If you need an extension, put the request in writing or call the officer. The response to the RFE must be sent by certified mail return receipt request in order to prove mailing should that become necessary.

Before leaving the interview, you should ask the officer how long it will take after the documents are turned in before the case will be completed. Ask how you should follow up, if there is no response for a while after you turn in the documents. Be sure you have their name and if possible their phone number.

Also keep track of the date of expiration of your fingerprints, which expire after fifteen months. If making an inquiry to request status of your case, also notify the INS that a fingerprint appointment letter is required.

If the case is approved and the passport is stamped or the green card received in the mail, the new permanent resident can contact Social Security to obtain an unrestricted card. The SS number will remain the same. It is not strictly necessary to obtain a new card but it would have its advantages such as in new employment situations.

THE DENIAL

NOTE: *If your application is denied, you definitely need to speak with an attorney or person qualified in immigration law.*

If the denial is in error, then a *motion to reopen* should be filed pointing out the mistake along with whatever documentary evidence might be required. The motion to reopen should be followed up with a phone call to the officer or an examinations supervisor. It is good practice to first file a motion to reopen for purposes of the record.

However, the vast majority of the time, a denial results in your file being sent to the Deportation Section for their review. A Notice to Appear (NTA) will likely be issued and served on the applicant. This means that the person has to appear in immigration court at a time to be set in the future.

In order for the INS to serve an applicant with the NTA, they must have the correct address. If you have moved and not notified the INS, that may prove too high a hurdle for the INS to serve a Notice to Appear given the number of cases they must process. (In most cities, the INS will have a huge file room full of cases to be processed for immigration proceedings.)

A further point of delay is the immigration court itself. The immigration court has a somewhat limited capacity to hear cases, there is a backlog. Once the NTA is served on the applicant and filed with the court, there is a wait of one year for a court date. However, once the case is before an immigration judge, it will proceed as quickly as possible.

Green Card Missing

If your case was approved at the interview, your green card should come in the mail after a period of time. At least, most of the time.

The biggest cause of a non-receipt of the green card is that you change your address. Most people will file a change of address notice with the post office, which is good for six months. However, the envelope with the green card contains an instruction to not forward to the new address. Sometimes, the envelope is forwarded anyway, but sometimes it is not.

If the envelope is not forwarded or otherwise cannot be delivered, it is sent back to the service center of the person's jurisdiction. It is kept there for approximately six months and then destroyed. If the card is destroyed, it will require that you go back for *ADIT processing*. ADIT processing refers to the process where the alien places his fingerprint and signature on a card that will eventually be made into his green card.

NOTE: *Unfortunately, regulations do not permit an attorney to receive a green card at his or her office.*

SERVICE CENTERS 18

A couple of points are relevant to a case that is at a service center. Depending on the backlog, the application will be decided on. If any information is missing or documentation incomplete, then a Request for Evidence (RFE) may be issued. You will then have an eighty-four day period to provide the required information.

NOTE: *This is a very strict deadline. Any response should be returned to the INS by overnight mail so that proof of mailing is available should the INS claim it was never received. You have generally one chance to comply with the RFE, so be sure you have enclosed all of the information. If it is not available, provide a detail explanation as to why.*

The adjustment process varies by service center. You will need to go the service center website to confirm the processing time before taking additional action.

If the processing time is past the time indicated on the receipt notice., wait an additional week or two. If nothing happens, you should call the number at the bottom of the receipt notice. It is possible to call the service center late at night when the phone lines are free. Eventually, you will be asked to punch in your case number including the three-letter service center designation as a number. (For example, "LIN" for the Lincoln service center is "546" on the keypad.)

You might get useful recorded information about your case. For example, the recording might say that an approval notice or request for evidence was sent.

To clear up processing problems, it is possible to call the service center and speak with an information officer. This is not an officer who will be deciding on the application. The information officer will not have access to the file and may only have the same information that is in the automated system.

A case will not be denied without allowing an opportunity to remedy the problem. While you may reapply in the event of a denial if the reason for denial can be overcome. You will need to be *in status* to do so unless the petition is grandfathered under Section 245(i).

If the case is granted, an *approval notice* will be mailed to the applicant. The applicant will be required to appear at his or her local INS office for ADIT processing.

IMMIGRATION COURT 19

If your case is denied at the INS, then you may find yourself placed into *removal proceedings* before the immigration court. The most important feature of the immigration court is that it is not part of the INS, but is a separate agency within the Department of Justice. The immigration judge (IJ) is not bound by a decision made by the INS and will seek to decide for himself based upon the court record. A proceeding before the immigration court is a civil rather than criminal proceeding, although the consequences of deportation may be much more severe than in a typical criminal case.

Before the law changed in 1996, proceedings before the immigration court used to be referred to as "deportation" rather than "removal proceedings." The name was changed to reflect the substantive changes in the law and to leave behind any case law associated with the term deportation.

The fact that your application may have been denied by the INS or the Asylum Office is of no concern to the IJ. In fact, you have gained credibility before the court because you affirmatively filed an application for relief. In other words, you applied for asylum on your own, as opposed to asking for it before the immigration court for the first time in a defensive posture to avoid or delay deportation.

NOTE: *If you have moved since your case was denied, it may be difficult for the INS to serve notice.*

Other than having your application denied, there are several other ways to land in immigration court. The other common way is to be apprehended by the INS as an *illegal alien* or as one who has been in contact with a law enforcement officer or criminal court. Even a green card holder who has committed crimes may be placed in proceedings. It is also not uncommon for a legal permanent resident who has acquired a criminal record to find themselves excluded from the U.S. upon re-entry if his or her record is checked by the border officer.

NOTE: *The court system is so backlogged that it may be a year before a court date can be scheduled, although this varies widely by locality.*

In reality the person who actually has a legitimate avenue for relief can fare very well in immigration court. For example, an asylum interview before the asylum office is a one-sided interview at the direction of the officer. However, before the immigration court, the same asylum applicant can not only put on a more effective case but also have the case decided by a more neutral and sympathetic person. Likewise, a marriage case denied by the INS will be treated more fairly and impartially by the immigration judge.

IMMIGRATION JUDGES

Naturally as human beings, immigration judges (IJ) exhibit a wide range of personality and inclinations to grant a case. An asylum application granted by one IJ might be laughed out of court by another IJ.

The IJs are unlike most judges you will see on TV. First of all, he or she is really an administrative law judge. They work for the Department of Justice, which is headed by the *Attorney General*, the country's top *prosecutor*. Thus, there is a central tension between the IJ's ultimate boss, the Attorney General, and the rights of an alien. (In contrast, a *federal judge* works for the *judiciary* which is a separate branch of the U.S.)

Previously, IJs were called *special inquiry officers*. Thus, they have wide power to interrupt and conduct their own questioning. A normal judge who is part of the judiciary, only runs the trial, decides questions of law, and sometimes questions of fact.

CHANGING JUDGES
It pays to know who your judge is. It is not possible to request a different judge in the same city. However, if your case is assigned to a tough judge, it may be worth your while to simply move to a different city and file a motion for change of venue with the original judge. If you have indeed moved, the motion will be granted and you will be scheduled for a master calendar hearing before the new judge. IJs are likely to grant such a motion because it means the case is marked off their docket and they have saved the several hours it might have taken for a hearing.

ATTORNEYS
Generally speaking, IJs are fair and decent people committed to upholding the law. However, the INS is represented in court by a trial attorney who is essentially *a prosecutor*. The trial attorneys unfortunately have little discretion to make their own decision regarding a case and therefore just oppose all but the most sympathetic cases. While they are personally likeable people, they can be counted on to oppose the majority of cases.

COMMON MISTAKES
The first mistake people often make regarding immigration court is that the IJ does not have absolute authority to do what is right or fair. Even if they are married to a U.S. citizen, or have U.S. citizen children, or have lived in the U.S. for twenty years and always pay their taxes, these facts may not be relevant. Sometimes a certain law decisively impacts their case and their personal circumstances, no matter how compelling, cannot change the outcome.

Another mistake is to think that because the IJ outwardly appears to be a likeable person, he or she will grant the case. There may be a difference between the outward demeanor of a judge and his or her leniency in rendering a decision.

HANDLING A COURT CASE

You should not be in immigration court without an immigration attorney. If your case is very simple, then it may be possible. But before doing so, you must consult with an attorney so that you understand the law and be sure you qualify. It is not enough that your friend had the same case and it was granted. A small fact that is different may make your case come out differently.

If you are going to proceed with your own case, you must ask at the filing window for a copy of the local rules of the court. It says how and when to file documents. You will be expected to follow these rules.

One feature of the immigration court that does make it possible to conduct your own hearing is that the *rules of evidence* are relaxed from the normal rules followed in a normal courtroom. In other words, *hearsay* statements are allowed into evidence, or documents do not necessarily need *foundation*. Therefore, a lot of objections that the prosecutor might normally make when a lay person conducts his or her own hearing that would not be appropriate before an IJ.

The principal trap is that it may seem easy to argue your case, that you are married to a U.S. citizen or have U.S. citizen children and should not be deported. However, the majority of what that the respondent will say in court will be absolutely irrelevant to any form of relief, no matter how important or just it might sound.

Even attorneys who are unfamiliar with immigration law but perhaps familiar with civil court procedure are at a complete loss to understand the procedure let alone figure out any avenue for relief. They too have a tendency to focus on the irrelevant portions of the respondent's situation.

TYPES OF HEARINGS There are two types of hearings in immigration court, the *master calendar* and *individual hearings*. It is easy to check on your hearing date and other case status information. Simply call 800-898-7180 and enter your A number. There are a series of five options of which the first gives you the date of your next hearing.

NOTICE TO APPEAR

An immigration case is initiated by a document called a *Notice to Appear* or *NTA*. If you consult with an attorney, you must be able to show this document to him or her. If you do not have it, then go to the immigration court that has your case and ask the court clerk to give you a copy. The important part of this form is that it states the grounds upon which you are removable from the U.S. and the facts that establish it.

You need to be prepared to proceed or at least have a good excuse. You may show up to court the first time and ask for time to find an attorney. Usually in this instance, the IJ will reset your master hearing in thirty or sixty days.

The IJ will not be willing to delay the case to allow a visa petition to be approved or a labor certification or some other favorable action. Continuances are hard to come by in immigration court. The IJ wants the case off his or her crowded docket.

THE MASTER CALENDAR HEARING

The following are a list of items that may come up at a master calendar hearing. They are written in formal English since this is how they will be referred to during the actual court proceeding. A respondent, through his attorney if he or she has one, will be asked to do at least some of the following:

- concede that he or she is the respondent named in the Notice to Appear;

- acknowledge that he or she is present in court with an attorney or acknowledge receipt of the list of free legal services programs required under the Code of Federal Regulations, Title 8, Section 242.2(d);.

- acknowledge proper service of the Notice to Appear;

- agree to the admission into the record of proceedings of the Notice to Appear as Exhibit 1;

- acknowledge that he or she has been advised by an attorney as to the nature and purpose of these deportation proceedings and of the respondent's rights, and that the respondent understands this advice;

- waive a formal reading and explanation of the charges contained in the Notice to Appear;

- admit all or some of the factual allegations or deny all or some factual allegations contained in the Notice to Appear;

- concede that the he or she is removable as charged in the Notice to Appear and on any Form I-261;

- designate a country as the country for removal purposes if necessary;

- specify of the following relief from removal he or she is eligible:

  - termination or administrative closure of proceedings;

  - adjustment of status;

  - asylum or withholding of deportation;

  - cancellation of removal;

  - waiver of grounds of removability or excludability pursuant to section(s) of the immigration and Nationality Act;

  - voluntary departure; or,

  - other;

- acknowledge that he or she understands that, unless otherwise ordered by the court, the respondent has thirty (30) days from the date hereof to file application(s) for all such relief, accompanied by all required supporting documents, in accordance with all applicable regulations;

- understand and agree that if the respondent fails to timely file any written application(s) for relief indicated above, the court will enter a decision on the record before it without further notice or hearing, and that no voluntary departure will be granted unless otherwise stipulated by the Service on the record or in writing;

- estimate the time required for the hearing;

- state that an interpreter is not required because the respondent speaks and understands English, OR request the court to order an interpreter proficient in the language for the individual calendar hearing; and,

- acknowledge that his attorney or the IJ has advised him or her of the consequences under Section 242B of the Act of failure to attend this removal proceeding, failure to depart voluntarily if the respondent has agreed or been allowed to do so, and failure to appear for removal at the time and place ordered.

The most important part of the master hearing is to determine which forms of relief the respondent is eligible for. The IJ actually has a responsibility to see what these might be. A case will be reopened by the Board of Immigration Appeals, if the IJ does not advise you as to your possible relief.

If the IJ discovers that you have an avenue for relief, then just listen to what he says. You must have paper with you and take very careful notes. Ask questions if you are unclear as to any instruction. Pay particular attention to which forms are required and when they should be filed. If a deadline is missed, the relief may be permanently cut off.

If later you discover that you forgot something the IJ said, you can go back to the court and listen to the tape recording of the hearing to listen again to what he or she said. Even if you still do not understand what he meant, the IJ would be impressed that you made that much effort to try to comply with the directions.

THE INDIVIDUAL HEARING

The *individual hearing* is the most critical aspect of one's immigration case, no matter how many twists and turns it has taken. Take care when preparing for the hearing. Problems and issues that might be raised by the INS should be anticipated as much as possible.

Applications for relief and supporting documents are due to the immigration court by the "*call-up date.*" This is the deadline set by the immigration judge in the particular case, or if one is not specifically set, then it is either ten or fourteen days prior to the hearing depending on the court's local operating rules. It is critical that all evidence and names of proposed witnesses be submitted to the court by this date or else there is a risk they will not be allowed into evidence at the hearing. Any motions, such as a motion for a continuance, must also be filed prior to the call-up date.

Preparation is important. If the supporting documentation is complete and convincing, and the alien is prepared to testify in detail about his or her case, then the odds of that case being approved are drastically increased. Too often it happens that a loose end to a case is not accounted for, and the entire case unravels.

DIRECT AND CROSS-EXAMINATION

On the hearing date, the IJ will hear the testimony of the alien and any witnesses and consider the documents submitted. The alien will first be questioned by his or her attorney in what is called a *direct examination.* The IJ will often interrupt with his or her own questions. At the end of the direct exam, the INS attorney will conduct a *cross-examination.* This cross examination is based on the testimony of the alien and documents contained in the record. At the end of the cross-exam, the alien may conduct a *re-direct* based on the cross-examination. In the same fashion, the testimony of any other witnesses will be heard.

At the end of the hearing, the alien or his or her attorney will be allowed to make *closing remarks.* These remarks may be critical to summarizing the testimony and addressing any damage done by the INS attorney during cross-examination.

ENDING THE HEARING

When the case is finished the judge will issue a decision, called an *order.* If the case is denied, the judge reads an oral decision into the record. It is important to take notes as to the basis for the denial. If the alien chooses to *appeal* the decision, it will be necessary to state the reasons for appeal on the *notice of appeal* form.

APPEAL

If an appeal is to be taken, the notice of appeal form must be received at the Board of Immigration Appeals within thirty days. This is a very strict deadline. It should be sent by overnight mail to ensure proper receipt. There is also a fee of $110 to be enclosed.

ADJUSTMENT OF STATUS GRANTED

If adjustment of status is granted, in order to receive a green card, the alien must complete ADIT processing through the local INS office. ADIT processing is the completion of the card that will be made into your green card by the service center. Until this happens, the person has not become a permanent resident (despite language to the contrary on the order).

FAMILY-BASED CASES

There are a few special considerations that may be crucial to a family-based case.

While it is possible to obtain adjustment of status through the immigration judge, you will require an approved and current I-130 petition. Unfortunately, the I-130 needs to be approved by the INS before the IJ can proceed with adjustment. Equally unfortunate, the IJ will be most impatient to finish the case and will not want to wait very long for the INS to complete processing of the case.

NOTE: *If a person is married after the date the NTA is served, then you are not guaranteed a continuance. Until recently there were long delays in processing I-130 petitions.*

A major advantage to being in immigration court is that if one has the approved I-130 petition, but the parties are separated, it is still possible to go into court and have the adjustment approved. However, there cannot be a divorce. But, since a divorce may take a substantial amount of time to complete, this scenario may work out.

Appeals and Beyond

There is often a worry on behalf of the alien that if the case is lost in the immigration court, the INS will take the person into custody. This is a rare occurrence. You are probably more likely to be taken into custody at an adjustment interview or a citizenship interview if you have a serious criminal record.

If your case is denied by the IJ, then you have the right to appeal your case to the Board of Immigration Appeals (BIA) located in Falls Church, Virginia just outside of Washington, D.C. The BIA is a separate agency within the Department of Justice.

The *notice of appeal* (Form EOIR-26) is due at the BIA within thirty days of the denial of your case. It does not matter when the documents are actually mailed. Even if you mail the documents by overnight mail the day before the due date. If the mail service makes a mistake and does not deliver through their own negligence, your appeal is terminated. Period. This is a very strict deadline to which there are no exceptions.

Except in an unusual case, you will not be making any appearance in front of this court. The court will make its decision based upon the *briefs* prepared by your attorney and the INS attorney and on the documents that are in the record of proceeding. The wait time is approximately six to twelve months for the transcripts to arrive in the mail along with a briefing schedule.

An advantage of the appeals process is that if you are waiting for a preference visa, your labor certificate to be approved, or your I-130 to be approved, it can give you a couple of years to allow that good stuff to happen.

REMOVAL ORDERS

If you are ordered removed by the Immigration Court you typically cannot return to the U.S. for ten years. In the case of a removal on criminal grounds, you will be ordered to be removed for twenty years. Realistically, the same criminal ground may prevent you from ever returning to the U.S. unless you get a waiver of inadmissibility approved, which is very difficult.

If a person returns to the U.S. after removal, they may be criminally prosecuted and face substantial sentence in a federal prison.

> *Warning:* Under a new operating procedure, the INS will be notifying the FBI of person ordered deported for entry into the National Crime Information Center (NCIC) database. This will allow local and state police to determine if an individual is subject to a deportation order. Someone now pulled over for even traffic violations, such as speeding, can now be easily checked for an immigration violation. Such a person then will likely be taken into custody and handed over to the INS. In such instances, a bond from immigration custody may be difficult to obtain.

LOSING YOUR GREEN CARD  20

This chapter discusses the different ways the green card or permanent residence status can be lost and the procedures to replace it.

MISPLACE

One can file the I-90 form with their local INS office and be processed for a new green card. The following should be brought in-person to the local INS office:

- Form I-90;

- filing fee of $130;

- two green card style photos;

- state-issued identification or foreign passport;

- copy of green card (if available);

- proof of name change (such as marriage certificate or divorce decree); and,

- fingerprint fee of $50 if now over 14 years of age.

However, if the individual is eligible for naturalization, then it may be cheaper and easier to save the filing fee and hassle and simply file the N-400 application without bothering to replace the green card. This is true if the permanent resident will not be travelling outside the U.S. or will not be needing the green card to show to their present or future employer. At the naturalization interview, the applicant will simply be asked to complete an affidavit saying that the green card is lost.

OUTSIDE U.S. FOR MORE THAN 6 MONTHS

A permanent resident of the U.S. is expected to permanently reside in the U.S. If a permanent resident seeks to enter the U.S. after an absence of less than six months, then admission is guaranteed with only one exception. That exception is if the resident has been convicted of a crime that makes them inadmissible.

If a permanent resident attempts to enter the U.S. after an absence of more than six months but less than one year, then they are no longer guaranteed readmission, and are considered to be an *applicant* for admission. As a practical matter, this should not cause any problem as long as the permanent resident has a residence in the U.S., has filed taxes every year, and was held up in his or her home country for reasons our of his or her control. The treatment the permanent resident gets may depend on the inspector who processes the entry. Further, such a permanent resident may be questioned about whether he or she is a public charge when he or she returns and the use of cash welfare or long-term care may be considered.

However, the INS depends upon an honor system to detect an impermissibly long absence from the U.S. At the present time, the INS is not able to maintain records as to absences from the U.S. of a permanent resident. The only evidence they will have is the testimony of the returning permanent resident.

If it is anticipated that an absence from the U.S. will be for more than one year, then a problem may develop. The permanent resident should apply for a re-entry permit, which does not guarantee re-entry but is another piece of evidence that they had no intention of abandoning their permanent residence.

CRIMINAL RECORD

Lawful permanent residents need to be careful to stay away from the criminal justice system. Many types of crimes that seem to be minor charges, may cause an alien to possibly lose his green card.

Any criminal conviction can have immigration consequences no matter whether its a misdemeanor, whether you have been in the U.S. for many years, or whether your wife and children and parents are all U.S. citizens. There are two basic categories of crimes that have an immigration consequence. One classification is *crimes involving moral turpitude* (CMIT),which include minor retail thefts. For a CIMT, an LPR can normally have a hearing before an immigration judge to show why they should not be deported.

The following crimes make a person deportable:

- conviction of one crime involving *moral turpitude* (CIMT) committed within five years of entry for which a sentence of one year may be imposed;

- conviction of two or more CIMTs;

- conviction of an aggravated felony;

- conviction of controlled substance violation;

- conviction of domestic violence;

- violation of a protection order;

- conviction of a firearms offense;

- false claim to U.S. citizenship; or,

- in very rare circumstances, use of cash welfare or long-term care within the first five years in the U.S. for an illness or disability that existed before adjustment *(public charge determination)*

The more serious type of crimes are *aggravated felonies*. These are listed in Section 101(a)(43) of the Immigration and Nationality Act (INA). When Congress first came up with the idea the aggravated felony classification in 1988, the list consisted of a few serious crimes, such as kidnapping and murder. However, Congress has been adding to the list every year so that now most felonies are aggravated felonies. Even worse, when Congress adds crimes to the list, the effect is *retroactive*. This means that even if at the time the person pled guilty the crime was not an aggravated felony, the fact that it was later added meant the person now had an aggravated felony for immigration purposes.

Further, in 1996, Congress removed section 212(c) relief for a person who had an aggravated felony on his or her record. The fact that you committed the crime when it was not an deportable offense, may not make a difference. LPRs even with a retroactive aggravated felony now not only had no way to avoid deportation but were effectively barred from returning to the U.S. at any time. Imagine having to tell a person, who now might have a family, of these harsh consequences for a crime which was often committed in his or her youth.

CRIMINAL ATTORNEYS

Unfortunately, not every criminal attorney is aware of immigration consequences. Too many times a green card holder never knew he or she would be deportable by pleading guilty to a certain crime. Anyone who has a green card and is arrested on a criminal charge, needs to consult with an *immigration lawyer* before proceeding with the criminal case.

PLEAS

Once a *plea* is made, there is almost no going back. In many states, the only possibility of reopening your case is if your lawyer gave you wrong advice. If he or she said "don't worry about being deported because you're married to a U.S. citizen" then you could reopen your case. However, if the immigration consequences were never discussed, as is usually the case, you are probably stuck with a conviction and its consequences. This differs by state so it is worth consulting with a criminal lawyer.

PARDONS

The only option may be to seek a *pardon* before the state governor. Most states have a prisoner review board that handles pardon applications. They will provide information on the pardon process. While the odds of a pardon are remote, you have a chance. If your crime is victimless, such as possession of a small amount of drugs, then there is at least some probability of success.

YOUR OPTIONS

You have many more options prior to your plea. For example, it is much better to plead guilty to *simple battery*, which has no immigration effect rather than *domestic battery*, which makes you deportable. Even if it means serving a short time in jail or longer probation, you are well advised to plead guilty rather than suffer immigration consequences in the future.

Further, there are strict provisions for mandatory custody of criminal aliens, even those with green cards. This means that if you are picked up by the INS, you may not be eligible for a *bond*.

THE BORDERS

If you leave the country, you could be denied entry if it is discovered that you have a criminal record at the border.

PREVENTING DEPORTATION

If an alien is in proceedings on account of a criminal record, he or she must consult with an immigration attorney to determine whether a *waiver* is available and the likelihood of it being granted in the local jurisdiction.

If the crime does not involve an aggravated felony, then a waiver may be possible. While an aggravated felony conviction automatically revokes permanent residence status, those with other removable offenses, such as CIMTs, may apply for *cancellation of removal.*

The following is filed in immigration court at the direction of the immigration judge to initiate the cancellation of removal case:

- Form EOIR-42A Application for Cancellation of Removal for Certain Permanent Residents filed with immigration court filing fee of $100;

- Form G325A (original to INS Attorney, copy to court); and,

- certificate of service.

To qualify for cancellation, the following must be shown at the hearing:
- you have been an LPR for five years;

- you have resided in the U.S. continuously for seven years after having been admitted in any status except *period of residence stops*:

  - after service of a Notice to Appear in immigration court; or,
  - when become inadmissible under section 212(a)(2) or removable under sections 237(a)(2) or (4);

- you have not been convicted of an aggravated felony;

- you were never before granted cancellation, suspension, or Section 212(c) relief;

- you can demonstrate positive factors:

  - evidence of hardship to respondent and family if removed;
  - existence of U.S. citizen spouse and children;
  - other family ties within U.S.;
  - residency of long duration in U.S.;
  - history of employment;
  - existence of property or business ties; or,
  - existence of value and service to the community.

- you have proof of genuine rehabilitation:

  - lack of commission of other crimes;
  - attendance at rehab programs;
  - statements of remorse;
  - evidence attesting to good character; or,
  - service in the armed forces.

- you can account for negative factors:

  - nature and underlying circumstances of crime;
  - other immigration violations;
  - other criminal record; or,
  - other evidence of bad character.

- If you have a drug offense or serious criminal conviction or record, you have to show *outstanding equities*.

The previous list is documentation that may be used to prove a cancellation of removal case. The principal form to be completed is the EOIR-42A. It is a detailed seven-page form requesting seemingly every possible personal history question. Before this application is filed with the court, it must be paid for at the local INS office. The immigration court does not accept any filing fees. In order to pay for an application at the INS cashier and receive it back, you will need to complete a routing slip and place it on top of the application. After the application is filed, supporting documents will be due to the court fourteen days prior to the hearing date. Go through the list of documents and compile as many as possible for filing.

NOTE: *The IJ can be expected to be fairly sympathetic to this type of case, particularly for a long-time permanent resident. Nonetheless, as much evidence as possible should be accumulated.*

NATURALIZATION 21

It is a good idea to file for citizenship as soon as you are eligible. There are a few criteria for eligibility:

Residency and Age. You must be a lawful permanent resident and at least 18 years of age.

Time as permanent resident. A person who has been a permanent resident for a minimum of five years (really four years nine months) may apply for citizenship. Those that obtained the green through marriage to a U.S. citizen, can apply three years (or two years nine months) if they are still married and residing with the U.S. citizen spouse. There are several other exceptions to the five-year rule.

Continuous residence in the U.S. The time as permanent resident described above may be broken by an absence from the U.S. of six months or longer. If the absence is less than one year but more than six months, it may be possible to argue that the continuous residence was not broken.

Physical presence in the U.S.. One must spend thirty months of the sixty months prior to the filing of the naturalization application actually living in the U.S.. This is only 18 months where the green card was obtained through marriage to a U.S. citizen.

Good moral character. One must have been a person of good moral character during the period of five years prior to filing and through the time the application is pending. *Good moral character* has been interpreted to mean character that measures up to the standards of average citizens of the community in which the applicant resides.

Not every criminal conviction breaks the good moral character requirement. A lawyer should be consulted if this is an issue. Any person with an aggravated felony under Section 101(a)(43) must not apply for citizenship as they are deportable with no possible relief in immigration court.

Grounds such as failure to pay child support, file income tax returns, or false testimony may be found to constitute lack of good moral character. Failure to register with the Selective Service may be a ground but only if the applicant *knowingly* failed to register—if a person did not know to register, then it is not a ground.

English and civic knowledge. The applicant must be able to speak, read and write English as well as pass a test of U.S. history and government. The applicant must answer six out of ten multiple choice questions correctly out of a list of questions. Those who have been a permanent resident for more than fifteen years and are over fifty-five years of age or have been a permanent resident for more than twenty years and are over fifty may take the civics test and conduct the interview with a translator.

NOTE: *A medical waiver on form N-648 may be submitted to waive this requirement.*

State residence. You must have resided for at least three months in the state in which the petition was filed.

For most countries, acquiring U.S. citizenship does not renounce the previous citizenship. The naturalized U.S. citizen simply becomes a dual citizen. However, there are numerous countries where this is not the case, for example, Germany, Japan and Australia. If there is any doubt, simply contact your country's embassy.

APPLICATION

The naturalization application is filed with the service center *jurisdiction* over the person's residence. An application consists of the following:

- Form N-400 application for naturalization;
- filing fee of $250;
- fingerprint fee of $50;
- copy of green card;
- two green card style photos; and,
- original *court dispositions*, if applicable.

The above listing consists of the few items to be filed along with the N-400 application. Simply attach one check or money order in the amount of $310 ($260+$50), a copy of the green card, and 2 green card style photos. If one has a criminal record, then original court dispositions obtained from the criminal clerk's office must be obtained. If the court is out of town it is possible to simply call the court and mail in payment.

The above application packet is mailed to the appropriate service center. See Appendix E for the correct address. The service center will process the application and then forward it to the appropriate local office for interview.

To change one's address prior to interview scheduling, call the National Customer Service line (800-375-5283).

THE INTERVIEW

The following documents should be brought to the interview, if applicable:

- green card;

- driver's license;

- passport;

- re-entry permit or refugee travel document;

- original court dispositions;

- original police records;

- proof of spouse's citizenship;

- proof of spouse's residence;

- proof of child support;

- tax forms or tax summary IRS Form 1722;

- proof of name change; and,

- marriage license.

If the application is approved by the INS officer, a *swear-in date* will be received in the mail. Typically, the swear-in ceremony is held four to six weeks after the interview. At that time, the naturalization will be granted.

FINDING AN 22
ATTORNEY

Unfortunately, there are too many instances of immigration lawyers who are not completely familiar with laws and procedures. The other side of the coin are those that are familiar with immigration practice but are too busy to do the work or pay close attention to the case. The problem is compounded by immigration clients who are often desperate to get their case completed and are willing to pay whatever it takes to whoever says the case is possible. An attorney may say a case is easy only because he is unaware of complicating factors.

Immigration law is a particularly difficult area in which to practice. The only constant in the immigration field is change. It is almost too difficult a field for a lawyer to practice part-time and be effective. Most competent general practice attorneys know to avoid immigration cases.

GETTING A REFERRAL

It can be almost impossible to evaluate whether an attorney is competent to practice immigration law. Therefore, the same rule applies when choosing any type of service provider, whether it be a contractor, plumber, doctor, or lawyer. The only way to find an immigration lawyer is by referral from someone who is very familiar with that person and his or her work. If you have another attorney that you trust, he or she should know an immigration attorney or can get a name from one of his colleagues.

Another excellent way to get a referral is through an ethnic association or organization. They often maintain referral lists or can give the name of an attorney familiar to them. These organizations often refer many cases and therefore have gotten feedback over the years about certain attorneys. Also, if an attorney knows a case was referred by a friend or organization, he or she knows that if a problem develops the word will spread to their community.

Each immigration court is required to maintain a list of local non-profit immigration service providers. You can pick this list up from the immigration court or possibly call and get a couple of phone numbers. These organizations generally provide competent legal help and are cheaper than a private attorney. If you prefer your own attorney, and cannot find one on your own, you should ask one of them for a referral. They should know of conscientious attorneys, particularly those that have helped out the organization on a reduced-fee basis.

Finally, if all else fails contact AILA—American Immigration Lawyers Association. This is the only immigration lawyer association. A referral through AILA should be fairly reliable.

MAKING THE DECISION

When you call an attorney to make an appointment, ask if there is a consultation fee. You should expect to pay one. It is very reasonable to pay a consultation fee for the initial meeting. You could definitely call around and find an attorney that does not charge a fee but keep in mind that you may get what you pay for.

Once you are in the attorney's office, there are certain questions you should ask:

● *What percentage of your practice is immigration? (Ideally, a majority of the attorney's practice should be immigration related.)*

APPENDIX E
BLANK FORMS

You may tear out these forms and use them, but it will be best if you make copies first in case you make a mistake. For additional information on these forms, go to the INS website at:

http://www.INS.gov

DO NOT WRITE IN THIS BLOCK - FOR EXAMINING OFFICE ONLY

A#	Action Stamp	Fee Stamp

Section of Law/Visa Category
- [ ] 201(b) Spouse - IR-1/CR-1
- [ ] 201(b) Child - IR-2/CR-2
- [ ] 201(b) Parent - IR-5
- [ ] 203(a)(1) Unm. S or D - F1-1
- [ ] 203(a)(2)(A)Spouse - F2-1
- [ ] 203(a)(2)(A) Child - F2-2
- [ ] 203(a)(2)(B) Unm. S or D - F2-4
- [ ] 203(a)(3) Married S or D - F3-1
- [ ] 203(a)(4) Brother/Sister - F4-1

Petition was filed on: _____ (priority date)
- [ ] Personal Interview
- [ ] Pet. [ ] Ben. " A" File Reviewed
- [ ] Field Investigation
- [ ] 203(a)(2)(A) Resolved
- [ ] Previously Forwarded
- [ ] I-485 Filed Simultaneously
- [ ] 204(g) Resolved
- [ ] 203(g) Resolved

Remarks:

A. Relationship   You are the petitioner; your relative is the beneficiary.

1. I am filing this petition for my:
[ ] Husband/Wife [ ] Parent [ ] Brother/Sister [ ] Child

2. Are you related by adoption?
[ ] Yes [ ] No

3. Did you gain permanent residence through adoption?
[ ] Yes [ ] No

B. Information about you

C. Information about your relative

1. Name (Family name in CAPS)   (First)   (Middle)

1. Name (Family name in CAPS)   (First)   (Middle)

2. Address (Number and Street)   **(Apt.No.)**

2. Address (Number and Street)   **(Apt. No.)**

(Town or City)   (State/Country)   (Zip/Postal Code)

(Town or City)   (State/Country)   (Zip/Postal Code)

3. Place of Birth (Town or City)   (State/Country)

3. Place of Birth (Town or City)   (State/Country)

4. Date of Birth (Month/Day/Year)

5. Gender [ ] Male [ ] Female

6. Marital Status [ ] Married [ ] Single [ ] Widowed [ ] Divorced

4. Date of Birth (Month/Day/Year)

5. Gender [ ] Male [ ] Female

6. Marital Status [ ] Married [ ] Single [ ] Widowed [ ] Divorced

7. Other Names Used (including maiden name)

7. Other Names Used (including maiden name)

8. Date and Place of Present Marriage (if married)

8. Date and Place of Present Marriage (if married)

9. Social Security Number (if any)   **10. Alien Registration Number**

9. Social Security Number (if any)   **10. Alien Registration Number**

11. Name(s) of Prior Husband(s)/Wive(s)   **12. Date(s) Marriage(s) Ended**

11. Name(s) of Prior Husband(s)/Wive(s)   **12. Date(s) Marriage(s) Ended**

13. If you are a U.S. citizen, complete the following:
My citizenship was acquired through (check one):
- [ ] Birth in the U.S.
- [ ] Naturalization. Give certificate number and date and place of issuance.

_____
- [ ] Parents. Have you obtained a certificate of citizenship in your own name?
  [ ] Yes. Give certificate number, date and place of issuance. [ ] No

13. Has your relative ever been in the U.S.? [ ] Yes [ ] No

14. If your relative is currently in the U.S., complete the following:
He or she arrived as a::
(visitor, student, stowaway, without inspection, etc.)

Arrival/Departure Record (I-94)   **Date arrived** (Month/Day/Year)

| | | | ▬ | | | | | | | |

Date authorized stay expired, or will expire, as shown on Form I-94 or I-95

15. Name and address of present employer (if any)

14a. If you are a lawful permanent resident alien, complete the following: Date and place of admission for, or adjustment to, lawful permanent residence and class of admission.

Date this employment began (Month/Day/Year)

14b. Did you gain permanent resident status through marriage to a United States citizen or lawful permanent resident?
[ ] Yes [ ] No

16. Has your relative ever been under immigration proceedings?
[ ] No [ ] Yes Where _____ When _____
[ ] Removal [ ] Exclusion/Deportation [ ] Recission [ ] Judicial Proceedings

INITIAL RECEIPT _____ RESUBMITTED _____ RELOCATED: Rec'd _____ Sent _____ COMPLETED: Appv'd _____ Denied _____ Ret'd _____

Form I-130 (Rev. 03/19/02) Y

C. Information about your alien relative (continued)

17. List husband/wife and all children of your relative.

(Name)	(Relationship)	(Date of Birth)	(Country of Birth)

18. Address in the United States where your relative intends to live.

(Street Address)	(Town or City)	(State)

19. Your relative's address abroad. (Include street, city, province and country)

Phone Number (if any)

20. If your relative's native alphabet is other than Roman letters, write his or her name and foreign address in the native alphabet.

(Name)   Address (Include street, city, province and country):

21. If filing for your husband/wife, give last address at which you lived together. (Include street, city, province, if any, and country):

From: To:
(Month) (Year)   (Month) (Year)

22. Complete the information below if your relative is in the United States and will apply for adjustment of status

Your relative is in the United States and will apply for adjustment of status to that of a lawful permanent resident at the office of the Immigration and

and Naturalization Service in _____ . If your relative is not eligible for adjustment of status, he or she
                                           (City)   (State)

will apply for a visa abroad at the American consular post in _____
                                                                    (City)   (Country)

NOTE: Designation of an American embassy or consulate outside the country of your relative's last residence does not guarantee acceptance for processing by that post. Acceptance is at the discretion of the designated embassy or consulate.

D. Other information

1. If separate petitions are also being submitted for other relatives, give names of each and relationship.

2. Have you ever filed a petition for this or any other alien before?   ☐ Yes   ☐ No

If "Yes," give name, place and date of filing and result.

WARNING: INS investigates claimed relationships and verifies the validity of documents. INS seeks criminal prosecutions when family relationships are falsified to obtain visas.

PENALTIES: By law, you may be imprisoned for not more than five years or fined $250,000, or both, for entering into a marriage contract for the purpose of evading any provision of the immigration laws. In addition, you may be fined up to $10,000 and imprisoned for up to five years, or both, for knowingly and willfully falsifying or concealing a material fact or using any false document in submitting this petition.

YOUR CERTIFICATION: I certify, under penalty of perjury under the laws of the United States of America, that the foregoing is true and correct. Furthermore, I authorize the release of any information from my records which the Immigration and Naturalization Service needs to determine eligibility for the benefit that I am seeking.

E. Signature of petitioner.

Date   Phone Number

F. Signature of person preparing this form, if other than the petitioner.

I declare that I prepared this document at the request of the person above and that it is based on all information of which I have any knowledge.

Print Name _____   Signature _____   Date _____

Address _____   G-28 ID or VOLAG Number, if any. _____

Form I-130 (Rev. 03/19/02) Y Page 2

U.S. Department of Justice
Immigration and Naturalization Service

OMB #1115-0005
Application for Travel Document

START HERE - Please Type or Print

Part 1. Information about you.

Family Name	Given Name	Middle Initial

Address - C/O

Street Number and Name		Apt. #
City	State or Province	
Country	ZIP/Postal Code	

Date of Birth (Month/Day/Year)	Country of Birth
Social Security #	A #

Part 2. Application Type (check one).

a. ☐ I am a permanent resident or conditional resident of the United States and I am applying for a Reentry Permit.

b. ☐ I now hold U.S. refugee or asylee status and I am applying for a Refugee Travel Document.

c. ☐ I am a permanent resident as a direct result of refugee or asylee status, and am applying for a Refugee Travel Document.

d. ☐ I am applying for an Advance Parole to allow me to return to the U.S. after temporary foreign travel.

e. ☐ I am outside the U.S. and am applying for an Advance Parole.

f. ☐ I am applying for an Advance Parole for another person who is outside the U.S. *Give the following information about that person:*

Family Name	Given Name	Middle Initial
Date of Birth (Month/Day/Year)	Country of Birth	

Foreign Address - C/O

Street Number and Name		Apt. #
City	State or Province	
Country	ZIP/Postal Code	

Part 3. Processing Information.

Date of Intended departure (Month/Day/Year)	Expected length of trip.

Are you, or any person included in this application, now in exclusion or deportation proceedings?

☐ No   ☐ Yes, at (give office name) _____

If applying for an Advance Parole Document, skip to Part 7.

Have you ever before been issued a Reentry Permit or Refugee Travel Document?

☐ No   ☐ Yes (give the following for the last document issued to you)

Date Issued	Disposition (attached, lost, etc.)

Form I-131 (Rev. 12/10/91) N   *Continued on back.*

- *Are you a member of AILA?* The AILA is the only immigration lawyers organization through which attorneys receive critical information pertaining to all aspects of immigration law practice and developments. A conscientious attorney also attends conferences and seminars sponsored by AILA. It is difficult to be a competent practitioner without being an AILA member. You can check for yourself at 202-216-2400. If he or she is not a member, you should send your business elsewhere unless you have a solid referral.

- *When are legal fees to be paid?* Under no circumstances should you pay the entire fee up front. A common fee arrangement is to pay half to start and the rest over time or when the case is complete.

- *Have you done cases like mine and with what result?* He or she should be able to say what the chances of your case succeeding are and on what grounds a denial is possible. You should take notes when you talk to your attorney.

- *What is the probability of my case being granted and what does it depend on?* In other words, you want to know why the case will not be granted.

- *Do I even need an attorney in the first place?* If the attorney is trustworthy, he should answer this question honestly. Your case may matter less to the attorney than you think. A busy attorney has his or her calendar filled anyway, so if he or she does not take your case, he or she will take someone else's. If he or she says you need a lawyer, ask how he or she will assist your case apart from filling out the forms.

- *Is there any way to reduce the attorney fee without compromising your case?* For example, does the attorney recommend that his or her role is to simply put the together the filing packet and then not appear at the INS interview. For citizenship cases with no complicating factors, an attorney's presence is not needed.

- *How is the fee calculated?* Most immigration cases are charged on what's called a flat fee basis, meaning you will pay one fee no matter how long the case takes. This is the safest method of charging. The other billing method is by the hour. Established attorneys typically charge very substantial fees per hour, $150 per hour and up. The time necessary for an immigration case can escalate very quickly if paying by the hour. However, an attorney should have a legal staff who can do must of the leg work.

- *When will the work be completed?* The flip side of finding a reputable attorney is that he or she is likely very busy. Before you entrust the attorney with the case or fee, you should get a timetable as to when the work will be done. Possibly you can negotiate a lower fee if the work takes longer than stated. Offer to pay the attorney the first half of the payment when the case is ready to file. Then you will come back to the office to pay the filing and legal fees. If a time deadline is involved, you must confirm with someone on his or her staff that the case was filed.

BEING A GOOD CLIENT

Just as you would like your attorney to be good, it is also in your best interests to be a good client.

The following are some helpful ideas:
- Ask for a receipt that states what work will be done and the fees to be charged.

- Keep copies of all payment receipts.

- Insist on retaining a copy of everything filed and all correspondence received on your behalf. Resist the urge to be lazy and think your attorney has a copy of everything, you needn't worry. You need to maintain your own file.

- Never leave original documents with your attorney.

- Make sure your attorney has your current address and phone numbers.

- Know under what name the attorney's office has filed the case and reference that name when you or your family calls.

- Designate one person from the family to be in contact with the attorney.

- Determine that either the attorney or the client will be in contact with the INS—not both.

- Seek as much assistance as possible from the attorney's staff rather than from the attorney. The attorney's legal staff is there to help you. You do not need to ask the attorney whether something was filed, ask the legal assistant who actually filed it.

- If you receive a letter from the INS which you don't understand, fax it to the attorney and ask for a call back from an assistant.

- Keep in touch with your attorney's office. Since some cases take years to complete, you should contact him at least every six months or so in case there are new legal developments. A busy attorney has many cases and cannot necessarily think of your case when a change in the law occurs.

Remember you are completely responsible for the work your lawyer does on your behalf. If a deadline is missed or a case improperly filed, you cannot say it was the fault of your attorney. Your only recourse is to prove that the attorney was negligent to the level of incompetence in what is called a *Matter of Lozada filing*, named after the Board of Immigration Appeals case that established a specific procedure. This does not mean that if your attorney simply made a mistake your case can be reopened or corrected. It has to be a mistake so *incompetent* that it falls to the level of *malpractice*. It is a tough standard to prove. You will also need to prove that he or she was contracted to do that work. Hopefully, this is evidenced on the payment receipts.

This chapter contains a few important but effective guidelines. If followed, then a foundation for a successful working relationship is established.

THE FUTURE OF **23**
IMMIGRATION
LAW

Congress is really tightening immigration law and making stricter policies. Here are some of the immigration reforms being seriously proposed at the time this book is published:

- *BIA reform*. The Attorney General is seeking to "reform" the Board of Immigration Appeals. This is the court that reviews adverse decisions from the Immigration Court who reviews decisions of applications filed with the INS or those picked up by the Deportation Section. As it is, it is very difficult to win an appeal at the BIA. Under the new more difficult proposed legal standard to prevail on an appeal, it may become impossible.

- *Regulations that allow the INS to obtain an automatic stay*. An *automatic stay* releases a detainee from custody on bond. The release of the alien is delayed under new law possibly for months—until the BIA decides the merits of the appeal.

- *Monitoring of attorney-INS detainee conversations*. This monitoring will occur where a determination is made that it is necessary to deter violence or terrorism.

- *B-1 or B-2 visitor admission*. Admission will be only for thirty days instead of 180.

Another law of interest is the U.S.A. Patriot Act. Enacted in the wake of the September 11 tragedy, it gives FBI new authority to search homes and offices and to monitor phone conversations and e-mail. It gives federal investigators greater access to personal records and affirms the government's right to detain noncitizens without charge.

While some reforms may be necessary, they should not be taken without careful consideration of their consequences. Many of the proposed reforms seek to limit rights and freedoms.

The biggest problem for would-be immigrants is that an extension of Section 245(i) is now on hold or will be enacted in limited form. Thus, many aliens will be barred from applying for adjustment in the U.S. Since they may be barred by unlawful presence from applying for permanent residence overseas as well, many out-of-status aliens are essentially trapped in the U.S.

GLOSSARY

A

"A" number. This can be an alien number, file number, green card number, or case number (especially in immigration court). Refers to the file number assigned in sequence by the INS to an alien who has applied for adjustment or has been apprehended by the INS. This is the permanent file number of the alien and will eventually appear on the work permit, green card, and naturalization certificate. This number must appear on all correspondence and applications filed with the INS.

ADIT processing. It stands for Alien Documentation, Identification and Telecommunication System. The process where an adjustment applicant places his or her signature and fingerprint on the I-89 card, which will be sent to a service center to be made into a green card. It is usually done at the INS interview.

adjudicate. This occurs when an INS officer makes a decision as to whether to grant or deny an application.

adjustment of status (AOS). Process where one becomes a permanent resident in the U.S. Since one has a previous status in the U.S., they are said to be changing their status to permanent residence.

adjustment application. See I-485 form.

admission. This occurs when an alien presents himself or herself for inspection to an immigration officer at a border or airport and whose entry was approved on a particular basis.

advance parole. Issued by either a local office or a service center, depending on where the adjustment application is, it is advance permission to return to the U.S. to resume processing of an adjustment application.

administrative appeal. An appeal filed at the local INS to the Administrative Appeals Unit in Washington within thirty days of a petition's denial.

administrative closure. A case that is not denied but is no longer pending.

affidavit. Any type of document written by the applicant or by a third party in support of the applicant and signed in front of a notary public.

affidavit of support. Important form required in a family-based adjustment case in which the petitioner agrees to reimburse the government if the person being adjusted requires federal benefits within ten years of adjustment or the person naturalizes.

aggravated felony. In the immigration this sense means any type of crime listed in Section 101(a)(43) of the INA, which includes many non-violent crimes and misdemeanors.

alien. One who is not a permanent resident but is present in the U.S. on a nonimmigrant visa, is out of status, or entered without inspection.

application support center (ASC). The facility that takes fingerprints of applicants.

amnesty. Time-limited benefit allowing adjustment of status that will issue out green cards based upon residence in the U.S. prior to a certain date.

approval notice. A notice from a service center stating a petition is approved. See I-797 form.

arrival/departure document. See I-94 form.

asylee. One who has been granted asylum either through the Asylum Office or by the immigration judge but who has not yet adjusted status to that of a permanent resident.

asylum. A showing that one has a well-founded fear of persecution on the basis of political opinion, religion, gender, nationality or membership in a particular social group. (A well-founded fear can be thought of as a 10% chance of severe harm.)

asylum officer. An employee of the INS who will conduct the initial administrative interview on an asylum application.

B

bag and baggage letter. (also known as a "run" letter.) A form letter sent by the Deportation Office asking an alien to appear at the their office with their luggage on a certain date to be deported.

beneficiary. The alien who will benefit (get to come to the U.S.)from the filing of a petition on his or her behalf by either a family member who is a U.S. citizen, or green card holder, or by a company making an appropriate job offer.

biographic information form. See G-325A form.

blue passport. See refugee travel document.

Board of Immigration Appeals (BIA). A separate office within the Executive Office of Immigration Review that administers appeals from the Immigration Court. It is located in Falls Church, Virginia, just outside Washington, D.C.

C

call-up date. Used in the Immigration Court to indicate when motions or supporting documents are due to the court. It is usually ten or fourteen days before the hearing.

cancellation of removal. Procedure available to one who is before the Immigration Court and can demonstrate that he has lived for ten years in the U.S., is a person of good moral character, and that there would be "extremely unusual hardship" to a U.S. citizen or LPR parent, spouse, or child if he or she was deported.

certificate of citizenship. Document given in place of a naturalization certificate to those born abroad to U.S. citizens, adopted by U.S. citizens, or children whose parents naturalized. Normally given to those who qualify for citizenship without first becoming a permanent resident.

change of status (COS). An application made on Form I-539 by one in the U.S. to change from one nonimmigrant status to another.

change of venue. Request of the applicant or by motion of a respondent to change the jurisdiction of the INS office or immigration court based on a change of address.

classification. Short code that appears on the green card and approval notice. It is the basis upon which one became a permanent resident.

clock. Generally, a running total of the number of days since an asylum application has been filed. It is used in determining when an asylum applicant may file a work permit application. The term is also used when accruing illegal presence.

Code of Federal Regulations (CFR). A multi-volume detailed interpretation of federal laws, including immigration laws.

conditional resident. One who has obtained conditional permanent residence through marriage to a U.S. citizen (where the marriage is less than two years old at the time of adjustment) or through a qualifying investment.

consulate. Office run by the U.S. Department of State and is a sub-office in a larger foreign country of the main embassy office. It is responsible for the issuance of immigrant and nonimmigrant visas to aliens for entry into the U.S. May also make determinations on U.S. citizenship.

conviction. A determination in a court case that someone broke the law and a sentence issued.

country reports. Detailed report of each foreign country published each February by the Department of State regarding human rights conditions in each country. These are heavily relied upon by immigration judges and asylum officers in deciding an asylum application.

crime involving moral turpitude (CIMT). There is no statutory definition, and it is somewhat in the "eye of the beholder." A CIMT within five years of adjustment or any two CIMTs at any time may make a person *removable*. There is a long list of CIMTs. A retail theft, for example, is a CIMT.

current visa. A visa where the priority date on the I-130 approval notice moves past the date reflected on the visa bulletin published by the Department of State.

cut-off date. The date on the Department of State's monthly visa chart that makes people whose priority date is before it eligible to apply for permanent residence.

D

deferred admission. Formerly, deferred inspection. Where a nonimmigrant or possibly lawful permanent residence had trouble re-entering the U.S. and must appear at the local INS office to clarify their status.

Department of Labor (DOL). Through its oversight of the labor certification process, it is responsible for providing determinations as to the availability of qualified U.S. workers for positions offered in many of the employment-based categories.

Department of State. Runs the embassies and consulates, which decide on immigrant and nonimmigrant visa applications. Also runs the Passport Office.

deportable. State where the alien is either being asked or may be asked in the future to leave the U.S.

deportation. This occurs when a person is physically taken by an INS Deportation officer to his or her native country, usually because either a deportation order or removal order from the immigration court exists.

deportation officer. An INS employee whose responsibility is to apprehend and deport illegal aliens from the U.S.

derivative beneficiary. One who obtains status on a visa petition not on account of their own standing but because of their relationship to the principal beneficiary, such as a child through his or her parent.

District Director (DD). The head official of the INS offices in a certain district that may include several states. The DD has considerable discretion and power over certain types of applications and waivers, such as humanitarian parole or extended voluntary departure.

diversity visa. (also known as the *visa lottery* or the *lottery*.) A green card lottery run by the Department of State where 100,000 people will be notified that they will be allowed to adjust status. However, only 50,000 visas are available.

duplicate petition. Normally filed where the original petition was lost or misplaced by the INS. In order to file the duplicate petition, one must have the original receipt number or a copy of the receipt notice in order to file the duplicate to the first filing.

E

embassy. The main office for the U.S. government located in a friendly foreign country.

employment authorization document (EAD). A photo identification card issued by the INS that evidences the holder's authorization to work in the U.S. and obtain a social security number.

entered without inspection (EWI, pronounced "eee-wee"). A person who entered the U.S. across the border from Mexico or Canada without being inspected by an immigration officer.

examinations section or exams. The typical name for the section of the INS that interviews adjustment applications

exclusion. This occurs when an LPR with a criminal record attempts to re-enter the country and is not allowed to enter.

Executive Office for Immigration Review (EOIR). A separate agency from the INS but also within the Department of Justice that runs the immigration court.

expedited case. Adjustment cases that are time-sensitive such as diversity visas, aging out (child about to turn 21), medical reasons, or other urgent reasons.

expungement. A criminal record where the person's name has been deleted from the records of a particular state.

extension of status (EOS). Where one applies for another term of status on the same type of nonimmigrant visa.

extreme hardship. The legal standard for different types of waivers, such as for unlawful presence or entry with a false passport. The hardship must be to a qualifying relative such as U.S. citizen or LPR parent or spouse.

F

file number.   See "A" number

filing receipt.   Small yellow cash register receipt attached to the receipt letter upon filing an adjustment case.

final order of removal (deportation).   An order to send a person out of the U.S. by the immigration judge that has not been appealed within the thirty-day period.

fingerprint clearance.   Required fingerprint check against FBI computer records prior to adjustment of status. Fingerprints must be taken within fifteen months prior to the date of adjustment or else the fingerprints will "expire" and have to be re-taken.

fingerprint card.   Until 1997, a card having fingerprints of an alien taken on it by a law enforcement entity or a credentialed private organization. INS took over the fingerprinting process to avoid fraud.

freedom of information act (FOIA).   Important law allowing anyone to obtain a copy of his or her file held at a governmental agency such as the INS.

Foreign Affairs Manual (referred to as the "FAM" - rhymes with "sam"). The regulations that apply to consular officers in adjudicating immigrant or nonimmigrant visas.

G

G-28.   Attorney appearance form. Blue form that must accompany any immigration application in order for an attorney to be officially entered as attorney of record and to receive copies of correspondence.

G-325A.   Detailed biographic information form that is required with an adjustment of status application and other petitions. One of the copies is sent to the embassy in the native country and another is sent to the CIA to perform records checks. Required for all adjustment applicants fourteen years of age and over.

grandfathered. One can apply for benefits under a favorable law which is now expired, such as Section 245(i).

green card holder. See lawful permanent resident.

green card number. See "A" number.

green card stamp. Also called I-551 stamp. Refers to the temporary stamp placed by an INS officer into a person's passport signifying his adjustment of status.

H

H-1B visa. The most popular temporary nonimmigrant visa, issued for a maximum of six years; most professional positions normally qualify; a job offer is required before can apply.

humanitarian parole. One is paroled into the U.S. for humanitarian reasons such as medical or for young children to reside with parents even if there isn't a visa number available.

I

I-20. Form issued by a school when a foreign student has enrolled and paid tuition.

I-94. Small white card stapled into one's passport upon admission into the U.S. on a nonimmigrant visa. It contains the date of expiration of the nonimmigrant visa.

I-161. See bag and baggage letter.

I-130. Visa petition form used for a family-sponsored immediate member or preference category.

I-140. Visa petition form used for an employment-based preference category.

I-212 waiver. Form needed to waive the effect of a removal or deportation order.

I-485. Adjustment of status form.

I-485 Supplement A. Form filed by those eligible for "mini-amnesty". You can only file it during certain times and you must be eligible. It is required by one who entered the country without documentation or who is out of status and is filing adjustment through a preference visa petition.

I-551. Another name for the green card.

I-551 stamp. See green card stamp.

I-601. See waiver.

I-765. Work permit application.

I-797. Also called a receipt notice or approval notice of action issued by a service center in regard to an immigrant or nonimmigrant visa application.

I-864. See affidavit of support.

illegal alien. One who is in the U.S. out of status or who entered without inspection.

immediate relative. Spouse, parent or child (under the age of 21) of a U.S. citizen. However, adopted children must have been adopted before the age of 16 and stepchildren before the age of 18.

immigrant visa (IV). Used when applying for permanent residence at an embassy or consulate.

immigrant visa packet. After the alien has been approved at an embassy or consulate, he or she is given a packet to present when arrive for inspection in the U.S. This packet must be presented to the INS officer for ADIT processing.

immigrant. Someone who has become a lawful permanent resident.

immigration court (EOIR). See Executive Office for Immigration Review.

immigration judge (IJ). An administrative law judge who is an employee of the Department of Justice.

Immigration and Nationality Act of 1952 (INA). The starting point of current immigration law; all immigration laws passed since then are amendments to the INA.

Immigration and Naturalization Service (INS). The agency of the Department of Justice that is responsible for enforcement of immigration laws within the U.S. and for decisions of eligibility for immigrant and nonimmigrant status and citizenship.

inadmissible. Any one of a number of grounds, such as criminal acts or medical conditions, that cause an alien not to be admitted to the U.S.

individual hearing. Type of hearing before the immigration court where the alien actually puts on his or her case over a one to three hour time period.

investigations section. Department composed of INS officers who are allowed to carry weapons, have arrest authority, and do investigations on fraudulent marriages, fraudulent businesses, alien smugglers, fraudulent documents and aliens involved in criminal and gang activities.

inspection. To be inspected by an immigration officer at an airport, or border, or on a ship. The officer will check to see that all documents are in order. The INS officer may admit, send the alien back, or refer the alien to deferred admission.

L

labor certification. An approved labor certification is a requirement for some employment-based adjustment applications. It is an actual recruitment of U.S. workers, under the supervision of the Department of Labor and a state employment security agency in order to establish that there is no U.S. worker who is ready, willing, able and qualified to take the position offered to an alien.

labor condition application (LCA). The first stage of a nonimmigrant H-1B petition; an LCA has nothing to do with a labor certification application.

late amnesty. Those illegal aliens that missed the 1988 deadline for amnesty applications and became part of several class-actions lawsuits against the INS such as LULAC or CSS. (Most late amnesty class members had a deadline of June 2002 to file for adjustment of status.)

lawful permanent resident (LPR). The most correct term for someone who has adjusted status through an immigrant visa.

legalization. The former process whereby aliens through the 1986 amnesty were first granted temporary residency then permanent residence.

LIFE Act. The most recent major legislation affecting immigration enacted in December 2000. Allows those who are out of status, entered EWI, or worked in the U.S. without INS authorization to adjust status through a family member or a labor certification filed before April 30, 2001.

lottery. See diversity visa.

M

mandamus. A petition filed in federal court to have a federal judge order the INS to take a certain action.

master calendar hearing (MCH). As opposed to the individual hearing, a brief housekeeping hearing before an immigration judge (IJ) at which the alien pleads to the Notice to Appear and states which relief he or she will apply for.

medical examination. An exam done by an INS or State Department approved physician and on a special form required prior to adjustment of status or to obtaining or to obtaining immigrant visa at an embassy or consulate.

motion. Any type of written request normally to the Immigration Court but also to an INS office or service center asking that agency to take a certain formal action.

motion to reopen. A common motion to make a previously denied or closed benefit pending again in order to obtain that benefit. There may be restrictions on the number of motions, when they may be filed and the basis for re-opening.

N

NACARA. (Nicaraguan Adjustment and Central American Relief Act.) Law that allows certain individuals from eastern Europe, former Soviet block countries, who entered the U.S. prior to 1991 and filed for asylum at that time to apply for suspension of deportation.

nationality. For immigration purposes, generally the same as citizenship.

National Visa Center (NVC). State Department office located in New Hampshire that stores approved visa petitions until they become current.

naturalization. Process whereby a green card holder becomes a U.S. citizen through filing a N-400 application.

naturalization certificate. A document given as evidence as having become a citizen of the U.S. by naturalization.

nonimmigrant visa (NIV). Any one of the several dozen visa types that permit one to stay in the U.S. for a temporary period for a specific purpose.

notice of action. See I-797.

notice to appear (NTA). Charging document that brings a person before the immigration court.

notice of intent to deny. Issued either for an I-130 petition or asylum application (where applicant is in valid nonimmigrant status) to give the applicant an opportunity to rebut and submit additional evidence.

O

onestop. When the I-130 and I-485 forms are filed at the same time normally with the local INS office if one is the beneficiary of an immediate visa petition.

out of status. (overstay.) One whose nonimmigrant status as set forth on the I-94 card or a subsequent extension has ended; or the person has violated the terms of the visa, for example, by engaging in unauthorized employment.

P

parole. Generally given to an alien outside the U.S. for humanitarian reasons or to an alien who is the U.S. who wishes to travel abroad and whose paperwork for adjustment is pending. Constitutes a lawful entry for purposes of applying for adjustment of status.

passport office. An office of the Department of State that issues passports and in doing so, may make decisions on U.S. citizenship.

permanent resident (LPR). See lawful permanent resident.

petitioner. The U.S. citizen or legal permanent resident or U.S. corporation filing on behalf of an alien beneficiary for either an immigrant or nonimmigrant visa

preference visa category. A family member other than an immediate relative and whose petition therefore requires a waiting period between the I-130 filing and the application for adjustment.

prevailing wage. Term used in an H-1B or labor certification application where the wage offered must be at least 95% of the average of those holding that position in that city or state.

principal applicant. The lead applicant in an adjustment or asylum application.

principal beneficiary. The main beneficiary of a visa petition, as opposed to a derivative beneficiary such as a minor child who obtains status through the principal.

priority date. (date of filing.) The date used to determine when a beneficiary of a visa petition is able to apply for adjustment of status.

proceedings. See removal proceedings.

R

receipt number. The case number assigned by a service center to a filing. The receipt number includes the first three letters of the Service Center and the year in which it was filed.

record of proceedings (rop). Formal name given to the court file in immigration court and the file upon which the Immigration Judge makes a decision.

reduction in recruitment (RIR). A relatively new fast track labor certification application where a company has already attempted to recruit a qualified worker and therefore does not need to go through supervised recruitment by the Department of Labor.

re-entry permit (often called the white passport). It is a document that lets an alien stay out of the country for over a year and up to two years without abandoning their permanent resident status.

refugee. One who is in the U.S. having been granted refugee status abroad, may apply for adjustment of status after one year in the U.S.

refugee travel document. Blue passport that replaces the passport from one's own country and is for refugees and asylees only. Does not function as a re-entry permit. Serves as advance parole for refugees and asylees.

registry. Anyone residing in the U.S. since before 1972 may be admitted as permanent residents if they can show good moral character.

regulations. See Code of Federal Regulations or Foreign Affairs Manual.

removable. An illegal alien or a lawful permanent resident who has violated immigration law by committing certain criminal acts or fraud and is subject to removal or deportation.

removal proceedings. One who is "in proceedings" is before the immigration court to determine whether he or she should be removed or deported.

remove conditions. The process by which the alien submits the proper form and evidence generally to a service center, showing that the marriage is bona fide or the alien has completed the investment requirements.

replacement agricultural workers (RAW). A program implemented after many agricultural workers became permanent residents through the 1986 amnesty.

request for evidence (RFE). Document issued by an INS office or service center requesting additional evidence or information to prove the alien's case.

resident alien. A permanent resident or someone on an extended non-immigrant visa, but not a tourist visa.

respondent. The name given to an alien who is in removal proceedings before the immigration court; similar to a defendant in a criminal proceeding.

routing slip. Form required in conjunction with an immigration court proceeding where an application must be paid for at the INS cashier prior to filing with the court. Form allows the INS cashier to return the paid application to the applicant so that it may be filed with the immigration court at the instruction of the immigration judge.

S

section 212(c) relief. Where a lawful permanent resident who has committed crimes involving moral turpitude but not an aggravated felony may seek to stop removal before an immigration judge upon a sufficient demonstration of the existence of certain positive factors or equities on his behalf.

section 245(i) eligible. One who is eligible to file the I-485A Supplement and pay the $1000 penalty and adjust status.

self-petition. An alien of extraordinary ability, a battered spouse or the widow or widower of a U.S. citizen who had been married to that citizen for at least two years.

service center. One of the several remote processing facilities. Each service center accepts certain petitions and application from people that live in the states within its jurisdiction.

signature card. Small card used for thumbprint in conjunction with an application for employment authorization at some service centers or possibly the I-89 card used in ADIT processing.

sponsor. An individual or company who is filing a petition on behalf of his or her relative or employee, or a joint sponsor who is filing an affidavit of support.

state employment security agency (SESA). Agency that operates with the Department of Labor to insure that there is no available U.S. worker for a particular position that is sought by an immigrant.

stay of deportation. An application made on form I-246 and filed with the Deportation Office to request that a scheduled deportation be delayed for extenuating circumstances.

stowaway. Person who entered illegally by travelling on a commercial transportation such as a train, bus or boat where a fare should have been paid.

T

temporary protected status (TPS). Status given to aliens of certain countries where there is war, famine, or natural disaster, such as hurricanes that allows the alien to work and obtain a social security number.

temporary resident alien. The correct term for someone granted the initial stage of the legalization process from the 1986 amnesty.

trial attorney. A prosecutor on behalf of the INS. An attorney employed by the INS to represent it in immigration court, among other duties.

U

undocumented alien. Someone who entered the U.S. illegally across a border without a visa.

unlawful presence. Time that an alien is in the U.S. illegally or out of status since April 1, 1997.

U.S. citizen (USC). Someone born in the U.S., someone born outside the U.S. to a U.S. citizen parent, or one who has naturalized or obtained a certificate of citizenship.

V

visa. Used by itself, it refers to one of the nonimmigrant temporary visas, of which the most common is the tourist B-2 visa.

visa bulletin. Information updated monthly by the Department of State available by mail, Internet, or phone showing which preference categories are currently available.

visa lottery. See diversity visa.

visa petition. Either the alien relative I-130 petition or the employment based I-140 petition filed on behalf of a beneficiary.

visa waiver. Entry into the U.S. without a visa from a changing list of approximately 20 countries whose citizens are known to respect U.S. immigration laws.

"V" visa. New benefit from LIFE Act that allows spouses or minor unmarried children of green card holders after 3 years wait on the I-130 petition to obtain lawful nonimmigrant status in the U.S. or enter the U.S. if abroad in order to wait the remaining years on their visa petition.

voluntary departure. Granted by an immigration judge or an INS officer where the alien agrees to leave the U.S. at his or her own expense by a certain date in lieu of deportation and the effects of a deportation order.

W

waiver. Generally, one of the several forms, such as I-212, I-601, I-602 or I-612, used to waive or negate a condition of inadmissibility such as entry on a false passport or criminal record. .

white card. See I-94.

white passport. See re-entry passport.

withholding of removal. Requires a showing that it is more likely than not that one faces persecution on the basis of political opinion, religion, gender, nationality or membership in a particular social group.

work permit. See employment authorization document.

Appendix A
INS Offices

Alabama:
INS Atlanta District
Martin Luther King Jr.
Federal Building
77 Forsyth Street SW, Room 111
Atlanta, GA 30303
404-331-0253

Alaska:
INS Anchorage District Office
620 East 10th Avenue, Suite 102
Anchorage, Alaska 99501
907-271-3521

Arizona:
INS Phoenix District Office
2035 North Central Avenue
Phoenix, AZ 85004
602-514-7799

INS Tucson Sub Office
South Country Club Road
Tucson, AZ 85706-5907
520-670-4624

Arkansas:
USINS
4991 Old Greenwood Road
Fort Smith, AR 72903
501-646-4721

California:
INS Los Angeles District Office
300 North Los Angeles Street,
Room 1001
Los Angeles, CA 90012
213-830-4940

USINS Fresno Sub Office
865 Fulton Mall
Fresno, CA 93721
559-487-5132

USINS Sacramento Sub Office
650 Capitol Mall
Sacramento, CA 95814
916-498-6480

U.S. Immigration &
Naturalization Service
34 Civic Center Plaza
Room 520
Santa Ana, CA 92701
714-972-6600

USINS San Diego District Office
U.S. Federal Building
880 Front Street, Suite 1234
San Diego, CA 92101
619-557-5645

INS San Francisco District Office
630 Sansome Street
San Francisco, CA 94111
415-844-5200

INS San Jose Sub Office
1887 Monterey Road
San Jose, CA 95112
408-918-4000

Colorado:
USINS Denver District Office
4730 Paris Street
Denver, CO 80239
303-371-0986

Connecticut:
USINS Hartford Sub Office
450 Main Street, 4th Floor
Hartford, CT 06103-3060
860-240-3050

Delaware:
USINS
1305 McD Drive
Dover, DE 19901
302-730-9311

District of Columbia:
USINS Washington
District Office
4420 N. Fairfax Drive
Arlington, VA 22203
202-307-1642

Florida:
Fort Lauderdale/Port Everglades
Sub Office
1800 Eller Drive, Suite 1401
P.O. Box 13054
Port Everglades Station
Fort Lauderdale, FL 33316
954-356-7790

USINS Miami District Office
7880 Biscayne Boulevard
Miami, FL 33138
305-762-3680

INS Jacksonville Sub Office
4121 Southpoint Boulevard
Jacksonville, FL 32216
904-232-2164

INS Orlando Sub Office
9403 Tradeport Drive
Orlando, FL 32827
407-855-1241

INS Tampa Sub Office
5524 West Cypress Street
Tampa, FL 33607-1708
813-637-3010

INS West Palm Beach Sub Office
301 Broadway, Suite 142
Riviera Beach, FL 33401
561-841-0498

Georgia:
INS Atlanta District
Martin Luther King Jr. Federal
Building
77 Forsyth Street SW, Room 111
Atlanta, GA 30303
404-331-0253

Hawaii:
USINS Honolulu District Office
595 Ala Moana Boulevard
Honolulu, HI 96813
808-532-3746

USINS Agana Sub Office
Sirena Plaza, Suite 100
108 Hernan Cortez Avenue
Hagatna, Guam 96910
671-472-7466

Idaho:
Boise Office Location:
USINS Boise Sub Office
1185 South Vinnell Way
Boise, ID 83709

Illinois:
USINS Chicago District Office
10 West Jackson Boulevard
Chicago, Illinois 60604
312-385-1820

*correspondence regarding adjust-
ment cases:*
U.S. I.N.S.
P.O. Box 3616
Chicago, IL 60690

*adjustment/work permit
applications:*
U.S. I.N.S.
P.O. Box A3462
Chicago, IL 60690-3462

Immigration and Naturalization
Service
Citizenship Office
539 S. LaSalle Street
Chicago, IL 60605
312-353-5440

Indiana:
Immigration and Naturalization
Service
Indianapolis Sub Office
950 N. Meridian St., Room 400
Indianapolis, Indiana 46204

Kansas:
USINS Wichita Satellite Office
271 West 3rd Street North, Suite
1050
Wichita, KS 67202-1212

Kentucky:
Gene Snyder U.S. Courthouse
and Customhouse
Room 390
601 West Broadway
Louisville, KY 40202
502-582-6526

Louisiana:

U.S. Department of Justice
Immigration and Naturalization
Service
701 Loyola Avenue,
Room T-8011
New Orleans, LA 70113
504-589-6521

Maine:

INS Portland, Maine
District Office
176 Gannett Drive
So. Portland, ME 04106
207-780-3399

Maryland:

INS Baltimore District
Fallon Federal Building
31 Hopkins Plaza
Baltimore, MD 21201
410-962-2010

Massachusetts:

USINS Boston District Office
John F. Kennedy Federal Building
Government Center
Boston, MA 02203
617-565-4274

Michigan:

INS Detroit District Office
333 Mt. Elliot
Detroit, MI 48207
313-568-6000

Minnesota:

INS St. Paul District
2901 Metro Drive, Suite 100
Bloomington, MN 55425
612-313-9020

Mississippi:

Dr. A. H. McCoy
Federal Building
100 West Capitol Street
Suite B-8
Jackson, Mississippi 39269

Missouri:

INS Kansas City District
9747 Northwest Conant Avenue
Kansas City, MO 64153
816-891-7422

INS St. Louis Sub Office
Robert A. Young Federal Building
1222 Spruce Street, Room 1.100
St. Louis, MO 63103-2815
314-539-2516

Montana:

USINS Helena District Office
2800 Skyway Drive
Helena, MT 59602
406-449-5220

Nebraska:

USINS Omaha District Office
3736 South 132nd Street
Omaha, NE 68144
402-697-1129

Information Office
13824 T Plaza (Millard Plaza)
Omaha, NE 68137

Nevada:

INS Las Vegas Sub Office
3373 Pepper Lane
Las Vegas, NV 89120-2739
702-451-3597

INS Reno Sub Office
1351 Corporate Boulevard
Reno, NV 89502
775-784-5427

New Hampshire:

USINS Manchester Office
803 Canal Street
Manchester, NH 03101
603-625-5276

New Jersey:

INS Newark District Office
Peter Rodino, Jr. Federal Building
970 Broad Street
Newark, NJ 07102
973-645-4421

INS Cherry Hill Sub Office
1886 Greentree Road
Cherry Hill, NJ 08003
609-424-7712

New Mexico:

INS Albuquerque Sub Office
1720 Randolph Road SE
Albuquerque, NM 87106
505-241-0450

New York:

(Mailing address:)
INS Buffalo District Office
Federal Center
130 Delaware Avenue
Buffalo, NY 14202
716-849-6760

USINS Albany Sub Office
1086 Troy-Schenectady Road
Latham, New York 12110
518-220-2100

INS New York City
District Office
26 Federal Plaza
New York City, NY 10278
212-264-5891

Rochester Satellite Office
Federal Building
100 State Street, Room 418
Rochester, NY 14614

Syracuse Satellite Office
412 South Warren Street
Syracuse, NY 13202

North Carolina:

INS Charlotte Sub Office
210 E. Woodlawn Road
Building 6, Suite 138 (Woodlawn
Green Office Complex)
Charlotte, NC 28217
704-672-6990

North Dakota:
INS St. Paul District
2901 Metro Drive, Suite 100
Bloomington, MN 55425
612-313-9020

Ohio:
INS Cleveland District
A.J.C. Federal Building
1240 East Ninth Street,
Room 1917
Cleveland, OH 44199
216-522-4766

INS Cincinnati Sub Office
J.W. Peck Federal Building
550 Main Street, Room 4001
Cincinnati, OH 45202
513-684-2412

INS Columbus Sub Office
Immigration & Naturalization
Service
50 W. Broad Street
Columbus, OH 43215
614-469-2900

Oklahoma:
USINS Oklahoma City
Sub Office
4149 Highline Boulevard,
Suite 300
Oklahoma City, OK 73108-2081
405-231-5944

Oregon:
USINS Portland, Oregon
District Office
511 NW Broadway
Portland, OR 97209
503-326-7585

Pennsylvania:
USINS Philadelphia
District Office
1600 Callowhill Street
Philadelphia, PA 19130
215-656-7150

USINS Pittsburgh Sub Office
Federal Building
1000 Liberty Avenue
Room 2130
Pittsburgh, PA 15222
412-395-4460

Puerto Rico and U.S. Virgin Islands:
(Street address:)
USINS San Juan District Office
San Patricio Office Center
7 Tabonuco Street, Suite 100
Guaynabo, Puerto Rico 00968
787-706-2343

(Mailing address:)
USINS San Juan District Office
P.O. Box 365068
San Juan, PR 00936

USINS Charlotte Amalie
Sub Office
Nisky Center, Suite 1A
First Floor South
Charlotte Amalie, St. Thomas
United States Virgin Islands
00802
340-774-1390

(Street address:)
Immigration and Naturalization
Service
Sunny Isle Shopping Center
Christiansted, St. Croix
United States Virgin Islands
00820

(Mailing address:)
Immigration and Naturalization
Service
P.O. Box 1468
Kingshill
St. Croix, USVI 00851
340-778-6559

Rhode Island:
USINS Providence Sub Office
200 Dyer Street
Providence, RI 02903
401-528-5528

South Carolina:
INS Charleston Office
170 Meeting Street, Fifth Floor
Charleston, SC 29401
843-727-4422

South Dakota:
INS St. Paul District
2901 Metro Drive, Suite 100
Bloomington, MN 55425
612-313-9020

Tennessee:
U.S. Department of Justice
Immigration and Naturalization
Service
701 Loyola Avenue
Room T-8011
New Orleans, LA 70113
504-589-6521

INS Memphis Sub Office
Suite 100
1341 Sycamore View Road
Memphis, TN 38134
901-544-0256

Texas:
U.S. Immigration and
Naturalization Service
8101 North Stemmons Freeway
Dallas, TX 75247
214-905-5800

USINS El Paso District Office
1545 Hawkins Boulevard
Suite 167
El Paso, TX 79925
915-225-1750

INS Harlingen District
2102 Teege Avenue
Harlingen, TX 78550
956-427-8592

Houston INS District Office
126 Northpoint
Houston, Texas 77060
281-774-4629

USINS San Antonio District
8940 Fourwinds Drive
San Antonio, TX 78239
210-967-7109

Utah:

USINS Salt Lake City Sub Office
5272 South College Drive, #100
Murray, UT 84123
801-265-0109

Vermont:

INS St. Albans Office
64 Gricebrook Road
St. Albans, VT 05478

Virginia:

USINS Washington
District Office
4420 N. Fairfax Drive
Arlington, VA 22203
202-307-1642

USINS Norfolk Sub Office
5280 Henneman Drive
Norfolk, VA 23513
757-858-7519

Washington:

USINS Seattle District Office
815 Airport Way South
Seattle, WA 98134
206-553-1332

USINS Spokane Sub Office
U.S. Courthouse
920 W. Riverside Room 691
Spokane, WA 99201
509-353-2761

(Street address:)
INS Yakima Sub Office
417 E. Chestnut
Yakima, WA 98901

(Mailing address:)
INS Yakima Sub Office
P.O. Box 78
Yakima, WA 98901

West Virginia:

210 Kanawha Blvd. West
Charleston, WV 25302

Wisconsin:

Immigration and Naturalization
Service
Milwaukee Sub Office
310 E. Knapp Street
Milwaukee, WI 53202
414-297-6365

Wyoming:

USINS Denver District Office
4730 Paris Street
Denver, CO 80239
303-371-0986

APPENDIX B
INS SERVICE CENTERS

This appendix contains contact information for the INS service centers. Four of these service centers are identical in that they each process all INS applications and differ by processing applications only from persons residing in their particular region of the U.S.

The fifth and newest center, the Missouri Service Center, is unique in that it is not responsible for any particular region or state but only processes the three new types of applications arising from the 2000 LIFE Act. No matter where one lives in the U.S., an applicant for a V or K visa will file their applications at this center.

When filing an application at a service center, care must be taken to address the envelope to the correct street address or post office box.

California

Jurisdiction over *Arizona, California, Guam, Hawaii, and Nevada.*

General Correspondence:

U.S. Department of Justice
Immigration and Naturalization
Service
California Service Center
P.O. Box 30111
Laguna Niguel, CA
92607-0111

Courier:

California Service Center
24000 Avila Road, 2nd Floor,
Room 2302
Laguna Niguel, CA 92677

U.S. Department of Justice
Immigration and
Naturalization Service
California Service Center
P.O. Box *(insert correct box number
listed below)*
Laguna Niguel, CA *(insert correct zip code
listed below)*

I-90:
P.O. Box 10090
Laguna Niguel, CA 92607-1009

I-90A (SAW):
P.O. Box 10190
Laguna Niguel, CA 92607-1019

I-129 (& related I-539s):
P.O. Box 10129
Laguna Niguel, CA 92607-1012

I-130/I-129F & EOIR-29:
P.O. Box 10130
Laguna Niguel, CA 92607-1013

I-140:
P.O. Box 10140
Laguna Niguel, CA 92607-1014

I-290A and I-290B:
P.O. Box 10290
Laguna Niguel, CA 92607-1029

I-360:
P.O. Box 10360
Laguna Niguel, CA 92607-1036

I-485:
P.O. Box 10485
Laguna Niguel, CA 92607-1048

I-526:
P.O. Box 10526
Laguna Niguel, CA 92607-1052

I-539:
P.O. Box 10539
Laguna Niguel, CA 92607-1053

I-589:
P.O. Box 10589
Laguna Niguel, CA 92607-1058

I-690:
P.O. Box 10690
Laguna Niguel, CA 92607-1069

I-694:
P.O. Box 10694
Laguna Niguel, CA 92607-1094

I-695:
P.O. Box 10695
Laguna Niguel, CA 92607-1095

I-698:
P.O. Box 10698
Laguna Niguel, CA 92607-1098

I-751:
P.O. Box 10751
Laguna Niguel, CA 92607-1075

I-765:
P.O. Box 10765
Laguna Niguel, CA 92607-1076

I-817:

P.O. Box 10817
Laguna Niguel, CA 92607-1081

I-821:

P.O. Box 10821
Laguna Niguel, CA 92607-1082

I-824:

Use the P.O. Box number for the type of
approved application or petition for
which action is being requested.

I-829:

P.O. Box 10526
Laguna Niguel, CA 92607-1052

N-400:

P.O. Box 10400
Laguna Niguel, CA 92607-1040

Walk-in Information Counter:

Chet Holifeld Federal Building
24000 Avila Road, 2nd Floor
Laguna Niguel, California
Open Monday through Friday
(9:00 AM to 2:30 PM) excluding holidays
949-831-8427

Missouri

Courier:

U.S. Immigration & Naturalization Service
1907 - 1909 S Blue Island Avenue
Chicago, IL 60608

V Visa:

U.S. Immigration & Naturalization Service
P.O. Box 7216
Chicago, IL 60680-7216

K visa:

U.S. Immigration & Naturalization Service
P.O. Box 7218
Chicago, IL 60680-7218

Legalization & Family Unity:

U.S. Immigration & Naturalization Service
P.O. Box 7219
Chicago, IL 60680-7219

Special information:

• There is no specific phone number for
this service center. Call the national customer service number 800-375-5283.

• Since all applications are scanned, there
should be no staples in any forms. Use
paperclips and binder clips.

• Write full name and "A" number on
back of photo with pencil or felt
marker, as there is greater chance of
photos becoming separated during
scanning process.

Nebraska

Jurisdiction over *Alaska, Colorado, Idaho,
Illinois, Indiana, Iowa, Kansas, Michigan,
Minnesota, Missouri, Montana, Nebraska,
North Dakota, Ohio, Oregon, South
Dakota, Utah, Washington, Wisconsin,
and Wyoming.*

Courier Delivery:
USINS
850 S Street (P.O. Box _____)
Lincoln, NE 68508 + 4 digit zip code

All applications should be sent to:
U.S. Department of Justice
Immigration and Naturalization Service
Nebraska Service Center
P.O. Box (Insert Correct Box Number)
Lincoln, NE (Insert Correct Zip Code)

General Correspondence:
P.O. Box 82521
Lincoln, NE 68501-2521

Forms:

I-102
P.O. Box 87102
Lincoln, NE 68501-7102

I-129
P.O. Box 87129
Lincoln, NE 68501-7129

I-129 (Premium Processing)
P.O. Box 87103
Lincoln, NE 68501-7103

I-129F
P.O. Box 87130
Lincoln, NE 68501-7130

I-130
P.O. Box 87130
Lincoln, NE 68501-7130

I-131
P.O. Box 87131
Lincoln, NE 68501-7131

I-140
P.O. Box 87140
Lincoln, NE 68501-7140

I-290
P.O. Box 87290
Lincoln, NE 68501-7290

I-360
P.O. Box 87360
Lincoln, NE 68501-7360

N-400
P.O. Box 87400
Lincoln, NE 68501-7400

I-485
P.O. Box 87209
Lincoln, NE 68501-7209

I-485
P.O. Box 87485
Lincoln, NE 68501-7485

I-539
P.O. Box 87539
Lincoln, NE 68501-7539

I-589
P.O. Box 87589
Lincoln, NE 68501-7589

I-694
P.O. Box 87698
Lincoln, NE 68501-7698

I-730

P.O. Box 87730

Lincoln, NE 68501-7730

I-751

P.O. Box 87751

Lincoln, NE 68501-7751

I-765

P.O. Box 87765

Lincoln, NE 68501-7765

I-817

P.O. Box 87817

Lincoln, NE 68501-7817

I-821

(ONLY for applicants from El Salvador, Honduras, and Nicaragua; all other TPS applicants file with the local INS offices)

P.O. Box 87821

Lincoln, NE 68501-7821

I-824

P.O. Box 87824

Lincoln, NE 68501-7824

402-323-7830

Texas

Jurisdiction over *Alabama, Arkansas, Florida, Georgia, Kentucky, Louisiana, Mississippi, New Mexico, North Carolina, Oklahoma, South Carolina, Tennessee, and Texas.*

General Correspondence:

USINS TSC

PO Box 851488

Mesquite, TX 75185-1488

Courier Delivery:

USINS TSC

4141 N. St. Augustine Rd.

Dallas, TX 75227

Forms:

I-131, I-824, I-102, I-539, I-698:

USINS TSC

PO Box 851182

Mesquite, TX 75185-1182

I-765:

USINS TSC

PO Box 851041

Mesquite, TX 75185-1041

I-485:

USINS TSC

PO Box 851804

Mesquite, TX 75185-1804

I-129

USINS TSC

PO Box 852211

Mesquite, TX 75185-2211

I-130

USINS TSC

PO Box 850919

Mesquite, TX 75185-0919

I-589

USINS TSC
PO Box 851892
Mesquite, TX 75185-1892

I-140, I-290 A&B, I-360, I-526, I-829:

USINS TSC
PO Box 852135
Mesquite, TX 75185-2135

I-129F, I-212, I-612, I-751, I-817:

USINS TSC
PO Box 850965
Mesquite, TX 75185-0965

N-400

USINS TSC
PO Box 851204
Mesquite, TX 75185-1204
214-381-1423

Vermont

Jurisdiction over Connecticut, Delaware, District of Columbia, Maine, Maryland, Massachusetts, New Hampshire, New Jersey, New York, Pennsylvania, Puerto Rico, Rhode Island, Vermont, Virgin Islands, Virginia, and West Virginia.

All applications other than N-400s:

U.S. Department of Justice
Immigration and Naturalization Service
Vermont Service Center
75 Lower Welden St.
Saint Albans, Vermont 05479

Form N-400

U.S. Department of Justice
Immigration and Naturalization Service
Vermont Service Center
75 Lower Welden St.
Saint Albans, Vermont 05479-9400
802-527-4913

Appendix C
Websites
and Contact
Information

Immigration & Naturalization Service (INS):

National Customer Service Center: 800-375-5283

INS Forms Line: 800-870-3676

http://www.ins.gov
(home page)

http://www.ins.gov/graphics/formsfee/forms
(forms, fees)

http://www.ins.gov/graphics/fieldoffices/alphaa.htm
(local offices and service centers)

http://www.ins.gov/graphics/howdoi/affsupp.htm#poverty
(poverty guidelines for affidavit of support form)

http://www.ins.gov/graphics/lawregs/index.htm
(INS manuals)

http://www.cdc.gov/ncidod/dq/pdf/ti-civil.pdf
(medical examination guidelines)

http://www.sss.gov
(Selective Service info: 847-688-6888)

Immigration Court (EOIR):

EOIR status line: 800-898-7180

BIA: 703-605-1007

http://www.usdoj.gov/eoir
(home page)

http://www.usdoj.gov/eoir/sibpages/fieldicmap.htm
(links to immigration courts)

http://www.usdoj.gov/eoir/vll/libindex.html
(BIA Practice Manual, BIA decisions)

http://www.usdoj.gov/eoir/efoia/foiafreq.htm
(asylum grant rates)

http://www.uscourts.gov
(links to federal courts)

http://www.findlaw.com
(links to federal and state statutes)

Department of State:

Visa Bulletin (recording): 202-663-1541

http://www.state.gov (home page)

http://www.foia.state.gov (reading room)

http://usembassy.state.gov (links to all embassies and consulates)

http://travel.state.gov (Visa Bulletin, Passport Agency, diversity visa) http://travel.state.gov/aos.html *(affidavit of support guidelines)*

http://www.state.gov/g/drl/hr *(country reports)*

Department of Labor:

http://www.doleta.gov

http://edc.dws.state ut.us/owl.asp *(prevailing wage information)*

http://workforcesecurity.doleta.gov/foreign/times.asp *(SESA and DOL processing times)*

http://www.onetcenter.org/ *(replacement for Dictionary of Occupational Titles)*

http://www.cgfns.org *(credential evaluation for health workers)*

http://www.bls.gov/oco *(Occupational Outlook Handbook)*

http://www.bls.gov/soc/socguide.htm *(Standard Occupational Classification)*

http://www.naics.com *(to obtain NAICS code for I-140)*

U.S. Congress:

http://www.house.gov/judiciary/privimm.pdf *(rules on private bills)*

http://www.senate.gov

Canadian immigration:

http://cicnet.ci.gc.ca/

http://www.Canada-congenbuffalo.org

Legal Assistance Organizations:

http://www.usdoj.gov/eoir/statspub/raroster.htm *(accredited legal assistance organizations)*

http://nlg.org/nip *(National Immigration Project: referrals, domestic violence info, useful links)*

http://nilc.org *(National Immigration Law Center)*

http://www.centerforhumanrights.org/AmnestyIndex.html *(updated info on late amnesty cases)*

Human Rights Organizations:
(proving asylum or hardship)

http://www.refugees.org/world/statistics/wrs02_tableindex.htm *(INS asylum grant rates by country, TPS)*

http://www.state.gov/g/drl/hr *(State Department country reports)*

http://www.ind.homeoffice.gov.uk *(country reports)*

http://www.unhchr.ch *(United Nations Human Rights Commission)*

http://www.asylumlaw.org

http://www.rferl.org *(Radio Free Europe)*

http://www.amnesty.org *(Amnesty International)*

http://www.hrw.org *(Human Rights Watch)*

Social Security Administration:

http://www.ssa.gov

Government Benefit Programs:

http://acf.dhhs.gov *(Department of Health and Human Services - assistance programs)*

http://www.servicelocator.org *(job assistance)*

http://www.fns.usda.gov *(WIC)*

http://www.hhs.gov *(Medicaid or TANF)*

Food stamps: 800-221-5689
http://www.govspot.com *(links to state, federal and foreign government sites)*

Appendix D
Fee Chart

Applications or petitions mailed, postmarked, or otherwise filed, on or after this date require the new fee. If you fail to include the correct fee your application or petition will be rejected by INS. The fee waiver request process is not affected by the fee difference.

I-17...........$230.00	I-360..........130.00	I-824 ....140.00
I-90.............130.00	1-485......... *	I-829 ....395.00
I-102..........100.00	I-526..........400.00	N-300..........60.00
I-129..........130.00	I-539..........140.00	N-336..........195.00
I-129F........110.00	I-600..........460.00	N-400..........260.00
I-130..........130.00	I-600A.......460.00	N-410..........50.00
I-131..........110.00	I-601..........195.00	N-455..........90.00
I-140..........135.00	I-612..........195.00	N-470..........95.00
I-191..........195.00	1-751.........145.00	N-565..........155.00
I-192..........195.00	I-765..........120.00	N-600..........185.00
I-193..........195.00	I-817..........140.00	N-643..........145.00
I-212..........195.00	N-644........80.00	I-246 ....155.00

*I-485

under the age of 14 . . . . 160.00
age 14 and older 255.00
refugees . . . . no fee

NOTE: *Filing fees listed above DO NOT include the $50.00 service fee for fingerprinting , or any other costs that may be associated with application for Immigration & Naturalization Benefits.*

NOTE: *$30.00 will be assessed for any checks returned to INS as unpayable.*

FC-023
01/16/02

Part 3. Processing Information. (continued)

Where do you want this travel document sent? (check one)

a. ☐ Address in Part 2, above

b. ☐ American Consulate at (give City and Country, below)

c. ☐ INS overseas office at (give City and Country, below)

    City   Country

If you checked b. or c., above, give your overseas address:

Part 4. Information about the Proposed Travel.

Purpose of trip. If you need more room, continue on a separate sheet of paper.	List the countries you intend to visit.

Part 5. Complete only if applying for a Reentry Permit.

Since becoming a Permanent Resident (or during the past five years, whichever is less) how much total time have you spent outside the United States?	☐ less than 6 months ☐ 2 to 3 years ☐ 6 months to 1 year ☐ 3 to 4 years ☐ 1 to 2 years ☐ more than 4 years	
Since you became a Permanent Resident, have you ever filed a federal income tax return as a nonresident, or failed to file a federal return because you considered yourself to be a nonresident? (if yes, give details on a separate sheet of paper).	☐ Yes ☐ No	

Part 6. Complete only if applying for a Refugee Travel Document.

Country from which you are a refugee or asylee:

If you answer yes to any of the following questions, explain on a separate sheet of paper.

Do you plan to travel to the above-named country?	☐ Yes	☐ No
Since you were accorded Refugee/Asylee status, have you ever: returned to the above-named country; applied for an/or obtained a national passport, passport renewal, or entry permit into this country; or applied for an/or received any benefit from such country (for example, health insurance benefits)?	☐ Yes	☐ No
Since being accorded Refugee/Asylee status, have you, by any legal procedure or voluntary act, re-acquired the nationality of the above-named country, acquired a new nationality, or been granted refugee or asylee status in any other country?	☐ Yes	☐ No

Part 7. Complete only if applying for an Advance Parole.

On a separate sheet of paper, please explain how you qualify for an Advance Parole and what circumstances warrant issuance of Advance Parole. Include copies of any documents you wish considered. (See instructions.)

For how may trips do you intend to use this document?   ☐ 1 trip   ☐ More than 1 trip
    If outside the U.S., at right give the U.S. Consulate or INS office you wish notified if this application is approved.

Part 8. Signature.
Read the information on penalties in the instructions before completing this section. You must file this application while in the United States if filing for a reentry permit or refugee travel document.

I certify under penalty of perjury under the laws of the United States of America that this petition, and the evidence submitted with it, is all true and correct. I authorize the release of any information from my records which the Immigration and Naturalization Service needs to determine eligibility for the benefit I am seeking.

Signature	Date	Daytime Telephone # ( )

Please Note: If you do not completely fill out this form, or fail to submit required documents listed in the instructions, you may not be found eligible for the requested document and this application will have to be denied.

Part 9. Signature of person preparing form if other than above. (sign below)

I declare that I prepared this application at the request of the above person and it is based on all information of which I have knowledge.

Signature	Print Your Name	Date

Firm Name and Address	Daytime Telephone # ( )

U.S. Department of Justice
Immigration and Naturalization Service

OMB No. 1115-0061

Immigrant Petition for Alien Worker

START HERE - Please Type or Print.

Part 1. Information about the person or organization filing this petition.

FOR INS USE ONLY
Receipt

If an individual is filing, use the top name line. Organizations should use the second line.

Family Name	Given Name	Middle Initial
Company or Organization		

Address - Attn:

Street Number and Name		Room
City	State or Province	
Country	Zip/Postal Code	

E-mail Address:

IRS Tax #	Social Security # (if any)

Part 2. Petition type.

This petition is being filed for (check one)

- a. ☐ An alien of extraordinary ability
- b. ☐ An outstanding professor or researcher
- c. ☐ A multinational executive or manager
- d. ☐ A member of the professions holding an advanced degree or an alien of exceptional ability (who is **NOT** seeking a National Interest Waiver.)
- e. ☐ A skilled worker (requiring at least two years of specialized training or experience) or professional (Item F- no longer available)
- g. ☐ Any other worker (requiring less than two years of training or experience)
- i. ☐ An alien applying for a national interest waiver (who **IS** a member of the professions holding an advanced degree or an alien of exceptional ability)

Classification:

- ☐ 203(b)(1)(A) Alien of Extraordinary Ability
- ☐ 203(b)(1)(B) Outstanding Professor or Researcher
- ☐ 203(b)(1)(C) Multi-national executive or manager
- ☐ 203(b)(2) Member of professions w/adv. degree or exceptional ability
- ☐ 203(b)(3) (A) (i) Skilled Worker
- ☐ 203(b)(3) (A) (ii) Professional
- ☐ 203(b)(3) (A) (iii) Other worker

Certification:

- ☐ National Interest Waiver (NIW)
- ☐ Schedule A, Group I
- ☐ Schedule A, Group II

Part 3. Information about the person you are filing for.

Family Name	Given Name	Middle Initial

Address - C/O

Street # and Name		Apt. #
City	State or Province	
Country	Zip/Postal Code	

E-mail Address:

Date of Birth (Month/Day/Year)	Country of Birth
Social Security # (if any)	A # (if any)

If in the U.S.

Date of Arrival (Month/Day/Year)	I-94 #
Current Nonimmigrant Status	Expires on (Month/Day/Year)

Priority Date	Consulate

Remarks

Action Block

Form I-140 (Rev. 12/04/01)N

Part 4. Processing Information.

Please complete the following for the person named in Part 3: (Check one)

☐ Alien will apply for a visa abroad at the American
Consulate in:　　City: _____

Foreign
Country: _____

☐ Alien is in the United States and will apply for adjustment of status to that of lawful permanent resident.

Alien's Country of Nationality: _____

Alien's country of current residence or, if now in the U.S., last permanent residence abroad: _____

If you provided a U.S. address in Part 3, print the person's foreign address: _____

If the person's native alphabet is other than Roman letters, write the person's foreign name and address in the native alphabet:

Are you filing any other petitions or applications with this one?	☐ No	☐ Yes-attach an explanation
Is the person you are filing for in removal proceedings?	☐ No	☐ Yes-attach an explanation
Has any immigrant visa petition ever been filed by or on behalf of this person?	☐ No	☐ Yes-attach an explanation

If you answered yes to any of these questions, please provide the case number, office location, date of decision and disposition of the decision on a separate sheet of paper.

Part 5. Additional information about the petitioner.

Type of petitioner (Check one).

☐ Employer　　☐ Self　　☐ Other (Explain, e.g., Permanent Resident, U.S Citizen or any other person filing on behalf of the alien.)

If a company, give the following:
Type of business

NAICS Code: ☐☐☐☐☐☐

Date Established	Current # of employees	Gross Annual Income	Net Annual Income
If an individual, give the following: Occupation		Annual Income	

Part 6. Basic information about the proposed employment.

Job title _____

SOC Code: ☐☐ — ☐☐☐☐

Nontechnical description of job _____

Address where the person will work
if different from address in Part 1. _____

Is this a full-time position?:	☐ Yes　☐ No (hours per week _____)	Wages per week $
Is this a permanent position?:	☐ Yes　☐ No	Is this a new position?　☐ Yes　☐ No

Part 7. Information on spouse and all children of the person you are filing for.

List husband/wife and all children related to the individual for whom the petition is being filed. Provide an attachment of additional family members, if needed.

(Name)	(Relationship)	(Date of Birth)	(Country of Birth)

Part 8. Signature.

Read the information on penalties in the instructions before completing this section. If someone helped you prepare this petition, he or she must complete Part 9.

I certify, under penalty of perjury under the laws of the United States of America, that this petition and the evidence submitted with it are all true and correct. I authorize the release of any information from my records which the Immigration and Naturalization Service needs to determine eligibility for the benefit I am seeking.

Petitioner's Signature	Print Name	Date	Daytime Telephone No.

E-mail Address:

Please Note: *If you do not completely fill out this form or fail to submit required documents listed in the instructions, you may not be found eligible for the requested benefit and this petition may be denied.*

Part 9. Signature of person preparing form, if other than above. *(Sign below)*

I declare that I prepared this petition at the request of the above person and it is based on all information of which I have knowledge.

Signature	Print Name	Date	Daytime Telephone No.

Firm's Name
and Address

E-mail Address:

To Be Completed by *Attorney or Representative, if any.*
☐ Fill in box if G-28 is attached to represent the petitioner.

VOLAG No.	ATTY State License No.

Attorney or Representative Signature:

Note: In the event of a Request for Evidence (RFE) may the INS contact you by Fax or E-mail: ☐ Yes ☐ No

Fax Number: E-mail Address:

(Family name)	(First name)	(Middle name)	☐ MALE ☐ FEMALE	BIRTHDATE (Mo.-Day-Yr.)	NATIONALITY	FILE NUMBER A-

ALL OTHER NAMES USED (Including names by previous marriages)	CITY AND COUNTRY OF BIRTH	SOCIAL SECURITY NO. (If any)

	FAMILY NAME	FIRST NAME	DATE	CITY AND COUNTRY OF BIRTH (If known)	CITY AND COUNTRY OF RESIDENCE.
FATHER					
MOTHER (Maiden name)					

HUSBAND (If none, so state) OR WIFE	FAMILY NAME (For wife, give maiden name)	FIRST NAME	BIRTHDATE	CITY & COUNTRY OF BIRTH	DATE OF MARRIAGE	PLACE OF MARRIAGE

FORMER HUSBANDS OR WIVES (if none, so state)

FAMILY NAME (For wife, give maiden name)	FIRST NAME	BIRTHDATE	DATE & PLACE OF MARRIAGE	DATE AND PLACE OF TERMINATION OF MARRIAGE

APPLICANT'S RESIDENCE LAST FIVE YEARS. LIST PRESENT ADDRESS FIRST

STREET AND NUMBER	CITY	PROVINCE OR STATE	COUNTRY	FROM MONTH	FROM YEAR	TO MONTH	TO YEAR
						PRESENT TIME	

APPLICANT'S LAST ADDRESS OUTSIDE THE UNITED STATES OF MORE THAN ONE YEAR

STREET AND NUMBER	CITY	PROVINCE OR STATE	COUNTRY	FROM MONTH	FROM YEAR	TO MONTH	TO YEAR

APPLICANT'S EMPLOYMENT LAST FIVE YEARS. (IF NONE, SO STATE) LIST PRESENT EMPLOYMENT FIRST

FULL NAME AND ADDRESS OF EMPLOYER	OCCUPATION (SPECIFY)	FROM MONTH	FROM YEAR	TO MONTH	TO YEAR
				PRESENT TIME	

Show below last occupation abroad if not shown above. (Include all information requested above.)					

THIS FORM IS SUBMITTED IN CONNECTION WITH APPLICATION FOR: ☐ NATURALIZATION ☐ STATUS AS PERMANENT RESIDENT ☐ OTHER (SPECIFY):	SIGNATURE OF APPLICANT	DATE
Submit all four pages of this form.	If your native alphabet is other than roman letters, write your name in your native alphabet here:	

PENALTIES: SEVERE PENALTIES ARE PROVIDED BY LAW FOR KNOWINGLY AND WILLFULLY FALSIFYING OR CONCEALING A MATERIAL FACT.

APPLICANT: BE SURE TO PUT YOUR NAME AND ALIEN REGISTRATION NUMBER IN THE BOX OUTLINED BY HEAVY BORDER BELOW.

COMPLETE THIS BOX (Family name)	(Given name)	(Middle name)	(Alien registration number)

(Family name)	(First name)	(Middle name)	☐ MALE ☐ FEMALE	BIRTHDATE (Mo.-Day-Yr.)	NATIONALITY	FILE NUMBER A-

ALL OTHER NAMES USED (Including names by previous marriages)	CITY AND COUNTRY OF BIRTH	SOCIAL SECURITY NO. (If any)

	FAMILY NAME	FIRST NAME	DATE, CITY AND COUNTRY OF BIRTH (If known)	CITY AND COUNTRY OF RESIDENCE
FATHER				
MOTHER (Maiden name)				

HUSBAND (If none, so state) OR WIFE	FAMILY NAME (For wife, give maiden name)	FIRST NAME	BIRTHDATE	CITY & COUNTRY OF BIRTH	DATE OF MARRIAGE	PLACE OF MARRIAGE

FORMER HUSBANDS OR WIVES (if none, so state)

FAMILY NAME (For wife, give maiden name)	FIRST NAME	BIRTHDATE	DATE & PLACE OF MARRIAGE	DATE AND PLACE OF TERMINATION OF MARRIAGE

APPLICANT'S RESIDENCE LAST FIVE YEARS. LIST PRESENT ADDRESS FIRST

STREET AND NUMBER	CITY	PROVINCE OR STATE	COUNTRY	FROM MONTH	YEAR	TO MONTH	YEAR
						PRESENT TIME	

APPLICANT'S LAST ADDRESS OUTSIDE THE UNITED STATES OF MORE THAN ONE YEAR

STREET AND NUMBER	CITY	PROVINCE OR STATE	COUNTRY	FROM MONTH	YEAR	TO MONTH	YEAR

APPLICANT'S EMPLOYMENT LAST FIVE YEARS. (IF NONE, SO STATE) LIST PRESENT EMPLOYMENT FIRST

FULL NAME AND ADDRESS OF EMPLOYER	OCCUPATION (SPECIFY)	FROM MONTH	YEAR	TO MONTH	YEAR
				PRESENT TIME	

Show below last occupation abroad if not shown above. (Include all information requested above.)				

THIS FORM IS SUBMITTED IN CONNECTION WITH APPLICATION FOR: ☐ NATURALIZATION ☐ STATUS AS PERMANENT RESIDENT ☐ OTHER (SPECIFY):	SIGNATURE OF APPLICANT	DATE

Submit all four pages of this form.	If your native alphabet is other than roman letters, write your name in your native alphabet here:

PENALTIES: SEVERE PENALTIES ARE PROVIDED BY LAW FOR KNOWINGLY AND WILLFULLY FALSIFYING OR CONCEALING A MATERIAL FACT.

APPLICANT:
BE SURE TO PUT YOUR NAME AND ALIEN REGISTRATION NUMBER IN THE BOX OUTLINED BY HEAVY BORDER BELOW.

COMPLETE THIS BOX (Family name)	(Given name)	(Middle name)	(Alien registration number)

(OTHER AGENCY USE)	INS USE (Office of Origin) OFFICE CODE: TYPE OF CASE: DATE:

(Family name)	(First name)	(Middle name)	☐ MALE ☐ FEMALE	BIRTHDATE (Mo.-Day-Yr.)	NATIONALITY	FILE NUMBER A-

ALL OTHER NAMES USED (Including names by previous marriages)	CITY AND COUNTRY OF BIRTH	SOCIAL SECURITY NO. (If any)

	FAMILY NAME	FIRST NAME	DATE, CITY AND COUNTRY OF BIRTH (If known)	CITY AND COUNTRY OF RESIDENCE
FATHER				
MOTHER (Maiden name)				

HUSBAND (If none, so state) OR WIFE	FAMILY NAME (For wife, give maiden name)	FIRST NAME	BIRTHDATE	CITY & COUNTRY OF BIRTH	DATE OF MARRIAGE	PLACE OF MARRIAGE

FORMER HUSBANDS OR WIVES (if none, so state) FAMILY NAME (For wife, give maiden name)	FIRST NAME	BIRTHDATE	DATE & PLACE OF MARRIAGE	DATE AND PLACE OF TERMINATION OF MARRIAGE

APPLICANT'S RESIDENCE LAST FIVE YEARS. LIST PRESENT ADDRESS FIRST

STREET AND NUMBER	CITY	PROVINCE OR STATE	COUNTRY	FROM MONTH	FROM YEAR	TO MONTH	TO YEAR
						PRESENT TIME	

APPLICANT'S LAST ADDRESS OUTSIDE THE UNITED STATES OF MORE THAN ONE YEAR

STREET AND NUMBER	CITY	PROVINCE OR STATE	COUNTRY	FROM MONTH	FROM YEAR	TO MONTH	TO YEAR

APPLICANT'S EMPLOYMENT LAST FIVE YEARS. (IF NONE, SO STATE) LIST PRESENT EMPLOYMENT FIRST

FULL NAME AND ADDRESS OF EMPLOYER	OCCUPATION (SPECIFY)	FROM MONTH	FROM YEAR	TO MONTH	TO YEAR
				PRESENT TIME	

Show below last occupation abroad if not shown above. (Include all information requested above.)

THIS FORM IS SUBMITTED IN CONNECTION WITH APPLICATION FOR: ☐ NATURALIZATION ☐ STATUS AS PERMANENT RESIDENT ☐ OTHER (SPECIFY):	SIGNATURE OF APPLICANT	DATE

Submit all four pages of this form. | If your native alphabet is other than roman letters, write your name in your native alphabet here:

PENALTIES: SEVERE PENALTIES ARE PROVIDED BY LAW FOR KNOWINGLY AND WILLFULLY FALSIFYING OR CONCEALING A MATERIAL FACT.

APPLICANT:
BE SURE TO PUT YOUR NAME AND ALIEN REGISTRATION NUMBER IN THE BOX OUTLINED BY HEAVY BORDER BELOW.

COMPLETE THIS BOX (Family name)	(Given name)	(Middle name)	(Alien registration number)

(OTHER AGENCY USE)	INS USE (Office of Origin) OFFICE CODE: TYPE OF CASE: DATE:

(Family name)	(First name)	(Middle name)	☐ MALE ☐ FEMALE	BIRTHDATE (Mo.-Day-Yr.)	NATIONALITY	FILE NUMBER A-

ALL OTHER NAMES USED (Including names by previous marriages)	CITY AND COUNTRY OF BIRTH	SOCIAL SECURITY NO. (If any)

	FAMILY NAME	FIRST NAME	DATE, CITY AND COUNTRY OF BIRTH (If known)	CITY AND COUNTRY OF RESIDENCE
FATHER				
MOTHER (Maiden name)				

HUSBAND (If none, so state) OR WIFE	FAMILY NAME (For wife, give maiden name)	FIRST NAME	BIRTHDATE	CITY & COUNTRY OF BIRTH	DATE OF MARRIAGE	PLACE OF MARRIAGE

FORMER HUSBANDS OR WIVES (if none, so state)

FAMILY NAME (For wife, give maiden name)	FIRST NAME	BIRTHDATE	DATE & PLACE OF MARRIAGE	DATE AND PLACE OF TERMINATION OF MARRIAGE

APPLICANT'S RESIDENCE LAST FIVE YEARS. LIST PRESENT ADDRESS FIRST

STREET AND NUMBER	CITY	PROVINCE OR STATE	COUNTRY	FROM MONTH	FROM YEAR	TO MONTH	TO YEAR
						PRESENT TIME	

APPLICANT'S LAST ADDRESS OUTSIDE THE UNITED STATES OF MORE THAN ONE YEAR

STREET AND NUMBER	CITY	PROVINCE OR STATE	COUNTRY	FROM MONTH	FROM YEAR	TO MONTH	TO YEAR

APPLICANT'S EMPLOYMENT LAST FIVE YEARS. (IF NONE, SO STATE) LIST PRESENT EMPLOYMENT FIRST

FULL NAME AND ADDRESS OF EMPLOYER	OCCUPATION (SPECIFY)	FROM MONTH	FROM YEAR	TO MONTH	TO YEAR
				PRESENT TIME	

Show below last occupation abroad if not shown above. (Include all information requested above.)

THIS FORM IS SUBMITTED IN CONNECTION WITH APPLICATION FOR: ☐ NATURALIZATION ☐ STATUS AS PERMANENT RESIDENT ☐ OTHER (SPECIFY):	SIGNATURE OF APPLICANT	DATE
Submit all four pages of this form.	If your native alphabet is other than roman letters, write your name in your native alphabet here:	

PENALTIES: SEVERE PENALTIES ARE PROVIDED BY LAW FOR KNOWINGLY AND WILLFULLY FALSIFYING OR CONCEALING A MATERIAL FACT.

APPLICANT: BE SURE TO PUT YOUR NAME AND ALIEN REGISTRATION NUMBER IN THE BOX OUTLINED BY HEAVY BORDER BELOW.

COMPLETE THIS BOX (Family name)	(Given name)	(Middle name)	(Alien registration number)

(OTHER AGENCY USE)	INS USE (Office of Origin) OFFICE CODE: TYPE OF CASE: DATE:

U.S. Department of Justice
Immigration and Naturalization Service

Petition for Amerasian, Widow(er), or Special Immigrant

START HERE - Please Type or Print

Part 1. Information about person or organization filing this petition. (Individuals should use the top name line; organizations should use the second line.) If you are a self-petitioning spouse or child and do not want INS to send notices about this petition to your home, you may show an alternate mailing address here. If you are filing for yourself and do not want to use an alternate mailing address, skip to part 2.

Family Name	Given Name	Middle Initial

Company or Organization Name

Address - C/O

Street Number and Name		Apt. #
City	State or Province	
Country	Zip/Postal Code	

U.S. Social Security #	A #	IRS Tax # (if any)

Part 2. Classification Requested (check one):

- a. ☐ Amerasian
- b. ☐ Widow(er) of a U.S. citizen who died within the past two (2) years
- c. ☐ Special Immigrant Juvenile
- d. ☐ Special Immigrant Religious Worker
- e. ☐ Special Immigrant based on employment with the Panama Canal Company, Canal Zone Government or U.S. Government in the Canal Zone
- f. ☐ Special Immigrant Physician
- g. ☐ Special Immigrant International Organization Employee or family member
- h. ☐ Special Immigrant Armed Forces Member
- i. ☐ Self-Petitioning Spouse of Abusive U.S. Citizen or Lawful Permanent Resident
- j. ☐ Self-Petitioning Child of Abusive U.S. Citizen or Lawful Permanent Resident
- k. ☐ Other, explain: _____

Part 3. Information about the person this petition is for.

Family Name	Given Name	Middle Initial

Address - C/O

Street Number and Name		Apt. #
City	State or Province	
Country	Zip/Postal Code	
Date of Birth (Month/Day/Year)	Country of Birth	
U.S. Social Security #	A # (if any)	

Marital Status: ☐ Single ☐ Married ☐ Divorced ☐ Widowed

Complete the items below if this person is in the United States:

Date of Arrival (Month/Day/Year)	I-94 #
Current Nonimmigrant Status	Expires on (Month/Day/Year)

Continued on back.

FOR INS USE ONLY

Returned	Receipt
Resubmitted	
Reloc Sent	
Reloc Rec'd	

☐ Petitioner/ Applicant Interviewed

☐ Beneficiary Interviewed

☐ I-485 Filed Concurrently
☐ Bene "A" File Reviewed

Classification

Consulate

Priority Date

Remarks:

Action Block

To Be Completed by Attorney or Representative, if any

☐ Fill in box if G-28 is attached to represent the applicant

VOLAG#

ATTY State License #

Part 4. Processing Information.

Below give to United States Consulate you want notified if this petition is approved and if any requested adjustment of status cannot be granted.

American Consulate: City	Country

If you gave a United States address in Part 3, print the person's foreign address below. If his/her native alphabet does not use Roman letters, print his/her name and foreign address in the native alphabet.

Name	Address

Sex of the person this petition is for.   ☐ Male   ☐ Female

Are you filing any other petitions or applications with this one?   ☐ No   ☐ Yes (How many? _____)

Is the person this petition is for in exclusion or deportation proceedings?   ☐ No   ☐ Yes (Explain an a separate sheet of paper)

Has the person this petition is for ever worked in the U.S. without permission? ☐ No   ☐ Yes (Explain an a separate sheet of paper)

Is an appilication for adjustment of status attached to this petition?   ☐ No   ☐ Yes

Part 5. Complete only if filing for an Amerasian.

Section A. Information about the mother of the Amerasian

Family Name	Given Name	Middle Initial

Living? ☐ No (Give date of death _____)   ☐ Yes (complete address line below)   ☐ Unknown (attach a full explanation)

Address

Section B. Information about the father of the Amerasian: If possible, attach a notarized statement from the father regarding parentage. Explain on separate paper any question you cannot fully answer in the space provided on this form.

Family Name	Given Name	Middle Initial

Date of Birth (Month/Day/Year)	Country of Birth

Living? ☐ No (give date of death _____)   ☐ Yes (complete address line below)   ☐ Unknown (attach a full explanation)

Home Address

Home Phone #	Work Phone #

At the time the Amerasian was conceived:

☐ The father was in the military (indicate branch of service below - and give service number here): _____

   ☐ Army   ☐ Air Force   ☐ Navy   ☐ Marine Corps   ☐ Coast Guard

☐ The father was a civilian employed abroad. Attach a list of names and addresses of organizations which employed him at that time.

☐ The father was not in the military, and was not a civilian employed abroad. (Attach a full explanation of the circumstances.)

Part 6. Complete only if filing for a Special Immigrant Juvenile Court Dependent.

Section A. Information about the Juvenile

List any other names used.

Answer the following questions regarding the person this petition is for. If you answer "no," explain on a separate sheet of paper.

Is he or she still dependent upon the juvenile court or still legally committed to or under the custody of an agency or department of a state?   ☐ No   ☐ Yes

Does he/she continue to be eligible for long term foster care?   ☐ No   ☐ Yes

Form I-360 (Rev. 09/11/00) Y Page 7

Continued on next page.

Part 7. Complete only if filing as a Widow/Widower, a Self-petitioning Spouse of an Abuser, or as a Self-petitioning Child of an Abuser.

Section A. Information about the U.S. citizen husband or wife who died or about the U.S. citizen or lawful permanent resident abuser.

Family Name	Given Name	Middle Initial

Date of Birth (Month/Day/Year)	Country of Birth	Date of Death (Month/Day/Year)

He or she is now, or was at time of death a (check one):

☐ U.S. citizen born in the United States.
☐ U.S. citizen born abroad to U.S. citizen parents.

☐ U.S. citizen through Naturalization *(Show A #)* _____
☐ U.S. lawful permanent resident *(Show A #)* _____
☐ Other, explain _____

Section B. Additional Information about you.

How many times have you been married?	How many times was the person in Section A married?	Give the date and place you and the person in Section A were married. *(If you are a self-petitioning child, write: "N/A")*

When did you live with the person named in Section A? From *(Month/Year)* _____ until *(Month/Year)* _____

If you are filing as a widow/widower, were you legally separated at the time of the U.S citizens's death? ☐ No ☐ Yes, *(attach explanation)*.

Give the last address at which you lived together with the person named in Section A, and show the last date that you lived together with that person at that address:

If you are filing as a self-petitioning spouse, have any of your children filed separate self-petitions? ☐ No ☐ Yes *(show child(ren)'s full names)*

Part 8. Information about the spouse and children of the person this petition is for. A widow/widower or a self-petitioning spouse of an abusive citizen or lawful permanent resident should also list the children of the deceased spouse or of the abuser.

A. Family Name	Given Name	Middle Initial	Date of Birth (Month/Day/Year)
Country of Birth	Relationship ☐ Spouse ☐ Child		A #

B. Family Name	Given Name	Middle Initial	Date of Birth (Month/Day/Year)
Country of Birth	Relationship ☐ Child		A #

C. Family Name	Given Name	Middle Initial	Date of Birth (Month/Day/Year)
Country of Birth	Relationship ☐ Child		A #

D. Family Name	Given Name	Middle Initial	Date of Birth (Month/Day/Year)
Country of Birth	Relationship ☐ Child		A #

E. Family Name	Given Name	Middle Initial	Date of Birth (Month/Day/Year)
Country of Birth	Relationship ☐ Child		A #

F. Family Name	Given Name	Middle Initial	Date of Birth (Month/Day/Year)
Country of Birth	Relationship ☐ Child		A #

G. Family Name		Given Name		Middle Initial	Date of Birth (Month/Day/Year)
Country of Birth		Relationship ☐ Child			A#
H. Family Name		Given Name		Middle Initial	Date of Birth (Month/Day/Year)
Country of Birth		Relationship ☐ Child			A#

Part 9. Signature.

Read the information on penalties in the instructions before completing this part. If you are going to file this petition at an INS office in the United States, sign below. If you are going to file it at a U.S. consulate or INS office overseas, sign in front of a U.S. INS or consular official.

I certify, or, if outside the United States, I swear or affirm, under penalty of perjury under the laws of the United States of America, that this petition and the evidence submitted with it is all true and correct. If filing this on behalf at an organization, I certify that I am empowered to do so by that organization. I authorize the release of any information from my records, or from the petitioning organization's records, which the Immigration and Naturalization Service needs to determine eligibility for the benefit being sought.

Signature	Date

Signature of INS or Consular Official	Print Name	Date

Please Note: If you do not completely fill out this form or fail to submit required documents listed in the instructions, the person(s) filed for may not be found eligible for a requested benefit and it may have to be denied.

Part 10. Signature of person preparing form if other than above. (sign below)

I declare that I prepared this application at the request of the above person and it is based on all information of which I have knowledge.

Signature	Print Your Name	Date

Firm Name and Address

U.S. Department of Justice
Immigration and Naturalization Service

Form I-485, Application to Register
Permanent Resident or Adjust Status

START HERE - Please Type or Print

Part 1.   Information About You.

Family Name	Given Name	Middle Initial

Address - C/O

Street Number and Name	Apt. #

City

State	Zip Code
Date of Birth (month/day/year)	Country of Birth
Social Security #	A # (if any)
Date of Last Arrival (month/day/year)	I-94 #
Current INS Status	Expires on (month/day/year)

Part 2.   Application Type. *(check one)*

I am applying for an adjustment to permanent resident status because:

a. ☐ an immigrant petition giving me an immediately available immigrant visa number has been approved. (Attach a copy of the approval notice-- or a relative, special immigrant juvenile or special immigrant military visa petition filed with this application that will give you an immediately available visa number, if approved.)

b. ☐ my spouse or parent applied for adjustment of status or was granted lawful permanent residence in an immigrant visa category that allows derivative status for spouses and children.

c. ☐ I entered as a K-1 fiance(e) of a U.S. citizen whom I married within 90 days of entry or I am the K-2 child of such a fiance(e). [Attach a copy of the fiance(e) petition approval notice and the marriage certificate.]

d. ☐ I was granted asylum or derivative asylum status as the spouse or child of a person granted asylum and am eligible for adjustment.

e. ☐ I am a native or citizen of Cuba admitted or paroled into the U.S. after January 1, 1959, and thereafter have been physically present in the U.S. for at least one year.

f. ☐ I am the husband, wife or minor unmarried child of a Cuban described in (e) and am residing with that person, and was admitted or paroled into the U.S. after January 1, 1959, and thereafter have been physically present in the U.S. for at least one year.

g. ☐ I have continuously resided in the U.S. since before January 1, 1972.

h. ☐ Other basis of eligibility. Explain. (If additional space is needed, use a separate piece of paper.)

_____

_____

I am already a permanent resident and am applying to have the date I was granted permanent residence adjusted to the date I originally arrived in the U.S. as a nonimmigrant or parolee, or as of May 2,1964, whichever date is later, and: *(Check one)*

i. ☐ I am a native or citizen of Cuba and meet the description in (e), above.

j. ☐ I am the husband, wife or minor unmarried child of a Cuban, and meet the description in (f), above.

FOR INS USE ONLY

Returned	Receipt
_____ _____	
Resubmitted _____ _____	
Reloc Sent _____ _____	
Reloc Rec'd _____ _____	
Applicant Interviewed	

Section of Law
☐ **Sec. 209(b), INA**
☐ **Sec. 13, Act of 9/11/57**
☐ **Sec. 245, INA**
☐ **Sec. 249, INA**
☐ **Sec. 2 Act of 11/2/66**
☐ **Sec. 2 Act of 11/2/66**
☐ **Other** _____

Country Chargeable

Eligibility Under Sec. 245
  Approved Visa Petition
  Dependent of Principal Alien
  Special Immigrant
  Other _____

Preference

Action Block

To be Completed by
Attorney or Representative, **if any**

☐ Fill in box if G-28 is attached to represent the applicant.

VOLAG #

ATTY State License #

Continued on back

Form I-485 (Rev. 02/07/00)N Page 1

Part 3. Processing Information.

A. City/Town/Village of Birth | Current Occupation

Your Mother's First Name | Your Father's First Name

Give your name exactly how it appears on your Arrival /Departure Record (Form 1-94)

Place of Last Entry Into the U.S. (City/State) | In what status did you last enter? *(Visitor, student, exchange alien, crewman, temporary worker, without inspection, etc.)*

Were you inspected by a U.S. Immigration Officer? ☐ Yes ☐ No

Nonimmigrant Visa Number | Consulate Where Visa Was Issued

Date Visa Was Issued (month/day/year) | Sex: ☐ Male ☐ Female | Marital Status ☐ Married ☐ Single ☐ Divorced ☐ Widowed

Have you ever before applied for permanent resident status in the U.S.? ☐ No ☐ Yes If you checked "Yes," give date and place of filing and final disposition.

B. List your present husband/wife and all your sons and daughters. (If you have none, write "none." If additional space is needed, use a separate piece of paper.)

Family Name	Given Name	Middle Initial	Date of Birth (month/day/year)
Country of Birth	Relationship	A #	Applying with You? ☐ Yes ☐ No
Family Name	Given Name	Middle Initial	Date of Birth (month/day/year)
Country of Birth	Relationship	A #	Applying with You? ☐ Yes ☐ No
Family Name	Given Name	Middle Initial	Date of Birth (month/day/year)
Country of Birth	Relationship	A #	Applying with You? ☐ Yes ☐ No
Family Name	Given Name	Middle Initial	Date of Birth (month/day/year)
Country of Birth	Relationship	A #	Applying with You? ☐ Yes ☐ No
Family Name	Given Name	Middle Initial	Date of Birth (month/day/year)
Country of Birth	Relationship	A #	Applying with You? ☐ Yes ☐ No

C. List your present and past membership in or affiliation with every political organization, association, fund, foundation, party, club, society or similar group in the United States or in other places since your 16th birthday. Include any foreign military service in this part. If none, write "none." Include the name(s) of the organization(s), location(s), dates of membership from and to, and the nature of the organization (s). If additional space is needed, use a separate piece of paper.

_____

_____

_____

_____

_____

_____

Part 3. Processing Information. *(Continued)*

Please answer the following questions. (If your answer is **"Yes"** to any one of these questions, explain on a separate piece of paper. Answering **"Yes"** does not necessarily mean that you are not entitled to adjust your status or register for permanent residence.)

1. Have you ever, in or outside the U. S.:
   a. knowingly committed any crime of moral turpitude or a drug-related offense for which you have not been arrested? ☐ Yes ☐ No
   b. been arrested, cited, charged, indicted, fined or imprisoned for breaking or violating any law or ordinance, excluding traffic violations? ☐ Yes ☐ No
   c. been the beneficiary of a pardon, amnesty, rehabilitation decree, other act of clemency or similar action? ☐ Yes ☐ No
   d. exercised diplomatic immunity to avoid prosecution for a criminal offense in the U. S.? ☐ Yes ☐ No

2. Have you received public assistance in the U.S. from any source, including the U.S. government or any state, county, city or municipality (other than emergency medical treatment), or are you likely to receive public assistance in the future? ☐ Yes ☐ No

3. Have you ever:
   a. within the past ten years been a prostitute or procured anyone for prostitution, or intend to engage in such activities in the future? ☐ Yes ☐ No
   b. engaged in any unlawful commercialized vice, including, but not limited to, illegal gambling? ☐ Yes ☐ No
   c. knowingly encouraged, induced, assisted, abetted or aided any alien to try to enter the U.S. illegally? ☐ Yes ☐ No
   d. illicitly trafficked in any controlled substance, or knowingly assisted, abetted or colluded in the illicit trafficking of any controlled substance? ☐ Yes ☐ No

4. Have you ever engaged in, conspired to engage in, or do you intend to engage in, or have you ever solicited membership or funds for, or have you through any means ever assisted or provided any type of material support to, any person or organization that has ever engaged or conspired to engage, in sabotage, kidnapping, political assassination, hijacking or any other form of terrorist activity? ☐ Yes ☐ No

5. Do you intend to engage in the U.S. in:
   a. espionage? ☐ Yes ☐ No
   b. any activity a purpose of which is opposition to, or the control or overthrow of, the government of the United States, by force, violence or other unlawful means? ☐ Yes ☐ No
   c. any activity to violate or evade any law prohibiting the export from the United States of goods, technology or sensitive information? ☐ Yes ☐ No

6. Have you ever been a member of, or in any way affiliated with, the Communist Party or any other totalitarian party? ☐ Yes ☐ No

7. Did you, during the period from March 23, 1933 to May 8, 1945, in association with either the Nazi Government of Germany or any organization or government associated or allied with the Nazi Government of Germany, ever order, incite, assist or otherwise participate in the persecution of any person because of race, religion, national origin or political opinion? ☐ Yes ☐ No

8. Have you ever engaged in genocide, or otherwise ordered, incited, assisted or otherwise participated in the killing of any person because of race, religion, nationality, ethnic origin or political opinion? ☐ Yes ☐ No

9. Have you ever been deported from the U.S., or removed from the U.S. at government expense, excluded within the past year, or are you now in exclusion or deportation proceedings? ☐ Yes ☐ No

10. Are you under a final order of civil penalty for violating section 274C of the Immigration and Nationality Act for use of fradulent documents or have you, by fraud or willful misrepresentation of a material fact, ever sought to procure, or procured, a visa, other documentation, entry into the U.S. or any immigration benefit? ☐ Yes ☐ No

11. Have you ever left the U.S. to avoid being drafted into the U.S. Armed Forces? ☐ Yes ☐ No

12. Have you ever been a J nonimmigrant exchange visitor who was subject to the two-year foreign residence requirement and not yet complied with that requirement or obtained a waiver? ☐ Yes ☐ No

13. Are you now withholding custody of a U.S. citizen child outside the U.S. from a person granted custody of the child? ☐ Yes ☐ No

14. Do you plan to practice polygamy in the U.S.? ☐ Yes ☐ No

Continued on back

Part 4. Signature. *(Read the information on penalties in the instructions before completing this section. You must file this application while in the United States.)*

I certify, under penalty of perjury under the laws of the United States of America, that this application and the evidence submitted with it is all true and correct. I authorize the release of any information from my records which the INS needs to determine eligibility for the benefit I am seeking.

Selective Service Registration. The following applies to you if you are a man at least 18 years old, but not yet 26 years old, who is required to register with the Selective Service System: I understand that my filing this adjustment of status application with the Immigration and Naturalization Service authorizes the INS to provide certain registration information to the Selective Service System in accordance with the Military Selective Service Act. Upon INS acceptance of my application, I authorize INS to transmit to the Selective Service System my name, current address, Social Security number, date of birth and the date I filed the application for the purpose of recording my Selective Service registration as of the filing date. If, however, the INS does not accept my application, I further understand that, if so required, I am responsible for registering with the Selective Service by other means, provided I have not yet reached age 26.

Signature	*Print Your Name*	*Date*	*Daytime Phone Number*

Please Note: *If you do not completely fill out this form or fail to submit required documents listed in the instructions, you may not be found eligible for the requested benefit and this application may be denied.*

Part 5. Signature of Person Preparing Form, If Other Than Above. *(Sign Below)*

I declare that I prepared this application at the request of the above person and it is based on all information of which I have knowledge.

Signature	*Print Your Name*	*Date*	*Daytime Phone Number*

Firm Name
and Address

START HERE - Please Type or Print

FOR INS USE ONLY

Part 1.   Information about applicant

Family Name	First Name	Middle Name

Address - C/O

Street Number and Name	Apt. Suite

City	State or Province

Country	Zip/Postal Code

INS A #	Date of Birth (month/day/year)	Country of Birth

FOR INS USE ONLY	
Returned	Receipt
Resubmitted	
Reloc Sent	
Reloc Rec'd	
Interviewed	
File Reviewed	Class of Adjustment Code:

Part 2.   Basis for eligibility (check one)

1. On Form I-485, Part 2. I checked application type (check one):

   a. ☐ An immigrant petition.   Go to #2.
   b. ☐ My spouse or parent applied.   Go to #2.
   c. ☐ I entered as a K-1 fiancé(e).   **Stop here. Do not file this form.**
   d. ☐ I was granted asylum.   **Stop here. Do not file this form.**
   e. ☐ I am a native or citizen of Cuba.   Go to #3.
   f. ☐ I am the husband, wife or child of a Cuban.   Go to #3.
   g. ☐ I have continuously resided in the U.S.   **Stop here. Do not file this form.**
   h. ☐ Other.   Go to #2.
   i. ☐ I am already a permanent resident.   **Stop here. Do not file this form.**
   j. ☐ I am already a permanent resident and am the husband, wife or unmarried child of a Cuban.   **Stop here. Do not file this form.**

To Be Completed by *Attorney or Representative, if any*
☐ Check if G-28 is attached showing you represent the petitioner
VOLAG#
ATTY State License #

2. I have filed Form I-360 and I am applying for adjustment of status as a special immigrant juvenile court dependent or a special immigrant who has served in the United States Armed Forces (check one).

   ☐ Yes **Stop here. Do not file this form.**   ☐ No Go to #3.

3. On Form I-485, Part 2, I checked block (e) or (f) and I last entered the United States legally after having been inspected and admitted or paroled. ☐ Yes **Stop here. Do not file this form.**   ☐ No Go to #11.

4. I last entered the United States (check one):

   ☐ As a stowaway.   Go to #11.   ☐ Legally without a visa as a visitor for tourism or business.   Go to #5.
   ☐ Legally as a crewman (D-1/D-2 visa). Go to #11.
   ☐ Without inspection.   Go to #11.   ☐ Legally as a parolee.   Go to #5.
   ☐ Legally in transit without visa status. Go to #11.   ☐ Legally with another type of visa (show type _____). Go to #5.

5. I last entered the United States legally without a visa as a visitor for tourism or business, and I am applying for adjustment of status as the spouse, unmarried child (under 21 years of age), parent, widow or widower of a United States citizen (check one).

   ☐ Yes **Stop here. Do not file this form.**   ☐ No   Go to #6.

6. I last entered the United States legally as a parolee, or with a visa (except as a crewman), or as a Canadian citizen without a visa, and I am applying for adjustment of status (check one)

   ☐ As the spouse, unmarried child (under 21 years of age), parent, widow or widower of a United States citizen. **Stop here. Do not file this form.**

   ☐ As a special immigrant retired international organization employee or family member of an international organization employee or as a special immigrant physician; and I have filed Form I-360. **Stop here. Do not file this form.**

   ☐ Under some other category. Go to #7.

Part 2. (continued)

7. I am a national of the (former) Soviet Union, Vietnam, Laos or Cambodia who last entered the United States legally as a public interest parolee after having been denied refugee status, and I am applying for adjustment of status under Public Law 101-167 *(check one)*.

☐ Yes **Stop here. Do not file this form.**   ☐ No **Go to #8.**

8. I have been employed in the United States after January 1, 1977 without INS authorization *(check one)*.

☐ Yes **Go to #9.**   ☐ No **Go to #10.**

9. I am applying for adjustment of status under the Immigration Nursing Relief Act (INRA). I was employed without INS authorization only on or before November 29, 1990, and I have always maintained a lawful immigration status while in the United States after November 5, 1986 *(check one)*:

☐ Yes **Stop here. Do not file this form.**   ☐ No **Go to #10.**

10.   I am now in lawful immigration status, and I have always maintained a lawful immigration status while in the United States after November 5, 1986 *(check one)*.

☐ Yes **Stop here. Do not file this form.**

☐ No, but I believe that INS will determine that my failure to be in or maintain a lawful immigration status was through no fault of my own or for technical reasons. **Stop here. Do not file this form.** Attach an explanation regarding this question to your Form I-485 application.

No   **Go to #11.**

11. I am unmarried and less than 17 years old *(check one)*.

☐ Yes **Stop here. File this form and Form I-485.** Pay only the fee required with Form I-485.
☐ No   **Go to #12.**

12. I am the unmarried child of a legalized alien and am less than 21 years old, or I am the spouse of a legalized alien, and I have attached a copy of my receipt or approval notice showing that I have properly filed Form I-817, Application for Voluntary Departure under the Family Unity Program *(check one)*.

☐ Yes **Stop here. File this form and Form I-485.** Pay only the fee required with Form I-485.
☐ No   **Go to #13.**

13. **File this form and Form I-485. You must pay the additional sum of :**

$ 220.00 - Fee required with Form I-485* and
$1,000.00 - Additional sum under section 245(i) of the Act

$1,220.00 - Total amount you must pay.

*If you filed Form I-485 separately, attach a copy of your filing receipt and pay only the additional sum of $1,000.00. In #11 and/or #12, show the answer you would have given on the date you filed Form I-485.

Part 3.   Signature. Read the information on penalties in the instructions before completing this section. If someone helped you prepare this petition, he or she must complete Part 4.

I certify, under penalty of perjury under the laws of the United States of America, that this application and the evidence submitted with it is all true and correct. I authorize the release of any information from my records which the Immigration and Naturalization Service needs to determine eligibility for the benefit I am seeking.

Signature	Print Your Name	Date	Daytime Telephone No.

Please Note: If you do not completely fill out this form or fail to submit required documents listed in the instructions, you may not be found eligible for the requested document and this application may be denied.

Part 4.   Signature of person preparing form, if other than above. *(Sign Below)*

I declare that I prepared this application at the request of the above person and it is based on all information of which I have knowledge.

Signature	Print Your Name	Date	Daytime Telephone No.

Firm Name
and Address

U.S. Department of Justice

Immigration and Naturalization Service

OMB No. 1115-0093; Expires 7/31/04

Application to Extend/Change Nonimmigrant Status

START HERE - Please Type or Print.

Part 1. Information about you.

Family Name	Given Name	Middle Initial

Address -
In care of -

Street Number and Name		Apt. #

City	State	Zip Code	Daytime Phone #

Country of Birth	Country of Citizenship

Date of Birth (MM/DD/YYYY)	Social Security # (if any)	A # (if any)

Date of Last Arrival Into the U.S.	I-94 #

Current Nonimmigrant Status	Expires on (MM/DD/YYYY)

Part 2. Application type. *(See instructions for fee.)*

1. I am applying for: *(Check one.)*
   a. ☐ An extension of stay in my current status.
   b. ☐ A change of status. The new status I am requesting is: _____
   c. ☐ Other: *(Describe grounds of eligibility.)* _____
2. Number of people included in this application: *(Check one.)*
   a. ☐ I am the only applicant.
   b. ☐ Members of my family are filing this application with me.
       The total number of people (including me) in the application is: _____
       (Complete the supplement for each co-applicant.)

Part 3. Processing information.

1. I/We request that my/our current or requested status be extended until (MM/DD/YYYY): _____
2. Is this application based on an extension or change of status already granted to your spouse, child or parent?
   ☐ No ☐ Yes, Receipt # _____
3. Is this application based on a separate petition or application to give your spouse, child or parent an extension or change of status? ☐ No ☐ Yes, filed with this I-539.
   ☐ Yes, filed previously and pending with INS. INS receipt number: _____
4. If you answered "Yes" to Question 3, give the name of the petitioner or applicant:

   If the petition or application is pending with INS, also give the following information:

Office filed at _____	Filed on (MM/DD/YYYY) _____

Part 4. Additional information.

1. For applicant #1, provide passport information: | Valid to: (MM/DD/YYYY)
   Country of Issuance

2. Foreign Address: Street Number and Name | Apt. #

City or Town	State or Province

Country	Zip/Postal Code

FOR INS USE ONLY

Returned	Receipt
Date	
Resubmitted	
Date	
Reloc Sent	
Date	
Reloc Rec'd	
Date	

☐ Applicant Interviewed on
_____
Date

☐ Extension Granted to (Date):
_____

Change of Status/Extension Granted
New Class: From (Date): _____
_____   To (Date): _____

If Denied:
☐ Still within period of stay
☐ S/D to: _____
☐ Place under docket control

Remarks:

Action Block

To be Completed by
Attorney or Representative, if any

☐ Fill in box if G-28 is attached to represent the applicant.

ATTY State License #

Form I-539 (Rev. 09/04/01)N *Prior versions may be used until 3/30/02*

Part 4. Additional information.

3. Answer the following questions. If you answer "Yes" to any question, explain on separate sheet of paper.	Yes	No
a. Are you, or any other person included on the application, an applicant for an immigrant visa?		
b. Has an immigrant petition ever been filed for you or for any other person included in this application?		
c. Has a Form I-485, Application to Register Permanent Residence or Adjust Status, ever been filed by you or by any other person included in this application?		
d. Have you, or any other person included in this application, ever been arrested or convicted of any criminal offense since last entering the U.S.?		
e. Have you, or any other person included in this application, done anything that violated the terms of the nonimmigrant status you now hold?		
f. Are you, or any other person included in this application, now in removal proceedings?		
g. Have you, or any other person included in this application, been employed in the U.S. since last admitted or granted an extension or change of status?		

- If you answered "Yes" to Question 3f, give the following information concerning the removal proceedings on the attached page entitled "**Part 4. Additional information. Page for answers to 3f and 3g.**" Include the name of the person in removal proceedings and information on jurisdiction, date proceedings began and status of proceedings.

- If you answered "No" to Question 3g, fully describe how you are supporting yourself on the attached page entitled "**Part 4. Additional information. Page for answers to 3f and 3g.**" Include the source, amount and basis for any income.

- If you answered "Yes" to Question 3g, fully describe the employment on the attached page entitled "**Part 4. Additional information. Page for answers to 3f and 3g.**" Include the name of the person employed, name and address of the employer, weekly income and whether the employment was specifically authorized by INS.

Part 5. Signature. *(Read the information on penalties in the instructions before completing this section. You must file this application while in the United States.)*

I certify, under penalty of perjury under the laws of the United States of America, that this application and the evidence submitted with it is all true and correct. I authorize the release of any information from my records which the Immigration and Naturalization Service needs to determine eligibility for the benefit I am seeking.

Signature	Print your Name	Date

Please note: *If you do not completely fill out this form, or fail to submit required documents listed in the instructions, you may not be found eligible for the requested benefit and this application will have to be denied.*

Part 6. Signature of person preparing form, if other than above. *(Sign below.)*

I declare that I prepared this application at the request of the above person and it is based on all information of which I have knowledge.

Signature	Print your Name	Date

Firm Name and Address	Daytime Phone Number *(Area Code and Number)*
	Fax Number *(Area Code and Number)*

(Please remember to enclose the mailing label with your application.)

Part 4. Additional information. Page for answers to 3f and 3g.

If you answered "Yes" to Question 3f in Part 4 on page 3 of this form, give the following information concerning the removal proceedings. Include the name of the person in removal proceedings and information on jurisdiction, date proceedings began and status of procedings.

If you answered "No" to Question 3g in Part 4 on page 3 of this form, fully describe how you are supporting yourself. Include the source, amount and basis for any income.

If you answered "Yes" to Question 3g in Part 4 on page 3 of this form, fully describe the employment. Include the name of the person employed, name and address of the employer, weekly income and whether the employment was specifically authorized by INS.

Supplement -1
Attach to Form I-539 when more than one person is included in the petition or application.
(List each person separately. Do not include the person named in the form.)

Family Name	Given Name	Middle Name	Date of Birth (MM/DD/YYYY)
Country of Birth	Country of Citizenship	Social Security # (if any)	A # (if any)
Date of Arrival (MM/DD/YYYY)		I-94 #	
Current Nonimmigrant Status:		Expires On (MM/DD/YYYY)	
Country Where Passport Issued		Expiration Date (MM/DD/YYYY)	

Family Name	Given Name	Middle Name	Date of Birth (MM/DD/YYYY)
Country of Birth	Country of Citizenship	Social Security # (if any)	A # (if any)
Date of Arrival (MM/DD/YYYY)		I-94 #	
Current Nonimmigrant Status:		Expires On (MM/DD/YYYY)	
Country Where Passport Issued		Expiration Date (MM/DD/YYYY)	

Family Name	Given Name	Middle Name	Date of Birth (MM/DD/YYYY)
Country of Birth	Country of Citizenship	Social Security # (if any)	A # (if any)
Date of Arrival (MM/DD/YYYY)		I-94 #	
Current Nonimmigrant Status:		Expires On (MM/DD/YYYY)	
Country Where Passport Issued		Expiration Date (MM/DD/YYYY)	

Family Name	Given Name	Middle Name	Date of Birth (MM/DD/YYYY)
Country of Birth	Country of Citizenship	Social Security # (if any)	A # (if any)
Date of Arrival (MM/DD/YYYY)		I-94 #	
Current Nonimmigrant Status:		Expires On (MM/DD/YYYY)	
Country Where Passport Issued		Expiration Date (MM/DD/YYYY)	

Family Name	Given Name	Middle Name	Date of Birth (MM/DD/YYYY)
Country of Birth	Country of Citizenship	Social Security # (if any)	A # (if any)
Date of Arrival (MM/DD/YYYY)		I-94 #	
Current Nonimmigrant Status:		Expires On (MM/DD/YYYY)	
Country Where Passport Issued		Expiration Date (MM/DD/YYYY)	

If you need additional space, attach a separate sheet(s) of paper.
Place your name, A # if any, date of birth, form number and application date at the top of the sheet(s) of paper.

U.S. Department of Justice
Immigration and Naturalization Service

Application for Asylum and for Withholding of Removal

Start Here - Please Type or Print. **USE BLACK INK. SEE THE SEPARATE INSTRUCTION PAMPHLET FOR INFORMATION ABOUT ELIGIBILITY AND HOW TO COMPLETE AND FILE THIS APPLICATION.** (Note: There is NO filing fee for this application.)

Please check the box if you also want to apply for withholding of removal under the Convention Against Torture. ☐

PART A. I.   INFORMATION ABOUT YOU

1. Alien Registration Number(s)(A#s)(If any)	2. Social Security No. (If any)

3. Complete Last Name	4. First Name	5. Middle Name

6. What other names have you used? *(Include maiden name and aliases.)*

7. Residence in the U.S. C/O	Telephone Number
Street Number and Name	Apt. No.

City	State	ZIP Code

8. Mailing Address in the U.S., if other than above	Telephone Number
Street Number and Name	Apt. No.

City	State	ZIP Code

9. Sex ☐ Male ☐ Female   10. Marital Status: ☐ Single ☐ Married ☐ Divorced ☐ Widowed

11. Date of Birth *(Mo/Day/Yr)*	12. City and Country of Birth

13. Present Nationality *(Citizenship)*	14. Nationality at Birth	15. Race, Ethnic or Tribal Group	16. Religion

17.   *Check the box, a through c that applies:*   a. ☐ I have never been in immigration court proceedings.
b. ☐ I am now in immigration court proceedings.   c. ☐ I am **not** now in immigration court proceedings, but I have been in the past.

18. *Complete 18 a through c.*
a. When did you last leave your country? *(Mo/Day/Yr)* _____   b. What is your current I-94 Number, if any? _____

c. Please list each entry to the U.S. beginning with your most recent entry.
   List date (Mo/Day/Yr), place, and your status for each entry. (Attach additional sheets as needed.)

Date _____ Place _____ Status _____ Date Status Expires _____
Date _____ Place _____ Status _____
Date _____ Place _____ Status _____
Date _____ Place _____ Status _____

19. What country issued your last passport or travel document?	20. Passport # Travel Document #	21. Expiration Date *(Mo/Day/Yr)*
22. What is your native language?	23. Are you fluent in English? ☐ Yes ☐ No	24. What other languages do you speak fluently?

FOR EOIR USE ONLY

FOR INS USE ONLY

Action:
Interview Date: _____
Decision:
__ Approval Date: _____
— Denial Date: _____
— Referral Date: _____
Asylum Officer ID# _____

Form I-589 (Rev. 10/18/01)N

PART A. II.   INFORMATION ABOUT YOUR SPOUSE AND CHILDREN

Your Spouse. ☐ I am not married. (Skip to *Your Children*, below.)

1. Alien Registration Number (A#) *(If any)*	2. Passport/ID Card No. *(If any)*	3. Date of Birth *(Mo/Day/Yr)*	4. Social Security No. *(If any)*
5. Complete Last Name	6. First Name	7. Middle Name	8. Maiden Name

9. Date of Marriage *(Mo/Day/Yr)*	10. Place of Marriage	11. City and Country of Birth

12. Nationality *(Citizenship)*	13. Race, Ethnic or Tribal Group	14. Sex ☐ Male ☐ Female

15. Is this person in the U.S.? ☐ Yes *(Complete blocks 16 to 24.)*   ☐ No *(Specify location)*

16. Place of last entry in the U.S. ?	17. Date of last entry in the U.S. *(Mo/Day/Yr)*	18. I-94 No. *(If any)*	19. Status when last admitted *(Visa type, if any)*

20. What is your spouse's current status?	21. What is the expiration date of his/her authorized stay, if any? *(Mo/Day/Yr)*	22. Is your spouse in immigration court proceedings? ☐ Yes ☐ No	23. If previously in the U.S., date of previous arrival *(Mo/Day/Yr)*

24.   If in the U.S., is your spouse to be included in this application? *(Check the appropriate box.)*

☐ Yes *(Attach one (1) photograph of your spouse in the upper right hand corner of page 9 on the extra copy of the application submitted for this person.)*

☐ No

Your Children. Please list **ALL** of your children, regardless of age, location, or marital status.

☐ I do not have any children. *(Skip to Part A. III., **Information about Your Background.**)*

☐ I do have children. Total number of children _____

(Use Supplement A Form I-589 or attach additional pages and documentation if you have more than four (4) children.)

1. Alien Registration Number (A#) *(If any)*	2. Passport/ID Card No. *(If any)*	3. Marital Status *(Married, Single, Divorced, Widowed)*	4. Social Security No. *(If any)*
5. Complete Last Name	6. First Name	7. Middle Name	8. Date of Birth *(Mo/Day/Yr)*

9. City and Country of Birth	10. Nationality *(Citizenship)*	11. Race, Ethnic or Tribal Group	12. Sex ☐ Male ☐ Female

13. Is this child in the U.S.? ☐ Yes *(Complete blocks 14 to 21.)*   ☐ No *(Specify Location)*

14. Place of last entry in the U.S.?	15. Date of last entry in the U.S.? *(Mo/Day/Yr)*	16. I-94 No. *(If any)*	17. Status when last admitted *(Visa type, if any)*

18. What is your child's current status?	19. What is the expiration date of his/her authorized stay, if any? *(Mo/Day/Yr)*	20. Is your child in immigration court proceedings? ☐ Yes ☐ No

21.   If in the U.S., is this child to be included in this application? *(Check the appropriate box.)*

☐ Yes *(Attach one (1) photograph of your child in the upper right hand corner of page 9 on the extra copy of the application submitted for this person.)*

☐ No

PART A. II. INFORMATION ABOUT YOUR SPOUSE AND CHILDREN Continued

1. Alien Registration Number (A#) *(If any)*	2. Passport/IDCard No. *(If any)*	3. Marital Status *(Married, Single, Divorced, Widowed)*	4. Social Security No. *(If any)*
5. Complete Last Name	6. First Name	7. Middle Name	8. Date of Birth *(Mo/Day/Yr)*
9. City and Country of Birth	10. Nationality *(Citizenship)*	11. Race, Ethnic or Tribal Group	12. Sex ☐ Male ☐ Female

13. Is this child in the U.S.? ☐ Yes *(Complete blocks 14 to 21.)* ☐ No *(Specify Location)*

14. Place of last entry in the U.S.?	15. Date of last entry in the U.S.? *(Mo/Day/Yr)*	16. I-94 No. *(If any)*	17. Status when last admitted *(Visa type, if any)*
18. What is your child's current status?	19. What is the expiration date of his/her authorized stay, *(if any)? (Mo/Day/Yr)*	20. Is your child in immigration court proceedings? ☐ Yes ☐ No	

21. If in the U.S., is this child to be included in this application? *(Check the appropriate box.)*
   ☐ Yes *(Attach one (1) photograph of your child in the upper right hand corner of page 9 on the extra copy of the application submitted for this person.)*
   ☐ No

1. Alien Registration Number (A#) *(If any)*	2. Passport/ID Card No. *(If any)*	3. Marital Status *(Married, Single, Divorced, Widowed)*	4. Social Security No. *(If any)*
5. Complete Last Name	6. First Name	7. Middle Name	8. Date of Birth *(Mo/Day/Yr)*
9. City and Country of Birth	10. Nationality *(Citizenship)*	11. Race, Ethnic or Tribal Group	12. Sex ☐ Male ☐ Female

13. Is this child in the U.S.? ☐ Yes *(Complete blocks 14 to 21.)* ☐ No *(Specify Location)*

14. Place of last entry in the U.S.?	15. Date of last entry in the U.S.? *(Mo/Day/Yr)*	16. I-94 No. *(If any)*	17. Status when last admitted *(Visa type, if any)*
18. What is your child's current status?	19. What is the expiration date of his/her authorized stay, if any? *(Mo/Day/Yr)*	20. Is your child in immigration court proceedings? ☐ Yes ☐ No	

21. If in the U.S., is this child to be included in this application? *(Check the appropriate box.)*
   ☐ Yes *(Attach one (1) photograph of your child in the upper right hand corner of page 9 on the extra copy of the application submitted for this person.)*
   ☐ No

1. Alien Registration Number (A#) *(If any)*	2. Passport/ID Card No. *(If any)*	3. Marital Status *(Married, Single, Divorced, Widowed)*	4. Social Security No. *(If any)*
5. Complete Last Name	6. First Name	7. Middle Name	8. Date of Birth *(Mo/Day/Yr)*
9. City and Country of Birth	10. Nationality *(Citizenship)*	11. Race, Ethnic or Tribal Group	12. Sex ☐ Male ☐ Female

13. Is this child in the U.S.? ☐ Yes *(Complete blocks 14 to 21.)* ☐ No *(Specify Location)*

14. Place of last entry in the U.S.?	15. Date of last entry in the U.S.? *(Mo/Day/Yr)*	16. I-94 No. *(If any)*	17. Status when last admitted *(Visa type, if any)*
18. What is your child's current status?	19. What is the expiration date of his/her authorized stay, if any? *(Mo/Day/Yr)*	20. Is your child in immigration court proceedings? ☐ Yes ☐ No	

21. If in the U.S., is this child to be included in this application? *(Check the appropriate box.)*
   ☐ Yes *(Attach one (1) photograph of your child in the upper right hand corner of page 9 on the extra copy of the application submitted for this person.)*
   ☐ No

Form I-589 (Rev. 10/18/01)N Page 3

PART A. III. INFORMATION ABOUT YOUR BACKGROUND

1. Please list your last address where you lived before coming to the U.S. If this is not the country where you fear persecution, also list the last address in the country where you fear persecution. *(List Address, City/Town, Department, Province, or State, and Country.)* *(Use Supplement B Form I-589 or additional sheets of paper if necessary.)*

Number and Street *(Provide if available)*	City/Town	Department, Province or State	Country	Dates From *(Mo/Yr)* To *(Mo/Yr)*

2. Provide the following information about your residences during the last five years. List your present address first. *(Use Supplement Form B or additional sheets of paper if necessary.)*

Number and Street	City/Town	Department, Province or State	Country	Dates From *(Mo/Yr)* To *(Mo/Yr)*

3. Provide the following information about your education, beginning with the most recent. *(Use Supplement B Form I-589 or additional sheets of paper if necessary.)*

Name of School	Type of School	Location (Address)	Attended From *(Mo/Yr)* To *(Mo/Yr)*

4. Provide the following information about your employment during the last five years. List your present employment first. *(Use Supplement Form B or additional sheets of paper if necessary.)*

Name and Address of Employer	Your Occupation	Dates From *(Mo/Yr)* To *(Mo/Yr)*

5. Provide the following information about your parents and siblings (brother and sisters). Check box if the person is deceased. *(Use Supplement B Form I-589 or additional sheets of paper if necessary.)*

Name	City/Town and Country of Birth	Current Location
Mother		☐ Deceased
Father		☐ Deceased
Siblings		☐ Deceased
		☐ Deceased

PART B. INFORMATION ABOUT YOUR APPLICATION

(Use Supplement B Form I-589 or attach additional sheets of paper as needed to complete your responses to the questions contained in PART B.)

When answering the following questions about your asylum or other protection claim (withholding of removal under 241(b)(3) of the Act or withholding of removal under the Convention Against Torture) you should provide a detailed and specific account of the basis of your claim to asylum or other protection. To the best of your ability, provide specific dates, places, and descriptions about each event or action described. You should attach documents evidencing the general conditions in the country from which you are seeking asylum or other protection and the specific facts on which you are relying to support your claim. If this documentation is unavailable or you are not providing this documentation with your application, please explain why in your responses to the following questions. Refer to Instructions, Part 1: Filing Instructions, Section II, "Basis of Eligibility," Parts A - D, Section V, "Completing the Form," Part B, and Section VII, "Additional Documents that You Should Submit" for more information on completing this section of the form.

1. Why are you applying for asylum or withholding of removal under section 241(b)(3) of the Act, or for withholding of removal under the Convention Against Torture? Check the appropriate box (es) below and then provide detailed answers to questions A and B below:

    I am seeking asylum or withholding of removal based on

    ☐ Race
    ☐ Religion
    ☐ Nationality
    ☐ Political opinion
    ☐ Membership in a particular social group
    ☐ Torture Convention

    A. Have you, your family, or close friends or colleagues ever experienced harm or mistreatment or threats in the past by anyone?
    ☐ No ☐ Yes If your answer is "Yes," explain in detail:

    1) What happened;
    2) When the harm or mistreatment or threats occurred;
    3) Who caused the harm or mistreatment or threats; and
    4) Why you believe the harm or mistreatment or threats occurred.

    B. Do you fear harm or mistreatment if you return to your home country?

    ☐ No ☐ Yes If your answer is "Yes," explain in detail:

    1) What harm or mistreatment you fear;
    2) Who you believe would harm or mistreat you; and
    3) Why you believe you would or could be harmed or mistreated.

PART B. INFORMATION ABOUT YOUR APPLICATION Continued

2. Have you or your family members ever been accused, charged, arrested, detained, interrogated, convicted and sentenced, or imprisoned in any country other than the United States?

☐ No ☐ Yes If "Yes," explain the circumstances and reasons for the action.

3. A. Have you or your family members ever belonged to or been associated with any organizations or groups in your home country, such as, but not limited to, a political party, student group, labor union, religious organization, military or paramilitary group, civil patrol, guerrilla organization, ethnic group, human rights group, or the press or media?

☐ No ☐ Yes If "Yes," describe for each person the level of participation, any leadership or other positions held, and the length of time you or your family members were involved in each organization or activity.

B. Do you or your family members continue to participate in any way in these organizations or groups?

☐ No ☐ Yes If "Yes," describe for each person, your or your family members' current level of participation, any leadership or other positions currently held, and the length of time you or your family members have been involved in each organization or group.

4. Are you afraid of being subjected to torture in your home country or any other country to which you may be returned?

☐ No ☐ Yes If "Yes," explain why you are afraid and describe the nature of the torture you fear, by whom, and why it would be inflicted.

PART C. ADDITIONAL INFORMATION ABOUT YOUR APPLICATION

(Use Supplement B Form I-589 or attach additional sheets of paper as needed to complete your responses to the questions contained in Part C.)

1. Have you, your spouse, your child(ren), your parents, or your siblings ever applied to the United States Government for refugee status, asylum, or withholding of removal? ☐ No ☐ Yes

    If "Yes" explain the decision and what happened to any status you, your spouse, your child(ren), your parents, or your siblings received as a result of that decision. Please indicate whether or not you were included in a parent or spouse's application. If so, please include your parent or spouse's A- number in your response. If you have been denied asylum by an Immigration Judge or the Board of Immigration Appeals, please describe any change(s) in conditions in your country or your own personal circumstances since the date of the denial that may affect your eligibility for asylum.

2. A. After leaving the country from which you are claiming asylum, did you or your spouse or child(ren), who are now in the United States, travel through or reside in any other country before entering the United States? ☐ No ☐ Yes

    B. Have you, your spouse, your child(ren), or other family members such as your parents or siblings ever applied for or received any lawful status in any country other than the one from which you are now claiming asylum? ☐ No ☐ Yes

    If "Yes" to either or both questions (2A and/or 2B), provide for each person the following: the name of each country and the length of stay; the person's status while there; the reasons for leaving; whether the person is entitled to return for lawful residence purposes; and whether the person applied for refugee status or for asylum while there, and, if not, why he or she did not do so.

3. Have you, your spouse, or child(ren) ever ordered, incited, assisted, or otherwise participated in causing harm or suffering to any person because of his or her race, religion, nationality, membership in a particular social group or belief in a particular political opinion?

    ☐ No ☐ Yes If "Yes," describe in detail each such incident and your own or your spouse's or child(ren)'s involvement.

PART C. ADDITIONAL INFORMATION ABOUT YOUR APPLICATION Continued

4. After you left the country where you were harmed or fear harm, did you return to that country?

☐ No ☐ Yes If "Yes," describe in detail the circumstances of your visit (for example, the date(s) of the trip(s), the purpose(s) of the trip(s), and the length of time you remained in that country for the visit(s)).

5. Are you filing the application more than one year after your last arrival in the United States?

☐No ☐Yes If "Yes," explain why you did not file within the first year after you arrived. You should be prepared to explain at your interview or hearing why you did not file your asylum application within the first year after you arrived. For guidance in answering this question, see Instructions, Part 1: Filing Instructions, Section V. "Completing the Form," Part C.

6. Have you or any member of your family included in the application ever committed any crime and/or been arrested, charged, convicted and sentenced for any crimes in the United States?

☐ No ☐ Yes If "Yes," for each instance, specify in your response what occurred and the circumstances; dates; length of sentence received; location; the duration of the detention or imprisonment; the reason(s) for the detention or conviction; any formal charges that were lodged against you or your relatives included in your application; the reason(s) for release. Attach documents referring to these incidents, if they are available, or an explanation of why documents are not available.

PART D.   YOUR SIGNATURE

After reading the information regarding penalties in the instructions, complete and sign below. If someone helped you prepare this application, he or she must complete Part E.

I certify, under penalty of perjury under the laws of the United States of America, that this application and the evidence submitted with it are all true and correct. Title 18, United States Code, Section 1546, provides in part: "Whoever knowingly makes under oath, or as permitted under penalty of perjury under Section 1746 of Title 28, United States Code, knowingly subscribes as true, any false statement with respect to a material fact in any application, affidavit, or knowingly presents any such application, affidavit, or other document required by the immigration laws or regulations prescribed thereunder, or knowingly presents any such application, affidavit, or other document containing any such false statement or which fails to contain any reasonable basis in law or fact - shall be fined in accordance with this title or imprisoned not more than five years, or both." I authorize the release of any information from my record which the Immigration and Naturalization Service needs to determine eligibility for the benefit I am seeking.

Staple your photograph here or the photograph of the family member to be included on the extra copy of the application submitted for that person.

WARNING: Applicants who are in the United States illegally are subject to removal if their asylum or withholding claims are not granted by an Asylum Officer or an Immigration Judge. Any information provided in completing this application may be used as a basis for the institution of, or as evidence in, removal proceedings even if the application is later withdrawn. Applicants determined to have knowingly made a frivolous application for asylum will be permanently ineligible for any benefits under the Immigration and Nationality Act. See 208(d)(6) of the Act and 8 CFR 208.20.

Print Complete Name | Write your name in your native alphabet

Did your spouse, parent, or child(ren) assist you in completing this application?   ☐ No ☐ Yes *(If "Yes," list the name and relationship.)*

_____ _____   _____ _____
        (Name)   *(Relationship)*   *(Name)*   *(Relationship)*

Did someone other than your spouse, parent, or child(ren) prepare this application?   ☐ No ☐ Yes *(If "Yes," complete Part E)*

Asylum applicants may be represented by counsel. Have you been provided with a list of persons who may be available to assist you, at little or no cost, with your asylum claim?   ☐ No ☐ Yes

Signature of Applicant *(The person in Part A. I.)*

[_____]   _____
     Sign your name so it all appears within the brackets   Date *(Mo/Day/Yr)*

PART E.   DECLARATION OF PERSON PREPARING FORM IF OTHER THAN APPLICANT, SPOUSE, PARENT OR CHILD

I declare that I have prepared this application at the request of the person named in Part D, that the responses provided are based on all information of which I have knowledge, or which was provided to me by the applicant and that the completed application was read to the applicant in his or her native language or a language he or she understands for verification before he or she signed the application in my presence. I am aware that the knowing placement of false information on the Form I-589 may also subject me to civil penalties under 8 U.S.C. 1324(c).

Signature of Preparer | Print Complete Name

Daytime Telephone Number ( ) | Address of Preparer: Street Number and Name

Apt. No. | City | State | ZIP Code

PART F.   TO BE COMPLETED AT INTERVIEW OR HEARING

You will be asked to complete this Part when you appear before an Asylum Officer of the Immigration and Naturalization Service (INS), or an Immigration Judge of the Executive Office for Immigration Review (EOIR) for examination.

I swear (affirm) that I know the contents of this application that I am signing, including the attached documents and supplements, that they are all true to the best of my knowledge taking into account correction(s) numbered _____ to _____ that were made by me or at my request.

Signed and sworn to before me by the above named applicant on:

_____   _____
      Signature of Applicant   Date *(Mo/Day/Yr)*

_____   _____
  Write Your Name in Your Native Alphabet   Signature of Asylum Officer or Immigration Judge

U.S. Department of Justice
Immigration and Naturalization Service

OMB No. 1115-0121

Refugee/Asylee Relative Petition

START HERE - Please Type or Print

Part 1.   Information about you.

Family Name	Given Name	Middle Name

Address - C/O

Street Number and Name	Apt.

City	State or Province

Country	ZIP/Postal Code	Sex: a. ☐ Male b. ☐ Female

Date of Birth (Month/Day/Year)	Country of Birth

A#	Social Security #

Other names used (including maiden name)

Present Status: (check one)
a. ☐ Refugee   ☐ Lawful Permanent Resident based on previous Refugee status
b. ☐ Asylee   ☐ Lawful Permanent Resident based on previous Asylee status

Date (Month/Day/Year) and Place Refugee or Asylee status was granted:

If granted Refugee status, Date (Month/Day/Year) and Place Admitted to the United States:

If Married, Date (Month/Day/Year) and Place of Present Marriage:

If Previously Married, Name(s) of Prior Spouse(s):

Date(s) Previous Marriage(s) Ended: (Month/Day/Year)

Part 2.   Information about the relationship.

The alien relative is my: a. ☐ Spouse
                             b. ☐ Unmarried child under 21 years of age

Number of relatives I am filing for: _____ (_____ of _____)

Part 3.   Information about your alien relative.   (If you are petitioning for more than one family member you must complete and file a separate Form I-730 for each additional family member.)

Family Name	Given Name	Middle Name

Address - C/O

Street Number and Name	Apt #

Form I-730 (Rev. 09/18/00) Y

Part 3. Information about your alien relative.   *Continue*

City	State or Providence	
Country	ZIP/Postal Code	Sex: a. ☐ Male b. ☐ Female
Date of Birth *(Month/Day/Year)*	Country of Birth	
Alien # *(If any)*	Social Security # *(If Any)*	

Other name(s) used *(including maiden name)*

If Married, Date *(Month/Day/Year)* and Place of Present Marriage:

If Previously Married, Name(s) of Prior Spouse(s):

Date(s) Previous Marriage(s) Ended: *(Month/Day/Year)*

Part 4.   Processing Information.

A. Check One:

    a. ☐ The person named in Part 3 is now in the United States.

    b. ☐ The person named in Part 3 is now outside the United States. (Please indicate the location of the American Consulate or Embassy where your relative will apply for a visa.)

    American Consulate/Embassy at: _____

                                                           City and Country

B. Is the person named in Part 3 in exclusion, deportation, or removal proceedings in the United States?

    a. ☐ No

    b. ☐ Yes (Please explain on a separate paper.)

Part 5. Signature.

Read the information on penalties in the instructions before completing this section and sign below. If someone helped you to prepare this petition, he or she must complete Part 6.

I certify or, if outside the United States, I swear or affirm, under penalty of perjury under the laws of the United States of America, that this petition and the evidence submitted with it, is all true and correct. I authorize the release of any information from my record which the Immigration and Naturalization Service needs to determine eligibility for the benefit I am seeking.

Signature	Print Name	Date	Daytime Telephone # ( )

Please Note: *If you do not completely fill out this form, or fail to submit the required documents listed in the instructions, your relative may not be found eligible for the requested benefit and this petition may be denied.*

Part 6. Signature of person preparing form if other than Petitioner above. *(Sign Below)*

I declare that I prepared this petition at the request of the above person and it is based on all of the information of which I have knowledge.

Signature	Print Name	Date	Daytime Telephone # ( )

*Firm Name
and Address*

OMB Approval No. 44-R1301

U.S. DEPARTMENT OF LABOR
Employment and Training Administration

APPLICATION
FOR
ALIEN EMPLOYMENT CERTIFICATION

IMPORTANT: READ CAREFULLY BEFORE COMPLETING THIS FORM

PRINT legibly in ink or use a typewriter. If you need more space to answer questions in this form, use a separate sheet. Identify each answer with the number of the corresponding question. SIGN AND DATE each sheet in original signature.

To knowingly furnish any false information in the preparation of this form and any supplement thereto or to aid, abet, or counsel another to do so is a felony punishable by $10,000 fine or 5 years in the penitentiary, or both (18 U.S.C. 1001)

PART A. OFFER OF EMPLOYMENT

1. Name of Alien   (Family name in capital letter, First, Middle, Maiden)

2. Present Address of Alien   (Number, Street, City and Town, State ZIP code or Province, Country)

3. Type of Visa   (If in U.S.)

The following information is submitted as an offer of employment.

4. Name of Employer   (Full name of Organization)

5. Telephone

6. Address   (Number, Street, City and Town, State ZIP code)

7. Address Where Alien Will Work   (if different from item 6)

8. Nature of Employer's Business Activity	9. Name of Job Title	10. Total Hours Per Week		11 Work Schedule (Hourly) a.m. p.m.	12. Rate of Pay	
		a. Basic	b. Overtime		a. Basic $ per _____	b. Overtime $ per hour

13. Describe Fully the job to be Performed   (Duties)

14. State in detail the MINIMUM education, training, and experience for a worker to perform satisfactorily the job duties described in item 13 above.

EDU-CATION (Enter number of years)	Grade School	High School	College	College Degree Required (specify)
				Major Field of Study

TRAIN-ING	No. Yrs.	No. Mos.	Type of Training

EXPERI-ENCE	Job Offered		Related Occupation	Related Occupation (specify)
	Number Yrs.	Mos.	Yrs.	Mos.

15. Other Special Requirements

16. Occupational Title of Person Who Will Be Alien's Immediate Supervisor

17. Number of Employees Alien Will Supervise

ENDORSEMENTS   (Make no entry in section - for Government use only)

Date Forms Received	
L.O.	S.O.
R.O.	N.O.
Ind. Code	Occ. Code
Occ. Title	

Replaces MA 7-50A, B and C (Apr. 1970 edition) which is obsolete.

ETA 750 (Oct. 1979)

18. COMPLETE ITEMS ONLY IF JOB IS TEMPORARY		19. IF JOB IS UNIONIZED (Complete)		
a. No. of Openings To Be Filled By Aliens Under Job Offer	b. Exact Dates You Expect To Employ Alien	a. Number of Local	b. Name of Local	
	From ___ To ___		c. City and State	

20. STATEMENT FOR LIVE-AT-WORK JOB OFFERS (Complete for Private Household ONLY)

a. Description of Residence		b. No. Persons residing at Place of Employment				c. Will free board and private room not shared with anyone be provided?	("X" one)
("X" one) ☐ House ☐ Apartment	Number of Rooms	Adults		Children	Ages		☐ YES ☐ NO
			BOYS				
			GIRLS				

21. DESCRIBE EFFORTS TO RECRUIT U.S. WORKERS AND THE RESULTS. (Specify Sources of Recruitment by Name)

22. Applications require various types of documentation. Please read Part II of the instructions to assure that appropriate supporting documentation is included with your application.

23. EMPLOYER CERTIFICATIONS

By virtue of my signature below, I HEREBY CERTIFY the following conditions of employment.

a. I have enough funds available to pay the wage or salary offered the alien.

b. The wage offered equals or exceeds the prevailing wage and I guarantee that, if a labor certification is granted, the wage paid to the alien when the alien begins work will equal or exceed the prevailing wage which is applicable at the time the alien begins work.

c. The wage offered is not based on commissions, bonuses, or other incentives, unless I guarantee a wage paid on a weekly, bi-weekly, or monthly basis.

d. I will be able to place the alien on the payroll on or before the date of the alien's proposed entrance into the United States.

e. The job opportunity does not involve unlawful discrimination by race, creed, color, national origin, age, sex, religion, handicap, or citizenship.

f. The job opportunity is not:

(1) Vacant because the former occupant is on strike or is being locked out in the course of a labor dispute involving a work stoppage.

(2) At issue in a labor dispute involving a work stoppage.

g. The job opportunity's terms, conditions and occupational environment are not contrary to Federal, State or local law.

h. The job opportunity has been and is clearly open to any qualified U.S. worker.

24. DECLARATIONS

DECLARATION OF EMPLOYER ➤ Pursuant to 28 U.S.C. 1746, I declare under penalty of perjury the foregoing is true and correct.

SIGNATURE	DATE

NAME (Type or Print)	TITLE

AUTHORIZATION OF AGENT OF EMPLOYER ➤ I HEREBY DESIGNATE the agent below to represent me for the purposes of labor certification and I TAKE FULL RESPONSIBILITY for accuracy of any representations made by my agent.

SIGNATURE OF EMPLOYER	DATE

NAME OF AGENT (Type or Print)	ADDRESS OF AGENT (Number, Street, City, State, ZIP code)

271

PART B. STATEMENT OF QUALIFICATIONS OF ALIEN

FOR ADVICE CONCERNING REQUIREMENTS FOR ALIEN EMPLOYMENT CERTIFICATION: If alien is in the U.S., contact nearest office of Immigration and Naturalization Service. If alien is outside U.S., contact nearest U.S. Consulate.

IMPORTANT: READ ATTACHED INSTRUCTIONS BEFORE COMPLETING THIS FORM.

Print legibly in ink or use a typewriter. If you need more space to fully answer any questions on this form, use a separate sheet. Identify each answer with the number of the corresponding question. Sign and date each sheet.

1. Name of Alien (Family name in capital letters)	First name	Middle name	Maiden name

2. Present Address (No., Street, City or Town, State or Province and ZIP code)	Country	3. Type of Visa (If in U.S.)

4. Alien's Birthdate (Month, Day, Year)	5. Birthplace (City or Town, State or Province)	Country	6. Present Nationality or Citizenship (Country)

7. Address in United States Where Alien Will Reside

8. Name and Address of Prospective Employer if Alien has job offer in U.S.	9. Occupation in which Alien is Seeking Work

10. "X" the appropriate box below and furnish the information required for the box marked

a. ☐ Alien will apply for a visa abroad at the American Consulate in ➤	City in Foreign Country	Foreign Country
b. ☐ Alien is in the United States and will apply for adjustment of status to that of a lawful permanent resident in the office of the Immigration and Naturalization Service at ➤	City	State

11. Names and Addresses of Schools, Colleges and Universities Attended (Include trade or vocational training facilities)	Field of Study	FROM		TO		Degrees or Certificates Received
		Month	Year	Month	Year	

SPECIAL QUALIFICATIONS AND SKILLS

12. Additional Qualifications and Skills Alien Possesses and Proficiency in the use of Tools, Machines or Equipment Which Would Help Establish if Alien Meets Requirements for Occupation in Item 9.

13. List Licenses (Professional, journeyman, etc.)

14. List Documents Attached Which are Submitted as Evidence that Alien Possesses the Education, Training, Experience, and Abilities Represented

Endorsements	DATE REC. DOL
	O.T. & C.
(Make no entry in this section - FOR Government Agency USE ONLY)	

(Items continued on next page)

15. WORK EXPERIENCE. List all jobs held during the last three (3) years. Also, list any other jobs related to the occupation for which the alien is seeking certification as indicated in item 9.

a. NAME AND ADDRESS OF EMPLOYER

NAME OF JOB	DATE STARTED Month	Year	DATE LEFT Month	Year	KIND OF BUSINESS

DESCRIBE IN DETAIL THE DUTIES PERFORMED, INCLUDING THE USE OF TOOLS, MACHINES OR EQUIPMENT	NO. OF HOURS PER WEEK

b. NAME AND ADDRESS OF EMPLOYER

NAME OF JOB	DATE STARTED Month	Year	DATE LEFT Month	Year	KIND OF BUSINESS

DESCRIBE IN DETAIL THE DUTIES PERFORMED, INCLUDING THE USE OF TOOLS, MACHINES OR EQUIPMENT	NO. OF HOURS PER WEEK

c. NAME AND ADDRESS OF EMPLOYER

NAME OF JOB	DATE STARTED Month	Year	DATE LEFT Month	Year	KIND OF BUSINESS

DESCRIBE IN DETAIL THE DUTIES PERFORMED, INCLUDING THE USE OF TOOLS, MACHINES OR EQUIPMENT	NO. OF HOURS PER WEEK

16. DECLARATIONS

DECLARATION OF ALIEN ➤ ➤ Pursuant to 28 U.S.C. 1746, I declare under penalty of perjury the foregoing is true and correct.

SIGNATURE OF ALIEN	DATE

AUTHORIZATION OF AGENT OF ALIEN ➤ ➤ I hereby designate the agent below to represent me for the purposes of labor certification and I take full responsibility for accuracy of any representations made by my agent.

SIGNATURE OF ALIEN	DATE

NAME OF AGENT (Type or print)	ADDRESS OF AGENT (No., Street, City, State, ZIP code)

273

15. WORK EXPERIENCE.
List all jobs held during the last three (3) years. Also, list any other jobs related to the occupation for which the alien is seeking certification as indicated in item 9.

d. NAME AND ADDRESS OF EMPLOYER

NAME OF JOB	DATE STARTED Month	Year	DATE LEFT Month	Year	KIND OF BUSINESS

DESCRIBE IN DETAIL THE DUTIES PERFORMED, INCLUDING THE USE OF TOOLS, MACHINES OR EQUIPMENT	NO. OF HOURS PER WEEK

e. NAME AND ADDRESS OF EMPLOYER

NAME OF JOB	DATE STARTED Month	Year	DATE LEFT Month	Year	KIND OF BUSINESS

DESCRIBE IN DETAIL THE DUTIES PERFORMED, INCLUDING THE USE OF TOOLS, MACHINES OR EQUIPMENT	NO. OF HOURS PER WEEK

f. NAME AND ADDRESS OF EMPLOYER

NAME OF JOB	DATE STARTED Month	Year	DATE LEFT Month	Year	KIND OF BUSINESS

DESCRIBE IN DETAIL THE DUTIES PERFORMED, INCLUDING THE USE OF TOOLS, MACHINES OR EQUIPMENT	NO. OF HOURS PER WEEK

16. DECLARATIONS

DECLARATION OF ALIEN ➤ ➤ Pursuant to 28 U.S.C. 1746, I declare under penalty of perjury the foregoing is true and correct.

SIGNATURE OF ALIEN	DATE

AUTHORIZATION OF AGENT OF ALIEN ➤ ➤ I hereby designate the agent below to represent me for the purposes of labor certification and I take full responsibility for accuracy of any representations made by my agent.

SIGNATURE OF ALIEN	DATE

NAME OF AGENT (Type or print)	ADDRESS OF AGENT (No., Street, City, State, ZIP code)

274

Do Not Write in This Block.

Remarks	Action Stamp	Fee Stamp
A#		
Applicant is filing under §274a.12 _____		

☐ Application Approved. Employment Authorized / Extended *(Circle One)* until _____ (Date).
_____ (Date).

Subject to the following conditions: _____

☐ Application Denied.
   ☐ Failed to establish eligibility under 8 CFR 274a.12 (a) or (c).
   ☐ Failed to establish economic necessity as required in 8 CFR 274a.12(c)(14), (18) and 8 CFR 214.2(f)

I am applying for:
   ☐ Permission to accept employment.
   ☐ Replacement *(of lost employment authorization document)*.
   ☐ Renewal of my permission to accept employment *(attach previous employment authorization document)*.

1. Name (Family Name in CAPS) (First) (Middle)

2. Other Names Used (Include Maiden Name)

3. Address in the United States (Number and Street) (Apt. Number)

(Town or City) (State/Country) (ZIP Code)

4. Country of Citizenship/Nationality

5. Place of Birth (Town or City) (State/Province) (Country)

6. Date of Birth   7. Sex ☐ Male ☐ Female

8. Marital Status ☐ Married ☐ Single ☐ Widowed ☐ Divorced

9. Social Security Number (Include all Numbers you have ever used) (if any)

10. Alien Registration Number (A-Number) or I-94 Number (if any)

11. Have you ever before applied for employment authorization from INS?
   ☐ Yes (If yes, complete below)   ☐ No
Which INS Office?   Date(s)

Results (Granted or Denied - attach all documentation)

12. Date of Last Entry into the U.S. (Month/Day/Year)

13. Place of Last Entry into the U.S.

14. Manner of Last Entry (Visitor, Student, etc.)

15. Current Immigration Status (Visitor, Student, etc.)

16. Go to Part 2 of the Instructions, Eligibility Categories. In the space below, place the letter and number of the category you selected from the instructions (For example, (a)(8), (c)(17)(iii), etc.).

Eligibility under 8 CFR 274a.12

(   ) (   ) (   )

Certification.

Your Certification: I certify, under penalty of perjury under the laws of the United States of America, that the foregoing is true and correct. Furthermore, I authorize the release of any information which the Immigration and Naturalization Service needs to determine eligibility for the benefit I am seeking. I have read the Instructions in Part 2 and have identified the appropriate eligibility category in Block 16.

Signature   Telephone Number   Date

Signature of Person Preparing Form, If Other Than Above: I declare that this document was prepared by me at the request of the applicant and is based on all information of which I have any knowledge.

Print Name   Address   *Signature*   Date

Initial Receipt	Resubmitted	Relocated		Completed		
		Rec'd	Sent	Approved	Denied	Returned

U.S. Department of Justice
Immigration and Naturalization Service

Affidavit of Support Under Section 213A of the Act

START HERE - Please Type or Print

Part 1.   Information on Sponsor   (You)

Last Name	First Name	Middle Name

Mailing Address *(Street Number and Name)*	Apt/Suite Number

City	State or Province

Country	ZIP/Postal Code	Telephone Number

Place of Residence if different from above *(Street Number and Name)*	Apt/Suite Number

City	State or Province

Country	ZIP/Postal Code	Telephone Number

Date of Birth *(Month, Day, Year)*	Place of Birth *(City, State, Country)*	Are you a U.S. Citizen? ☐ Yes ☐ No

Social Security Number	A-Number *(If any)*

FOR AGENCY USE ONLY

This Affidavit	Receipt
[ ] Meets	
[ ] Does not meet	
Requirements of Section 213A	

Officer or I.J. Signature

Location

Date

Part 2.   Basis for Filing Affidavit of Support

I am filing this affidavit of support because *(check one):*

a. ☐ I filed/am filing the alien relative petition.

b. ☐ I filed/am filing an alien worker petition on behalf of the intending

immigrant, who is related to me as my _____ .
(relationship)

c. ☐ I have ownership interest of at least 5% _____ .
(name of entity which filed visa petition)

which filed an alien worker petition on behalf of the intending

immigrant, who is related to me as my _____ .
(relationship)

d. ☐ I am a joint sponsor willing to accept the legal obligations with any other sponsor(s).

Part 3.   Information on the Immigrant(s) You Are Sponsoring

Last Name	First Name	Middle Name

Date of Birth *(Month, Day, Year)*	Sex ☐ Male ☐ Female	Social Security Number *(If any)*

Country of Citizenship	A-Number *(If any)*

Current Address *(Street Number and Name)*	Apt/Suite Number	City

State/Province	Country	ZIP/Postal Code	Telephone Number

List any spouse and/or children immigrating with the immigrant named above in this Part: *(Use additional sheet of paper if necessary.)*

Name	Relationship to Sponsored Immigrant			Date of Birth			A-Number *(If any)*	Social Security *(If any)*
	Spouse	Son	Daughter	Mo.	Day	Yr.		

Form I-864 (Rev. 11/05/01)Y

Part 4.   Eligibility to Sponsor

To be a sponsor you must be a U.S. citizen or national or a lawful permanent resident. If you are not the petitioning relative, you must provide proof of status. To prove status, U.S. citizens or nationals must attach a copy of a document proving status, such as a U.S. passport, birth certificate, or certificate of naturalization, and lawful permanent residents must attach a copy of both sides of their Permanent Resident Card (Form I-551).

The determination of your eligibility to sponsor an immigrant will be based on an evaluation of your demonstrated ability to maintain an annual income at or above 125 percent of the Federal poverty line (100 percent if you are a petitioner sponsoring your spouse or child and you are on active duty in the U.S. Armed Forces). The assessment of your ability to maintain an adequate income will include your current employment, household size, and household income as shown on the Federal income tax returns for the 3 most recent tax years. Assets that are readily converted to cash and that can be made available for the support of sponsored immigrants if necessary, including any such assets of the immigrant(s) you are sponsoring, may also be considered.

The greatest weight in determining eligibility will be placed on current employment and household income. If a petitioner is unable to demonstrate ability to meet the stated income and asset requirements, a joint sponsor who *can* meet the income and asset requirements is needed. Failure to provide adequate evidence of income and/or assets or an affidavit of support completed by a joint sponsor will result in denial of the immigrant's application for an immigrant visa or adjustment to permanent resident status.

A. Sponsor's Employment

I am: 1. ☐ Employed by _____ *(Provide evidence of employment)*

Annual salary _____ or hourly wage $ _____ *(for _____ hours per week)*

2. ☐ Self employed _____ *(Name of business)*

Nature of employment or business _____

3. ☐ Unemployed or retired since _____

B. Sponsor's Household Size   **Number**

1. Number of persons (related to you by birth, marriage, or adoption) living in your residence, including yourself *(Do NOT include persons being sponsored in this affidavit.)*   _____

2. Number of immigrants being sponsored in this affidavit *(Include all persons in Part 3.)*   _____

3. Number of immigrants **NOT** living in your household whom you are obligated to support under a previously signed Form I-864.   _____

4. Number of persons who are otherwise dependent on you, as claimed in your tax return for the most recent tax year.   _____

5. Total household size. *(Add lines 1 through 4.)*   **Total**   _____

List persons below who are included in lines 1 or 3 for whom you previously have submitted INS Form I-864, *if your support obligation has not terminated.*

(If additional space is needed, use additional paper)

Name	A-Number	Date Affidavit of Support Signed	Relationship

C. Sponsor's Annual Household Income

Enter total unadjusted income from your Federal income tax return for the most recent tax year below. If you last filed a joint income tax return but are using only your *own* income to qualify, list total earnings from your W-2 Forms, or, *if* necessary to reach the required income for your household size, include income from other sources listed on your tax return. If your *individual* income does not meet the income requirement for your household size, you may also list total income for anyone related to you by birth, marriage, or adoption currently living with you in your residence if they have lived in your residence for the previous 6 months, or any person shown as a dependent on your Federal income tax return for the most recent tax year, even if not living in the household. For their income to be considered, household members or dependents must be willing to make their income available for support of the sponsored immigrant(s) and to complete and sign Form I-864A, Contract Between Sponsor and Household Member. A sponsored immigrant/household member only need complete Form I-864A if his or her income will be used to determine your ability to support a spouse and/or children immigrating with him or her.

You must attach evidence of current employment and copies of income tax returns as filed with the IRS for the most recent 3 tax years for yourself and all persons whose income is listed below. See "Required Evidence" in Instructions. Income from all 3 years will be considered in determining your ability to support the immigrant(s) you are sponsoring.

☐ I filed a single/separate tax return for the most recent tax year.

☐ I filed a joint return for the most recent tax year which includes only my own income.

☐ I filed a joint return for the most recent tax year which includes income for my spouse and myself.

  ☐ I am submitting documentation of my individual income (Forms W-2 and 1099).

  ☐ I am qualifying using my spouse's income; my spouse is submitting a Form I-864A.

Indicate most recent tax year

_____
(tax year)

Sponsor's individual income $ _____

or

Sponsor and spouse's combined income $ _____
(If spouse's income is to be considered, spouse must submit Form I-864A.)

Income of other qualifying persons.
(List names; include spouse if applicable. Each person must complete Form I-864A.)

_____ $ _____

_____ $ _____

_____ $ _____

Total Household Income $ _____

Explain on separate sheet of paper if you or any of the above listed individuals were not required to file Federal income tax returns for the most recent 3 years, or if other explanation of income, employment, or evidence is necessary.

D. Determination of Eligibility Based on Income

1. ☐ I am subject to the 125 percent of poverty line requirement for sponsors.
    ☐ I am subject to the 100 percent of poverty line requirement for sponsors on active duty in the U.S. Armed Forces sponsoring their spouse or child.

2.   Sponsor's total household size, from Part 4.B., line 5   _____ .

3.   Minimum income requirement from the Poverty Guidelines chart for the year of _____ is $ _____
      for this household size.   *(year)*

If you are currently employed and your household income for your household size is equal to or greater than the applicable poverty line requirement (from line D.3.), you do not need to list assets (Parts 4.E. and 5) or have a joint sponsor (Part 6) unless you are requested to do so by a Consular or Immigration Officer. You may skip to Part 7, Use of the Affidavit of Support to Overcome Public Charge Ground of Admissibility. **Otherwise, you should continue with Part 4.E.**

Part 4.   Eligibility to Sponsor   (Continued)

E. Sponsor's Assets and Liabilities

Your assets and those of your qualifying household members and dependents may be used to demonstrate ability to maintain an income at or above 125 percent (or 100 percent, if applicable) of the poverty line *if* they are available for the support of the sponsored immigrant(s) and can readily be converted into cash within 1 year. The household member, other than the immigrant(s) you are sponsoring, must complete and sign Form I-864A, Contract Between Sponsor and Household Member. List the cash value of each asset *after* any debts or liens are subtracted. Supporting evidence must be attached to establish location, ownership, date of acquisition, and value of each asset listed, including any liens and liabilities related to each asset listed. See "Evidence of Assets" in Instructions.

Type of Asset	Cash Value of Assets (Subtract any debts)
Savings deposits	$
Stocks, bonds, certificates of deposit	$
Life insurance cash value	$
Real estate	$
Other (specify)	$
Total Cash Value of Assets	$ _____

Part 5.   Immigrant's Assets and Offsetting Liabilities

The sponsored immigrant's assets may also be used in support of your ability to maintain income at or above 125 percent of the poverty line *if* the assets are or will be available in the United States for the support of the sponsored immigrant(s) and can readily be converted into cash within 1 year.

The sponsored immigrant should provide information on his or her assets in a format similar to part 4.E. above. Supporting evidence must be attached to establish location, ownership, and value of each asset listed, including any liens and liabilities for each asset listed. See "Evidence of Assets" in Instructions.

Part 6.   Joint Sponsors

If household income and assets do not meet the appropriate poverty line for your household size, a joint sponsor is required. There may be more than one joint sponsor, but each joint sponsor must individually meet the 125 percent of poverty line requirement based on his or her household income and/or assets, including any assets of the sponsored immigrant. By submitting a separate Affidavit of Support under Section 213A of the Act (Form I-864), a joint sponsor accepts joint responsibility with the petitioner for the sponsored immigrant(s) until they become U.S. citizens, can be credited with 40 quarters of work, leave the United States permanently, or die.

Part 7.   Use of the Affidavit of Support to Overcome Public Charge Ground of Inadmissibility

Section 212(a)(4)(C) of the Immigration and Nationality Act provides that an alien seeking permanent residence as an immediate relative (including an orphan), as a family-sponsored immigrant, or as an alien who will accompany or follow to join another alien is considered to be likely to become a public charge and is inadmissible to the United States unless a sponsor submits a legally enforceable affidavit of support on behalf of the alien. Section 212(a)(4)(D) imposes the same requirement on an employment-based immigrant, and those aliens who accompany or follow to join the employment-based immigrant, if the employment-based immigrant will be employed by a relative, or by a firm in which a relative owns a significant interest. Separate affidavits of support are required for family members at the time they immigrate if they are not included on this affidavit of support or do not apply for an immigrant visa or adjustment of status within 6 months of the date this affidavit of support is originally signed. The sponsor must provide the sponsored immigrant(s) whatever support is necessary to maintain them at an income that is at least 125 percent of the Federal poverty guidelines.

> *I submit this affidavit of support in consideration of the sponsored immigrant(s) not being found inadmissible to the United States under section 212(a)(4)(C) (or 212(a)(4)(D) for an employment-based immigrant) and to enable the sponsored immigrant(s) to overcome this ground of inadmissibility. I agree to provide the sponsored immigrant(s) whatever support is necessary to maintain the sponsored immigrant(s) at an income that is at least 125 percent of the Federal poverty guidelines. I understand that my obligation will continue until my death or the sponsored immigrant(s) have become U.S. citizens, can be credited with 40 quarters of work, depart the United States permanently, or die.*

Notice of Change of Address.

Sponsors are required to provide written notice of any change of address within 30 days of the change in address until the sponsored immigrant(s) have become U.S. citizens, can be credited with 40 quarters of work, depart the United States permanently, or die. To comply with this requirement, the sponsor must complete INS Form I-865. Failure to give this notice may subject the sponsor to the civil penalty established under section 213A(d)(2) which ranges from $250 to $2,000, unless the failure to report occurred with the knowledge that the sponsored immigrant(s) had received means-tested public benefits, in which case the penalty ranges from $2,000 to $5,000.

> *If my address changes for any reason before my obligations under this affidavit of support terminate, I will complete and file INS Form I-865, Sponsor's Notice of Change of Address, within 30 days of the change of address. I understand that failure to give this notice may subject me to civil penalties.*

Means-tested Public Benefit Prohibitions and Exceptions.

Under section 403(a) of Public Law 104-193 (Welfare Reform Act), aliens lawfully admitted for permanent residence in the United States, with certain exceptions, are ineligible for most Federally-funded means-tested public benefits during their first 5 years in the United States. This provision does not apply to public benefits specified in section 403(c) of the Welfare Reform Act or to State public benefits, including emergency Medicaid; short-term, non-cash emergency relief; services provided under the National School Lunch and Child Nutrition Acts; immunizations and testing and treatment for communicable diseases; student assistance under the Higher Education Act and the Public Health Service Act; certain forms of foster-care or adoption assistance under the Social Security Act; Head Start programs; means-tested programs under the Elementary and Secondary Education Act; and Job Training Partnership Act programs.

Consideration of Sponsor's Income in Determining Eligibility for Benefits.

If a permanent resident alien is no longer statutorily barred from a Federally-funded means-tested public benefit program and applies for such a benefit, the income and resources of the sponsor and the sponsor's spouse will be considered (or deemed) to be the income and resources of the sponsored immigrant in determining the immigrant's eligibility for Federal means-tested public benefits. Any State or local government may also choose to consider (or deem) the income and resources of the sponsor and the sponsor's spouse to be the income and resources of the immigrant for the purposes of determining eligibility for their means-tested public benefits. The attribution of the income and resources of the sponsor and the sponsor's spouse to the immigrant will continue until the immigrant becomes a U.S. citizen or has worked or can be credited with 40 qualifying quarters of work, provided that the immigrant or the worker crediting the quarters to the immigrant has not received any Federal means-tested public benefit during any creditable quarter for any period after December 31, 1996.

> *I understand that, under section 213A of the Immigration and Nationality Act (the Act), as amended, this affidavit of support constitutes a contract between me and the U.S. Government. This contract is designed to protect the United States Government, and State and local government agencies or private entities that provide means-tested public benefits, from having to pay benefits to or on behalf of the sponsored immigrant(s), for as long as I am obligated to support them under this affidavit of support. I understand that the sponsored immigrants, or any Federal, State, local, or private entity that pays any means-tested benefit to or on behalf of the sponsored immigrant(s), are entitled to sue me if I fail to meet my obligations under this affidavit of support, as defined by section 213A and INS regulations.*

Civil Action to Enforce.

If the immigrant on whose behalf this affidavit of support is executed receives any Federal, State, or local means-tested public benefit before this obligation terminates, the Federal, State, or local agency or private entity may request reimbursement from the sponsor who signed this affidavit. If the sponsor fails to honor the request for reimbursement, the agency may sue the sponsor in any U.S. District Court or any State court with jurisdiction of civil actions for breach of contract. INS will provide names, addresses, and Social Security account numbers of sponsors to benefit-providing agencies for this purpose. Sponsors may also be liable for paying the costs of collection, including legal fees.

I acknowledge that section 213A(a)(1)(B) of the Act grants the sponsored immigrant(s) and any Federal, State, local, or private agency that pays any means-tested public benefit to or on behalf of the sponsored immigrant(s) standing to sue me for failing to meet my obligations under this affidavit of support. I agree to submit to the personal jurisdiction of any court of the United States or of any State, territory, or possession of the United States if the court has subject matter jurisdiction of a civil lawsuit to enforce this affidavit of support. I agree that no lawsuit to enforce this affidavit of support shall be barred by any statute of limitations that might otherwise apply, so long as the plaintiff initiates the civil lawsuit no later than ten (10) years after the date on which a sponsored immigrant last received any means-tested public benefits.

Collection of Judgment.

I acknowledge that a plaintiff may seek specific performance of my support obligation. Furthermore, any money judgment against me based on this affidavit of support may be collected through the use of a judgment lien under 28 U.S.C 3201, a writ of execution under 28 U.S.C 3203, a judicial installment payment order under 28 U.S.C 3204, garnishment under 28 U.S.C 3205, or through the use of any corresponding remedy under State law. I may also be held liable for costs of collection, including attorney fees.

Concluding Provisions.

I, _____, certify under penalty of perjury under the laws of the United States that:

(a) I know the contents of this affidavit of support signed by me;

(b) All the statements in this affidavit of support are true and correct;

(c) I make this affidavit of support for the consideration stated in Part 7, freely, and without any mental reservation or purpose of evasion;

(d) Income tax returns submitted in support of this affidavit are true copies of the returns filed with the Internal Revenue Service; and

(e) Any other evidence submitted is true and correct.

_____   _____
(Sponsor's Signature)   *(Date)*

Subscribed and sworn to (or affirmed) before me this

_____ day of _____, _____
                              (Month)   *(Year)*

at _____ .

My commission expires on _____ .

_____
(Signature of Notary Public or Officer Administering Oath)

_____
(Title)

I certify under penalty of perjury under the laws of the United States that I prepared this affidavit of support at the sponsor's request, and that this affidavit of support is based on all information of which I have knowledge.

Signature	Print Your Name	Date	Daytime Telephone Number

Firm Name and Address

DIVERSITY VISA APPLICATION

ATTACH RECENT PHOTOGRAPH OF THE APPLICANT, THE APPLICANT'S SPOUSE AND ALL CHILDREN (2" x 2"). SEPARATE PHOTOS MUST BE ATTACHED FOR EACH FAMILY MEMBER. PRINT THE NAME AND DATE OF BIRTH OF EACH FAMILY MEMBER ON THE BACK OF EACH PHOTO.

A.	NAME _____ LAST FIRST MIDDLE

B.	DATE OF BIRTH _____
	                             DAY/MONTH/YEAR
	
	 PLACE OF BIRTH _____
	                (CITY, PROVINCE OR OTHER POLITICAL SUBDIVISION, AND COUNTRY)

C.	APPLICANT'S NATIVE COUNTRY IF DIFFERENT FROM COUNTRY OF BIRTH _____
D.	INFORMATION CONCERNING SPOUSE FULL NAME DATE OF BIRTH PLACE OF BIRTH (LAST/FIRST/MIDDLE) (D/M/Y) (CITY, POLITICAL SUBDIVISION, AND COUNTRY) _____
E.	INFORMATION CONCERNING CHILDREN FULL NAME DATE OF BIRTH PLACE OF BIRTH (LAST/FIRST/MIDDLE) (D/M/Y) (CITY, POLITICAL SUBDIVISION, AND COUNTRY) _____ _____ _____ _____ (ATTACH INFORMATION ON ADDITIONAL CHILDREN AS NEEDED)
F.	CURRENT MAILING ADDRESS AND PHONE NUMBER _____ NO. AND NAME OF STREET APARTMENT NO. _____ CITY STATE/PROVINCE/COUNTRY ZIP CODE _____ TELEPHONE NO.
G.	SIGNATURE _____

OMB #1125-0001

Application for Cancellation of Removal and Adjustment of Status for Certain Nonpermanent Residents

PLEASE READ ADVICE AND INSTRUCTIONS BEFORE FILLING IN FORM

PLEASE TYPE OR PRINT

Fee Stamp

PART 1 - INFORMATION ABOUT YOURSELF

1) My present true name is: *(Last, First, Middle)*	2) Alien Registration Number:
3) My name given at birth was: *(Last, First, Middle)*	4) Birth Place: *(City, Country)*

5) Date of Birth: *(Month, Day, Year)*	6) Gender: ☐ Male ☐ Female	7) Height:	8) Hair Color:	9) Eye Color:
10) Current Nationality & Citizenship:	11) Social Security Number:	12) Home Phone Number: ( )		13) Work Phone Number: ( )

14) I currently reside at:	15) I have been known by these additional name(s):
Apt. number and/or in care of	
Number and Street	
City or Town State ZIP Code	

16) I have resided in the following locations in the United States (List PRESENT ADDRESS FIRST, and work back in time for at least 10 years.)

Street and Number - Apt. or Room# - City or Town - State - ZIP Code	Resided From: *(Month, Day, Year)*	Resided To: *(Month, Day, Year)*
		PRESENT

PART 2 - INFORMATION ABOUT THIS APPLICATION

17) I, the undersigned, hereby request that my removal be cancelled under the provisions of section 240A(b) of the Immigration and Nationality Act (INA). I believe that I am eligible for cancellation of removal because: (check all that apply)

☐ My removal would result in exceptional and extremely unusual hardship to my: *(Place a USC in the space if the family member is a citizen of the United States, an L if the family member is a lawful permanent resident of the United States, an X if the family member is neither and leave BLANK if not applicable.)*

_____ **Husband** _____ **Wife** _____ **Father** _____ **Mother** _____ **Child or Children.**

With the exception of absences described in question #25, I have resided in the United States since:
(Month, Day, Year) _____ .

☐ I, or my child, have been battered or subjected to extreme cruelty by a United States citizen or lawful permanent resident spouse or parent.

With the exception of absences described in question #25, I have resided in the United States since:
(Month, Day, Year) _____ .

PART 3 - INFORMATION ABOUT YOUR PRESENCE IN THE UNITED STATES

18) I first arrived in the United States under the name of: *(Last, First, Middle)*

19) I first arrived in the United States on: *(Month, Day, Year)*

20) Place or port of first arrival: *(Place or Port, City, and State)*

21) I arrived: ☐ as a lawful permanent resident, ☐ as a Visitor, ☐ as a Student, ☐ without inspection, or ☐ Other *(Place an X in the correct box, if Other is selected please explain)*:

22) If admitted as a nonimmigrant, period for which admitted: *(Month, Day, Year)*   to

23) My last extension of stay in the United States expired on: *(Month, Day, Year)*

24) If not inspected or if arrival occurred at other than a regular port, describe the circumstances as accurately as possible:

25) Since the date of my first arrival I departed from and returned to the United States at the following places and on the following dates:
(Please list all departures regardless of how briefly you were absent from the United States)
If you have never departed from the United States since your original date of arrival, please mark an X in the box: ☐

	Port of Departure *(Place or Port, City and State)*	Departure Date *(Month, Day, Year)*	Purpose of Travel	Destination
1	Port of Return *(Place or Port, City and State)*	Return Date *(Month, Day, Year)*	Manner of Return	Inspected & Admitted? ☐ Yes ☐ No
2	Port of Departure *(Place or Port, City and State)*	Departure Date *(Month, Day, Year)*	Purpose of Travel	Destination
	Port of Return *(Place or Port, City and State)*	Return Date *(Month, Day, Year)*	Manner of Return	Inspected & Admitted? ☐ Yes ☐ No

26) Have you ever departed the United States: a) under an order of deportation, exclusion or removal? ------------ ☐ Yes ☐ No

b) pursuant to a grant of voluntary departure? ----------------------- ☐ Yes ☐ No

PART 4 - INFORMATION ABOUT YOUR MARITAL STATUS AND SPOUSE *(Continued on page 3)*

27) I am not married: ☐
I am married: ☐

28) If married, the name of my spouse is: *(Last, First, Middle)*

29) Date of marriage: *(Month, Day, Year)*

30) The marriage took place in: *(City and Country)*

31) Birth place of spouse: *(City and Country)*

32) My spouse currently resides at:

Apt. number and/or in care of

Number and Street

City or Town   State/Country   ZIP Code

33) Birth date of spouse: *(Month, Day, Year)*

34) My spouse is a citizen of: *(Country)*

35) If your spouse is other than a native born United States citizen, answer the following:

He/she arrived in the United States at: *(City and State)* _____ .

He/she arrived in the United States on: *(Month, Day, Year)* _____ .

His/her alien registration number is: A# _____ .

He/she was naturalized on *(Month, Day, Year)* _____ at _____ .
(City and State)

36) My spouse ☐ - is ☐ - is not employed. If employed, please give salary and the name and address of the place(s) of employment.

Full Name and Address of Employer	Earnings Per Week *(Approximate)*
	$
	$
	$

Form EOIR-42B
4/97

PART 4 - INFORMATION ABOUT YOUR MARITAL STATUS AND SPOUSE *(Continued)*

37) I ☐ - have ☐ - have not been previously married: *(If previously married, list the name of each prior spouse, the dates on which each marriage began and ended, the place where the marriage terminated, and describe how each marriage ended.)*

Name of prior spouse: *(Last, First, Middle)*	Date marriage began: Date marriage ended:	Place marriage ended: *(City and Country)*	Description or manner of how marriage was terminated or ended:

38) My present spouse ☐ - has ☐ - has not been previously married: *(If previously married, list the name of each prior spouse, the dates on which the marriage began and ended, the place where the marriage terminated, and describe how each marriage ended.)*

Name of prior spouse: *(Last, First, Middle)*	Date marriage began: Date marriage ended:	Place marriage ended: *(City and Country)*	Description or manner of how marriage was terminated or ended:

39) Have you been ordered by any court, or are otherwise under any legal obligation, to provide child support and/or spousal maintenance as a result of a separation and/or divorce?   ☐ - Yes   ☐ - No

PART 5 - INFORMATION ABOUT YOUR EMPLOYMENT AND FINANCIAL STATUS

40) Since my arrival into the United States, I have been employed by the following - named persons or firms: *(Please begin with present employment and work back in time. Any periods of unemployment or school attendance should be specified.)*

Full Name and Address of Employer	Earnings Per Week *(Approximate)*	Type of Work Performed	Employed From: *(Month, Day, Year)*	Employed To: *(Month, Day, Year)*
	$			PRESENT
	$			
	$			

41) If self-employed, describe the nature of the business, the name of the business, its address, and net income derived therefrom:

42) My assets (and if married my spouse's assets) in the United States and other countries, not including clothing and household necessities, are:

Self		Jointly Owned with Spouse	
Cash, Stocks, and Bonds — — — — — — —	$	Cash, Stocks, and Bonds — — — — — — —	$
Real Estate — — — — — — — — —	$	Real Estate — — — — — — — — —	$
Automobile (value minus amount owed) — — —	$	Automobile (value minus amount owed) — — —	$
Other (describe on line below) — — — — —	$	Other (describe on line below) — — — — —	$
_____ TOTAL	$	_____ TOTAL	$

43) I ☐ - have ☐ - have not received public or private relief or assistance (e.g. Welfare, Unemployment Benefits, Medicaid, ADC, etc.). If you have, please give full details including the type of relief or assistance received, date for which relief or assistance was received, place, and amount received during this time: _____

44) Please list each of the years in which you have filed an income tax return with the Internal Revenue Service: _____

Form EOIR-42B
4/97

45) I have _____ (Number of) children. Please list information for each child below, include assets and earnings information for children over the age of sixteen who have separate incomes:

Name of Child: *(Last, First, Middle)* Child's Alien Registration Number:	Citizen of What Country: Birth Date: *(Month, Day, Year)*	Now Residing At: *(City and Country)* Birth Place: *(City and Country)*	Immigration Status of Child?
A#:			
Estimated Total of Assets: $ _____	Estimated Average Weekly Earnings: $ _____		
A#:			
Estimated Total of Assets: $ _____	Estimated Average Weekly Earnings: $ _____		
A#:			
Estimated Total of Assets: $ _____	Estimated Average Weekly Earnings: $ _____		

46) If your application is denied, would your spouse and all of your children accompany you to your:

Country of Birth - ☐ Yes ☐ No

Country of Nationality - ☐ Yes ☐ No

Country of Last Residence - ☐ Yes ☐ No

If you answered "NO" to any of the responses, please explain: _____

_____

_____

47) Members of my family, including my spouse and/or child(ren) ☐ - have ☐ - have not received public or private relief or assistance (e.g., Unemployment Benefits, Welfare, Medicaid, ADC, etc.). If any member of your immediate family has received such relief or assistance, please give full details including identity of person(s) receiving relief or assistance, dates for which relief or assistance was received, place, and amount received during this time: _____

_____

_____

_____

48) Please give the requested information about your parents, brothers, sisters, aunts, uncles, and grandparents. As to residence, show street address, city, and state, if in the United States; otherwise show only country:

Name: *(Last, First, Middle)* Alien Registration Number:	Citizen of What Country: Birth Date: *(Month, Day, Year)*	Relationship to Me: Birth Place: *(City and Country)*	Immigration Status of Listed Relative
A#:	/ /		
Complete Address of Current Residence: _____			
A#:	/ /		
Complete Address of Current Residence: _____			

IF THIS APPLICATION IS BASED ON HARDSHIP TO A PARENT OR PARENTS, QUESTIONS 49 TO 52 MUST BE ANSWERED.

49) As to such parent who is not a citizen of the United States, give the date and place of arrival in the United States including full details as to the date, manner and terms of admission into the United States:

_____

_____

_____

50) My father ☐ - is ☐ - is not employed. If employed, please give salary and the name and address of the place(s) of employment.

Full Name and Address of Employer	Earnings Per Week *(Approximate)*
	$

51) My mother ☐ - is ☐ - is not employed. If employed, please give salary and the name and address of the place(s) of employment.

Full Name and Address of Employer	Earnings Per Week *(Approximate)*
	$

52) My parent's assets in the United States and other countries not including clothing and household necessities are:

Assets of father consist of the following:

Cash, Stocks, and Bonds — — — — — — —$ _____
Real Estate — — — — — — — — — —$ _____
Automobile (value minus amount owed) — —$ _____
Other (describe on line below) — — — — —$ _____

_____ **TOTAL** $ _____

Assets of mother consist of the following:

Cash, Stocks, and Bonds — — — — — — —$ _____
Real Estate — — — — — — — — — —$ _____
Automobile (value minus amount owed) — —$ _____
Other (describe on line below) — — — — —$ _____

_____ **TOTAL** $ _____

PART 7 - MISCELLANEOUS INFORMATION *(Continued on page 6)*

53) I ☐ - have ☐ - have not entered the United States as a crewman after June 30, 1964.

54) I ☐ - have ☐ - have not been admitted as, or after arrival into the United States acquired the status of, an exchange alien.

55) I ☐ - have ☐ - have not submitted address reports as required by section 265 of the Immigration and Nationality Act.

56) I ☐ - have ☐ - have never (either in the United States or in any foreign country) been arrested, summoned into court as a defendant, convicted, fined, imprisoned, placed on probation, or forfeited collateral for an act involving a felony, misdemeanor, or breach of any public law or ordinance (including, but not limited to, traffic violations or driving incidents involving alcohol). *(If answer is in the affirmative, please give a brief description of each offense including the name and location of the offense, date of conviction, any penalty imposed, any sentence imposed, and the time actually served).* _____

_____

_____

_____

57) Have you ever served in the Armed Forces of the United States? ☐ - Yes ☐ - No. If "Yes", please state branch *(Army, Navy, etc.)* and service number. _____

Place of entry on duty: *(Place, City, and State)* _____

Date of entry on duty: *(Month, Day, Year)* _____. Date of discharge: *(Month, Day, Year)* _____.

Type of discharge *(Honorable, Dishonorable, etc.):* _____

I served in active duty status from: *(Month, Day, Year)* _____ to *(Month, Day, Year)* _____

58) Have you ever left the United States or the jurisdiction of the district where you registered for the draft to avoid being drafted into the military or naval forces of the United States?

☐ Yes ☐ No

Form EOIR-42B
4/97

IF THIS APPLICATION IS BASED ON HARDSHIP TO A PARENT OR PARENTS, QUESTIONS 49 TO 52 MUST BE ANSWERED.

49) As to such parent who is not a citizen of the United States, give the date and place of arrival in the United States including full
details as to the date, manner and terms of admission into the United States:

_____

_____

_____

50) My father ☐ - is ☐ - is not employed. If employed, please give salary and the name and address of the place(s) of employment.

Full Name and Address of Employer	Earnings Per Week *(Approximate)*
	$

51) My mother ☐ - is ☐ - is not employed. If employed, please give salary and the name and address of the place(s) of employment.

Full Name and Address of Employer	Earnings Per Week *(Approximate)*
	$

52) My parent's assets in the United States and other countries not including clothing and household necessities are:

Assets of father consist of the following:

Cash, Stocks, and Bonds — — — — — — —$ _____

Real Estate — — — — — — — — — — —$ _____

Automobile (value minus amount owed) — —$ _____

Other (describe on line below) — — — — —$ _____

_____ **TOTAL $** _____

Assets of mother consist of the following:

Cash, Stocks, and Bonds — — — — — — —$ _____

Real Estate — — — — — — — — — — —$ _____

Automobile (value minus amount owed) — — $ _____

Other (describe on line below) — — — — —$ _____

_____ **TOTAL $** _____

53) I ☐ - have ☐ - have not   entered the United States as a crewman after June 30, 1964.

54) I ☐ - have ☐ - have not   been admitted as, or after arrival into the United States acquired the status of, an exchange alien.

55) I ☐ - have ☐ - have not   submitted address reports as required by section 265 of the Immigration and Nationality Act.

56) I ☐ - have ☐ - have never (either in the United States or in any foreign country) been arrested, summoned into court as a defendant,
convicted, fined, imprisoned, placed on probation, or forfeited collateral for an act involving a felony, misdemeanor, or breach of any public
law or ordinance (including, but not limited to, traffic violations or driving incidents involving alcohol). *(If answer is in the affirmative,
please give a brief description of each offense including the name and location of the offense, date of conviction, any penalty imposed,
any sentence imposed, and the time actually served).* _____

_____

_____

_____

57) Have you ever served in the Armed Forces of the United States? ☐ - Yes ☐ - No. If "Yes", please state branch *(Army, Navy,
etc.)* and service number. _____

Place of entry on duty: *(Place, City, and State)* _____

Date of entry on duty: *(Month, Day, Year)* _____. Date of discharge: *(Month, Day, Year)* _____.

Type of discharge *(Honorable, Dishonorable, etc.)*: _____

I served in active duty status from: *(Month, Day, Year)* _____ to *(Month, Day, Year)* _____.

58) Have you ever left the United States or the jurisdiction of the district where you registered for the draft to avoid being drafted into
the military or naval forces of the United States?

☐ Yes ☐ No

59) Have you ever deserted from the military or naval forces of the United States while the United States was at war? ☐ Yes ☐ No

60) If male, did you register under the Selective Service (Draft) Law of 1917, 1918, 1948, 1951, or later Draft Laws? ☐ Yes ☐ No
If "Yes," please give date, Selective Service number, local draft board number, and your last draft classification:_____
_____

61) Were you ever exempted from service because of conscientious objection, alienage, or any other reason? ☐ Yes ☐ No

62) Please list your present or past membership in or affiliation with every political organization, association, fund, foundation, party, club, society, or similar group in the United States or any other place since your 16th birthday. Include any foreign military service in this part. If none, write "NONE". Include the name of the organization, location, nature of the organization, and the dates of membership.

Name of Organization	Location of Organization	Nature of Organization	Member From: *(Month, Day, Year)*	Member To: *(Month, Day, Year)*

63) Have you ever:

☐ Yes ☐ No been ordered deported or removed?
☐ Yes ☐ No overstayed a grant of voluntary departure from an Immigration Judge or the Immigration and Naturalization Service (INS)?
☐ Yes ☐ No failed to appear for removal or deportation?

64) Have you ever been:

☐ Yes ☐ No a habitual drinker?
☐ Yes ☐ No one whose income is derived principally from illegal gambling?
☐ Yes ☐ No one who has given false testimony for the purpose of obtaining immigration benefits?
☐ Yes ☐ No engaged in prostitution or unlawful commercialized vice?
☐ Yes ☐ No involved in a serious criminal offense and asserted immunity from prosecution?
☐ Yes ☐ No a polygamist?
☐ Yes ☐ No one who aided and/or abetted another to enter the United States illegally?
☐ Yes ☐ No a trafficker of a controlled substance, or a knowing assister, abettor, conspirator, or colluder with others in any such controlled substance offense (not including a single offense of simple possesion of 30 grams or less of marijuana)?
☐ Yes ☐ No inadmissible or deportable on security-related grounds under sections 212(a)(3) or 237(a)(4) of the INA?
☐ Yes ☐ No one who has ordered, incited, assisted, or otherwise participated in the persecution of an individual on account of his or her race, religion, nationality, membership in a particular social group, or political opinion?
☐ Yes ☐ No a person previously granted relief under sections 212(c) or 244(a) of the INA or whose removal has previously been cancelled under section 240A of the INA?

64) Are you: ☐ Yes ☐ No the beneficiary of an approved visa petition?
If yes, can you: ☐ Yes ☐ No arrange a trip outside the United States to obtain an immigrant visa. If no, please explain:
_____
_____
_____
_____

Please use a separate sheet for additional entries.

Form EOIR-42B
4/97

65) The following certificates or other supporting documents are attached hereto as a part of this application: *(Refer to the Instruction Sheet for documents which **should be attached**).*

_____   _____

_____   _____

_____   _____

_____   _____

_____   _____

_____   _____

_____   _____

_____   _____

_____   _____

_____   _____

_____   _____

_____   _____

APPLICATION NOT TO BE SIGNED BELOW UNTIL APPLICANT APPEARS BEFORE AN IMMIGRATION JUDGE

I do swear (affirm) that the contents of the above application, including the documents attached hereto, are true to the best of my knowledge, and that this application is now signed by me with my full, true name.

_____
(Complete and true signature of applicant or parent or guardian)

Subscribed and sworn to before me by the above-named applicant at _____

_____
Immigration Judge

_____
Date: (Month, Day, Year)

CERTIFICATE OF SERVICE

I hereby certify that a copy of the foregoing was: ☐ - delivered in person,   ☐ - mailed first class, postage prepaid   on

_____ *(Month, Day, Year)*   to   _____
(INS District Counsel and Address)

_____

_____
Signature of Applicant (or attorney or representative)

Form EOIR-42B
4/97

CERTIFICATION BY TRANSLATOR

I, _____, certify that I am fluent in the English and _____ languages, that I am competent to perform this translation and that the above is an accurate translation of the document entitled _____.

_____   _____
Date   Signature

INDEX